ELIZABETH RICE

RITUALS
OF
SEPARATION

A SOUTH KOREAN MEMOIR OF
IDENTITY AND BELONGING

FOR KAREN ~
    I COUNT IT AS ONE OF LIFE'S GREATEST
BLESSINGS TO MEET SOMEONE AND FROM THAT
MOMENT FEEL LIKE WE'VE BEEN FRIENDS FOREVER.
YOU'RE FUN, FUNNY, KIND, AND SO MANY GOOD
THINGS, AND I LOVED HANGING OUT WITH YOU.
I'LL BE THINKING OF YOU AS YOU NAVIGATE YOUR
NEXT LIFE STEPS + I'M HAPPY TO KNOW I'VE
GOT A NEW FRIEND.
            LOVE YOU -
               LIZ

    P.S. HOW ABOUT NOW?

The author gratefully acknowledges and gives special thanks for the permission
of artist Minouk Lim to use "Rituals of Separation" as the title of this book.

Book cover design by Catherine Breer
Book design by Elizabeth Rice
Cover photography by Elizabeth Rice
See notes for chapter photo credits and source citations

Copyright © 2016 by Elizabeth Rice

ISBN 978-0692815892

This is a work of non-fiction. A few names have been changed to protect
privacy or to make the story easier to follow.

TOJANG
PRESS

To my parents, who gave their hearts to Korea.

To Kim Kap-gil, who loved me unconditionally.

For my childhood friends of Korea,
who each, in their own way, share this story.

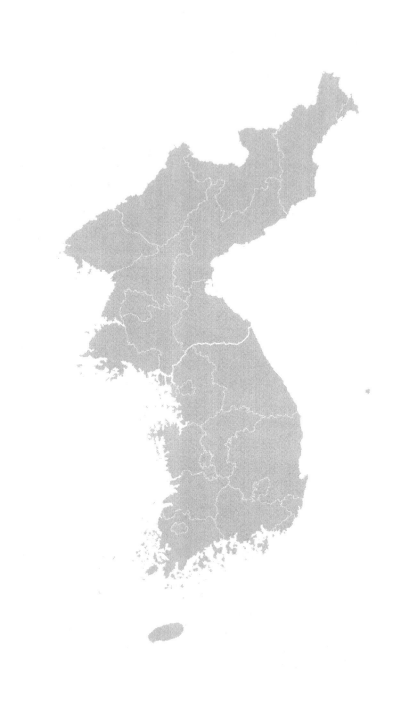

A Note About Romanization

Hangul, the Korean alphabet, is phonetic. Throughout history, linguists have developed different methods to express the best English pronunciation for Korean sounds that do not have an exact English match. When my family was living in Korea, the McCune–Reischauer system was used to represent the phonetic pronunciation of Korean. For example, I grew up knowing the cities of Taegu, Pusan, Kwang Ju, and Taechon. Now, since a new system is in place, those same cities are known in English as Daegu, Busan, Gwang Ju, and Daecheon. Of course the Korean spelling and pronunciation hasn't changed, just the representation of those words in English.

Imagine if Toledo one day became Doledo, or Pennsylvania was suddenly written, Bennsylvania. For the sake of historical accuracy and to reflect the particular time we lived in Korea, the Korean words in this book are represented using the McCune-Reischauer system, in the way they were spelled in the years we lived there.

A note about Korean personal names. Korean names are written with the family name first, followed by the given name. For example, my father's Korean name is Na Ui Son. In the United States, he would be called Ui Son Na, or Mr. Na. Sometimes given names are hyphenated in English. Sometimes they are not. My father's Korean name could be written as Ui-Son, Ui Son, or Ui-son. Sometimes it comes down to a matter of personal preference. For the sake of consistency, the Korean names in this book are represented using the Ui-son format, or in the way an individual has chosen for him or herself.

Special thanks to Professor Hangtae Cho of University of Minnesota's Asian Languages and Literature program for reviewing the romanization used in this book. Any errors or deviations from the McCune-Reischauer system are entirely the fault of the author.

"Nietzsche was said to have wept as he embraced
a downtrodden horse,
but I want to weep, embracing places.

I am weeping,
hugging a place as the protagonist of a tragedy.

I am inventing rituals for, and keeping records of,
moments of separation."

—MINOUK LIM

SITTING BY THE TRAIL

*"We all know the story about the man
who sat by the trail too long,
and then it grew over,
and he could never find his way again.*

*We can never forget what has happened,
but we cannot go back.
Nor can we just sit beside the trail."*

—CHIEF POUNDMAKER

Hi Lizzy,

How are you?

This morning we saw a new building in Yonhi-dong and we were very surprised. Because it is located instead of your child house.

Our funny house on the hill is gone. Persimmon tree, fired green garden, and Mom's kitchen, all gone.

Time flies fast. You tell Mom and Dad.

We think and talk about you all the time. Send news soon again.

Bye!
Myong-ju

My childhood house is gone. It was bulldozed and replaced with a nondescript apartment building. Two of our other Seoul homes will fall to the wrecking ball this year. This is the way of life when you come from a city that changes so fast people say it has "liquid architecture." Sometimes it feels like I had a liquid childhood. So how did it feel so steadfast and rooted, so unwavering?

I feel a lump settle in my throat as I read Myong-ju's email. I picture the warm floor of my parents' bedroom. I remember the comfort of slipping under Mom's thick *ibul* blanket after school, the way the fabric of the rainbow-colored silk of the *yo* mattress moved easily against the rice-paper covered surface. I see the long view of western Seoul from our yard above the valley road, and the tangle of one-story homes and businesses that stretched out for miles into the horizon. As if it was just yesterday, I see the single persimmon tree outside the living room window, and the two tall gingkos that stood like sentinels guarding our Nissan station wagon. And now it's all gone.

What did they do with the gingko trees when they took down our house? Is the persimmon tree that gave us such soft, orange fruit, year after year, now in a heap of concrete and dust somewhere outside the city? Is the thick rice paper of our floors crumpled there, too? And where is Ajumoni today?

But there is too much loss in this image. Too much heartbreak. I don't want to dwell on what is gone. But sometimes it seems to be all I can do. Maybe I carry some measure of *han*, the collective ache and unresolved resentment Koreans are said to carry from enduring centuries of hardship. Or maybe I'm just longing to go home, to talk to Ajumoni, to pluck a persimmon from our tree.

Myong-ju's mother was in her thirties when she came to work for us. Recently widowed, she desperately needed employment so she could keep her three young children. One day Ajumoni told me the story of her husband's death. She used her shirtsleeves to wipe away falling tears, as if in wiping them away she could reverse his death. *Maum* is the Korean word for heart. But the word, like so much about Korea, is untranslatable into English. *Maum* is the deepest place of the soul, part mind, part spirit center.

"*Maumi apayo.*" Ajumoni said as she patted her hand to her chest. My heart hurts.

She didn't hide her sorrow from me in the same way she didn't suppress her infectious laughter when it came. By the age of six, when she came into my life, I had lived five of my six years in South Korea. I was accustomed to Ajumoni's open lament and easy amusement. I was familiar with her way of expressing pain and loss and I knew it was different from the way my grandparents expressed theirs. They kept their sorrows private. Their conflicts were hidden behind closed doors. I held and balanced each way inside of me. I was a little American girl with a Korean heart, at home in a country of open tears.

I never imagined that years would pass when I wouldn't see Ajumoni. I never imagined a day would come I wouldn't walk the hillsides of Yonhi-dong or pass the centuries old city gates that defined the limits of my universe. For sixteen years the air of Korea filled my lungs and the ways of that land settled into my heart.

When my family left Korea, I carried my love for Ajumoni with me. I carried the morning mist that materialized in the pine forests of Saddleback Mountain, and the chatter of the blue and white *kkachi*, the magpie who called to me each morning from the tree outside my bedroom window. I carried the expat community who helped raise me, aunts, uncles, and cousins by circumstance, so-called "foreigners" who called Korea home. I carried my international school friends, the only people in the world who shared my particular identity. I carried the story of my parents, humble people of humor and great life spirit who not only chose to leave behind lives of privilege, but ended up walking arm in arm with Koreans fighting for human rights and democracy. People who answered a calling to be missionaries and then challenged the idea of what being a missionary was all about. I carried the story of eight men hung for no reason, and the tragedy of one country split in two.

In my twenties, I began to dream about Korea. I walked through open markets of knockoff Nikes, nylon backpacks, and stacks of dried fish. Men pulled carts of nappa cabbages and thick taffy along city roads. Middle-aged ladies in starched yellow uniforms peddled yogurt carts through my old neighborhood like carry-on luggage. The night was beginning to feel more real than the day. I was five again, skipping past mounds of spent *yontan* charcoal briquettes. Our house appeared around the corner as if my family never left Korea. Mom was there, and Ajumoni too, laughing as she added sesame oil to a simmering stew. I was carrying my longing for Korea like a *chigae* a-frame of heavy stones. Instead of sticks of firewood, I carried a childhood. Each stone was a memory I couldn't put down. *Maumi apayo.*

I began to count up the number of years I had lived in the U.S. and measure them against the number of years I had lived in Korea. I felt reassured when I calculated the greater balance was spent in Korea. But the balance was shifting. Could I keep or lose the Korean part of me through simple mathematics? Could the most fundamental part of me slip away over time? Was all of me still there if a part of me was hidden behind light hair, green-blue eyes, and native English ability?

I knew identity wasn't like this. I knew that deep inside of me was a person, anchored and fixed, formed by family, genetics, learned rituals, and environment. I also knew that when people looked at me they saw the obvious, because this is what we all do. We categorize others by their appearance to make sense of the world. We categorize others to make sense of ourselves. "Where are you from?" people ask, again and again.

I'm a *miguksaram* in Korea. An American. In Costa Rica, I learned to say *"soy gringa."* When I lived in Zambia I was a *muzungu*, the general term used for white person, which literally means, maybe too fittingly in my case, "someone who roams around aimlessly." But I carry a person inside of me. My outside doesn't tell my full story of belonging. My face and passport only tell a part of my internal truth. They misrepresent the story.

My grief dug in stubbornly as I moved from state to state, trying to get my life back. When ten years passed without going to Korea, I wept into a plate of *chapchae* noodles when I heard the clanging, percussive beat of the age-old Farmer's Dance begin in a St. Paul, Minnesota music hall. Ten years felt like a lifetime. It almost felt like I never lived in Korea, that Korea didn't exist, even when every fiber of my being was telling me otherwise. Even as I felt my salty tears fall at the sound of a Korean harvest dance. I was sitting by the trail. And the trail was growing over.

My childhood that felt so rooted and permanent was a house of cards. When my family left Korea, the complex world that formed me into the person I was dropped to the floor, card by card. In the U.S. I was a hidden immigrant living in a country I didn't belong to. I was a foreigner living in a land that was supposed to be mine. And I missed Korea so much I ached inside.

I was nine months old when my parents moved to South Korea. They were a social-action oriented couple eager to do something to help a country recovering from a devastating century. Their decision to move across the seas was made with hearts as big and as good as I would ever know. They knew very little about Korea. They didn't speak the language. The only foreign country they had visited was Canada, just over the Rainbow Bridge from their New York hometown. They knew to expect culture shock. The Presbyterian Mission prepared them, during a six month orientation, to expect the difficult process called acculturation and the lonely condition called homesickness. They hoped and prayed their four young children would adjust. They were especially worried about their oldest boy, who they anticipated might bear this life change more than any of us. What they didn't know is that their decision to move across the world would turn our sense of cultural and national identity on its head.

More than our family story changed the day we landed in Seoul. The needle of my internal cultural compass swung into a new position. When we left Korea, it would not budge back. All that I carried with me from my childhood, all that Korea had instilled in me, was held closely in my heart. I was silently grieving for a country and a life left behind. And how could I explain the depth of this loss to people who did not know that place? I was longing for so many things at once. For the grime of a frenetic ancient city. For a lady who knew the unbearable loss of permanent separation. For a people of grace and coarseness who hoped when hope was all they had.

I come from New York lawyers and Vermont gentlemen farmers. My ancestors are Hosbachs and Beldens, Rices and Ransoms. These people are a fundamental part of me, too. But my heart belongs to a nation of rising and falling dynasties, industrial factories, and army general dictators. I am from a thin place, where the boundary between heaven and earth, light and dark, and good and evil, was always like a fine thread of silk.

In the densely packed hills of Seoul, time-worn tile roofs lifted elegantly towards the sky, cracking against the concrete walls of industrialization. The black shingles were formed from clay. The mud was pulled through the muck of a harvested rice paddy. I still know their shape. I can still picture the pattern of lines they formed when laid from peak to eave. I remember the vivid colors of the painted halls of Kyung Bok Palace and the feel of thick white rubber *komusin* shoes on my feet. I know these things like I know the lines on my own hand.

Human beings have rituals of separation for a reason. We play bagpipes. We carry shrouded bodies through the streets of our towns and cities. We burn flesh and sinew into pyres flicking spirits into ashen air. Rituals of separation tell us we must begin to let go. They help us heal. They tell us who we are and where we come from. Rituals of separation show us how our people mourn and how our people begin to move on. Rituals of separation are rituals of thanksgiving.

After we left Korea, I balanced precariously between two lives, unsure how to go back and unable to move forward. I had to come to terms with all I had seen in those years. I had to look into the ways of the people and places that formed me and find myself, like a pebble sorted from rice. And I learned to pick up the pieces of an unrooted adulthood time and time again. For what is lost can't always be recovered. Sometimes the only way to move on is to learn to let go, to be deeply grateful for what we had, to know we will never be the same for what we have seen. To learn that maybe, just maybe, our fractured parts do, after all, make a whole.

COMPASS POINT

*"There are two kinds of people:
those who are content where they are,
and those who say,
'Let's go and see what's on the other side of the hill.'
When we do that, of course, there is a cost."*

—HENRIETTA BOGGS
First Lady of the Revolution, Spark Media

Connecticut, 1965

Dear Friends far and wide,

Two acts of grace form the substance of our letter. The first occurred four days ago. We received word from our mission board that we have been appointed to represent our denomination and country as missionaries in Korea in 1966.

Our tentative sailing date is August. Upon our arrival there, we will spend eighteen months in Seoul learning the Korean language. We look toward this new challenge with mingled feelings—joy, a little fear, some sorrow at leaving this parish and so many familiar things. But we do believe this is an expression of God's will for us, and we go in that confidence.

The second act of grace occurred on November 6, 1965, when, at long last, a girl baby came into our family. Elizabeth Jeanne Rice was born that night, and ever since then there has been a little extra whiff of sweetness in the air. Sue carried Elizabeth well, and has swung back into her normal life with comparative ease. Our sons, Ricky, now 8, Chris, now 5, and Mark Peter, now 3, have already formed a protective threesome of big brothers about their new sister.

Our new address after January will be Missionary Orientation Center, Stony Point, N.Y. Write us there. We look forward to a Korean Christmas next year, and to a re-strengthening of these ties which bind us all to you, who mean so much to us. In your faith and friendship, we are strong. Pray for us, as we for you.

Happy Christmas,
Randy, Sue, Ricky, Chris, Mark, and Elizabeth

South Korea was never my country by birthright or ancestry. There was no *hojok*, no family registry on which my grandfathers' names were written down. The place that is my motherland is not, after all, my mother's land. I am eligible for membership in the Daughters of the American Revolution.

The first hard evidence of Korea in my life was when I was nine months old, when our passports were stamped, "Admitted: Republic of Korea. September 15, 1966." My mother held me in her arms as our mission-issue Land Rover crossed the Han River Bridge into Seoul. Like many of my childhood friends, I entered into Korea obliviously, too young to experience culture shock, too young to have to adjust or acclimate, all of those things humans usually do when we enter a new place. But there is a story before my birth and before the time of my first memories, a story that explains why my heart is half Korean.

Missionaries often said they felt *called* to places, as if it happened by God-magic. I always imagined it as if the phone rang and it was God, telling Mom and Dad in concise terms where to go and what to do. And because I believed calling was magical, I thought of our transition from the U.S. to Korea as easy, as if we, the sons and daughters of New York business people, were meant to be living on an East Asian peninsula. Mom and Dad had been *called*, after all. So had all the other missionary families. What more evidence did I need?

I was too young to remember my family anxiously lining up for what would be the first of sixteen years of annual inoculations for typhoid fever, smallpox, cholera, and TB. I don't remember

Mom and Dad packing our shipping crates with clothes, furniture, toys, books, and a five-year supply of Tide, or the six months we lived at the progressive missionary think tank and training center known as Stony Point. I was too young to know about teary airport good-byes, our American family, or to really understand what it meant that we might belong anywhere other than Korea. But, like I said, my ancestors' names are not written into any Korean family registry.

I was born across the world from Korea in a place called Connecticut. I was the fourth and last child of a friendly young Presbyterian minister named Randy Rice and his outgoing wife named Sue. Both sides of my father's family had lived in the United States for generations, running general stores in Vermont and serving as doctors in Ransomville, New York. One side of Mom's family came from Germany, the other came from England. One of my great-grandfathers ran a shoe store in Jersey City. Another worked in the auto industry and raised his children in the Detroit suburbs. Eventually some member of each family made their way to Niagara Falls and the nearby town of Lewiston, where they made a name for themselves in insurance and real estate.

My parents grew up in homes of quality furniture, well-stocked liquor cabinets, and set meal times. Part of the same social circle, they played badminton and golf at the Niagara Falls Country Club and joined high school fraternities and sororities. They were of that world, born into it, and fundamentally shaped by it. But after they graduated from college and got married the story began to change. The ancestral ship began to veer off course, and it would take me and my brothers with it.

Mom and Dad didn't talk about finding a fine house with a big yard in a neighborhood near a good school. They wanted to help people. They wanted to go somewhere they could make a difference. For me, Lewiston, New York was always the place my parents chose to leave behind. The act of leaving was an act of breaking away. Dad gave up a guaranteed place at the successful family business to become a minister. He wasn't cut out for deal-making. In fact, he hated business work. Mom had a heart for social work. In business-oriented families like ours this was not great news. I always wondered if it might have been more acceptable had they joined the circus.

In each move further away, my parents stretched themselves. I heard the stories when I grew older, when one day I asked how it was we got to Korea. Dad told me how he and Mom moved to Pittsburgh so he could attend seminary. Their first home was a third floor walk-up apartment in a low-income area of Pittsburgh's inner city core. The house across the street from their apartment building literally had a red light shining in the window. Mom couldn't open the refrigerator door in their tiny kitchen when she got past six months of her first pregnancy, which they both found to be hilarious.

Downwardly-mobile, they moved from that cramped apartment into a housing project with a few other young, idealist seminary couples to learn about the challenges low-income people faced. They reached out to people of different social classes, races, and faiths. Dad served for a year in the department of student religious affairs at University of Michigan, working with students and alongside missionaries recently home from China, and other internationally-minded folks.

They befriended a couple from Sri Lanka and college students from Israel and Kenya. Dad grew close to a leader of the local civil rights movement in Pittsburgh. Becoming part of a faith community didn't close down my parents' world. It opened it up. I can see now that by the time South Korea became an idea they held a fundamental belief that their faith required them to feed the hungry and invite the stranger in. These weren't just words in a hymn or verses to recite at church. They really believed this was required of them.

In 1964, my parents heard Dr. Martin Luther King, Jr. speak, calling people to action in the civil rights movement. Driving home that day they agreed they needed to do something. They would make a habit out of agreeing they needed to do something. During Freedom Summer, not long after the bodies of three young civil rights workers were found in an earthen Mississippi dam, Dad traveled to Hattiesburg as a part of a major drive to educate and register voters. When seminary was over, my parents served for two years at a church in a decaying Ohio mining town. In Amsterdam they learned about the perils of small town politics and added a third boy to their growing family. After two years in Ohio, they moved to Connecticut, where my father took a ministerial position at a church in the town of Bridgeport.

During these years they wrote letters home about their new life. Dad talked cheerily about making peach pie and cooking chuck roast. He talked about each of his children, their likes and dislikes, their singular personalities. He told my grandparents about all he and Mom were learning. They wrestled with the line between Christianity and nationality, the dangers of nuclear war, and the roots of deep racial divisions in the U.S. I can tell you, after visiting Lewiston more than a few times, that these were not issues my parents were brought up to talk about from their houses high upon the Niagara escarpment. These were subject matters, in that patriotic world of social clubs and set tee times, that were not commonly discussed.

But a bigger sea change was on the horizon. Grace Choi, a woman at their Connecticut church, told them about her country. Her father, Reverend Choi Go-dok, was a prominent Presbyterian minister in Seoul. My parents watched a slide show presented by a medical missionary to South Korea. Dr. Sibley, a tall, down-to-earth surgeon trained at Dartmouth Medical School, told them about his work providing medical expertise to a country recovering slowly from a terrible war. And Mom, being Mom, saw the pictures of the rugged countryside, and the TB patients, and she thought to herself, "It looks beautiful there."

By 1966, my parents had been married for ten years. They had worked in three churches and lived in three different states. That year, with four young children to raise, they took their biggest leap of faith and signed up for a five-year term as missionaries to South Korea. By the time I was nine months old our airline tickets and passports were in hand and my short stint as a "normal" American child was over. From the moment our plane touched down on a landing strip in a green sea of rice paddy fields, nothing would or could ever be the same.

For as long as I remember I believed my parents' decision to go to Korea was rooted in a mythical idea of calling. But I don't know if I think of it as calling anymore. Calling makes it sound simple and easy. What Mom and Dad did wasn't simple or easy. They walked away from something. They broke an ancestral chain. They left behind parents, siblings, friends, a way of life, and the only country they knew.

It's a strange privilege to be able to leave comfort and stability behind. You have to be given something in life to choose to give it up. Mom and Dad never characterized walking away from their old life as a sacrifice or some great thing they did. This was the life they chose, the life they wanted to live, and it always seemed to me to be the life they were meant to live. I never heard them talk misty-eyed about what could have been. They chose to live a life they were not handed. They decided to raise their children on a peninsula of poverty and division in a far away part of the world they knew little about, because they wanted to. That was their real story. And in doing so, they irrevocably changed mine. In September of 1966 my compass point swung into a new position.

SANTOKKI

산토끼 토끼야
어디를 가느냐?
깡충깡충 뛰면서
어디를 가느냐?

Mountain bunny, bunny
Where are you going?
Bouncing, bouncing,
as you're running.
Where are you going?

A few years after we arrived in Korea, *National Geographic* published an article called "South Korea: Success Story in Asia." The country's rapid industrialization and war recovery was making record books. In 1966, the country did not quite look like a place of miracles. But of course, what a place looks like is a relative thing.

My parents looked out over the muddy banks of the Han River and watched women beat their clothes clean against rocks as their children ran along nearby sandbanks. They stood near the edge of Cheonggyecheon Stream in downtown Seoul and saw sewage spilling from the dilapidated, stilted shacks of former war refugee families from the north. Beggars with missing limbs hobbled in torn rags through city markets. Mom and Dad could better understand when they saw these people and these parts of the city, that only thirteen years had passed since someone who walked the war-torn peninsula said, "This land is the most devastated land on earth."

But the low lying city of sorrow was becoming a city of hope. Seoul was rebuilding, expanding, and improving its infrastructure. The country was emerging from years of poverty and instability. A wide boulevard led from the grand, Renaissance style City Hall to Kyung Bok Kung, the five-hundred-year-old palace of Korea's last nobles. The House of Yi was deposed by Japanese colonialists in the first decade of the 20th century, and the expansive palace grounds had long ago become a city park, making it a perfect place for family picnics alongside lotus-pond pavilions once used to host court banquets.

It would take some years before I understood that our industrious, cheerful downtown core was recently marked by cavernous shell holes and much of the city was left in ruins. I thought Admiral Yi and his turtle boat statue had been there forever, that my city had always looked like this. But Bando Hotel Arcade, busy open markets, full universities, and the well-to-do customers once again climbing the grand staircase of Shinsegae Department Store told the story of Seoul's re-emergence as much as Cheonggyecheon told the story of its recent tragedy. Growing up in Korea during this time shaped what I came to believe about almost everything. I knew something good could emerge from broken places. And I understood a place of growing peace could carry immeasurable underlying sorrow and turbulence.

We arrived in Seoul on an evening of torrential, unseasonal rains. The airport welcome of Reverend Choi and his family was an unannounced surprise that deeply touched my parents. It meant so much to Mom and Dad that people who didn't personally know them had traveled across the city to welcome us into their country. This first gesture spoke volumes about the Korean capacity to show kindness and concern. The arrival of a representative from the mission community was an expected official pickup that deeply relieved my parents. From that moment on, with these two blessings, I became something in-between. I was entering into a childhood of blurred cultural lines, and in that moment of arrival I began to unconsciously reconcile, balance, and become shaped by two different worlds.

We moved into a neighborhood of rice paddy fields, sloped hills, open markets, and corner stores. Our house was in Sodaemun, the West District of Seoul, in the shadow of Ansan, the mountain missionaries called Saddleback. Our two-story, stone home sat in a wooded area in back of the campus of Yonsei, a prominent university founded by pioneering missionaries. My brothers' foreign school was a ten minute walk away. In the morning, the steady *tak-tak-tak* of the hollow wooden *moktak* gong and the chants of early rising monks at the Buddhist temple up the hill commenced the day. The honks of buses and taxis soon joined in the chorus of a bustling neighborhood at peace, a capital city on the rise.

Mom and Dad cobbled together incoherent conversations about buying groceries and making meals with our new staff. Mrs. Kim was our maid and Mr. No was the person missionaries called the "outside man." My parents tried to figure out just where the market was, and what they might buy there without speaking any Korean. Mr. No was aghast when Dad tried to work in the yard. Mrs. Kim laughed when Mom stepped into the kitchen to cook, shooing her away. My parents had always done these things for themselves. They were industrious people who liked doing things for themselves. But there were new rules to follow, a different set of protocols to learn to live by.

Within the first few months Mom contracted dysentery from eating contaminated fruit, Chris's asthma worsened because the house was so musty, the drains clogged, and Mr. No fell asleep on security patrol. But we had a large, comfortable home, kind and patient people to help us, and an extensive community of expats and Koreans who quickly opened up their hearts to us. If only every emigrating family had it this easy.

One morning, a few weeks later, my parents walked down our driveway to the forested lane that led through campus to Yonsei's well respected language school. Rick and Chris took the same lane past college buildings and through pine trees, walking further through the campus to Seoul Foreign School, where my oldest brothers joined a tight and diverse kindergarten through high school community of missionary, business, and diplomat kids.

After my parents and big brothers left, Mrs. Kim's niece, the woman I soon called big sister, leaned over and swung me onto her back. *Onni* held me there as she pulled a thick quilt *podaegi* around both of us, wrapping me tightly in place. While my parents were away learning a new language, and my two oldest brothers were making new friends, *Onni* and Mrs. Kim carried me like they were once carried, like their mothers and grandmothers had been carried. Not from a culture of high chairs, they didn't put me down to eat. Not from a people of cribs and prams, they didn't put me down to sleep. Mom was worried I would become bow-legged. She asked Dad, after finding me in this cozy position again and again upon returning home in the afternoon, "Honey, how will Elizabeth learn to walk?"

Baby-wearing was a way to keep children close and safe while shopping in the market, washing clothes, and bending into a rice paddy. But I know I felt more than practicality to this gesture, to the way I was held close to Mrs. Kim, heartbeat to heartbeat. This practice was part of a larger sentiment that I began to unconsciously feel then, an unspoken understanding that humans needed and wanted to be physically close to the people who loved and cared for them.

My family had crossed the world, and there was insecurity in crossing from one life to the next. But I was safe and secure. I had as much loving care as any child could ask for. I was marking a cake with a B with Mom and I was asking the mountain rabbit where he was going, singing, "*Santokki, tokkiya, odirul kanunya?*"

The challenges ahead for my parents would not include putting food on the table and making ends meet. There would be a lean missionary budget to manage, and my parents almost went into debt their first year paying the school fees for Mrs. Kim and Mr. No's children. But they found this all extremely and starkly relative when they saw rag pickers sort through our garbage. They passed tents in the neighborhood below us, hovels where families somehow seemed to manage to survive and make some sort of life, even in the bitter cold of winter. They heard stories of orphan children who roamed the city after the War ended, "dust of the streets" they were called. Like the widows, the severely disabled, and the broken families, these children were collateral damage of a war of proxy, a war that changed everything.

Onni had known heartache my family did not know. One day, she told my parents a story. When North Korea attacked Seoul in 1950, she and her brother ran out of the house to find safety. In that one moment of confusion they were separated. She never saw him again. She didn't know if he was dead, if he was wounded, or if he was still alive somewhere north of the DMZ border line that separated one Korea into two.

I was too young to ask questions then, to say, "Big sister, are you still sad? Big sister, what was your brother like? How many days, weeks, months, and years did you look for him? Do you look for him still?" I was too young to understand she carried sorrow in her heart as she carried me on her back.

Mom told me that on some days, when my parents were away, Mrs. Kim took me to her home. We left by the old farmer's path, following the same trail I walked for sixteen years when I cut through Yonsei, until one day the path gave way to a large dormitory hall. Down the hill from the ivy-covered buildings, green hedges, and stone missionary homes of Yonsei, was the world of Seoul. Tile and tin roof homes met the walls of makeshift shacks. Fried fish odors and pit toilet smells, dish clanks, and thousands of years of a common way of life linked one house to the next. Young girls took turns jumping over long, stretched rubber bands. Boys stood in small circles, using the instep of their feet to pass tasseled *chegi* hacky sacks high into the air.

The low walls surrounding homes gave privacy to the *madang*, the courtyard where women washed clothes, dried red peppers in the sun, and prepared winter *kimchi* in large batches. When fall came, the women of each family turned high mounds of salted nappa cabbage heads into the spicy, fermented dish so essential to life that a woman's ability to handle the affairs of her household was said to be measured by its tastefulness.

I began to love the taste of Mrs. Kim's fermented cabbage. I walked on chubby toddler legs between the large brown crocks that lined her courtyard, squatting down next to earthenware *onggi* vessels that held the homemade condiments fundamental to Korean cooking, the condiments that soon became as much a part of me as Mrs. Kim's language did. The *kanjang* soy sauce she sprinkled onto my rice. The deep red *kochujang* paste too spicy for my baby tongue. The *toenjang* soy bean paste whose acrid odor drifted lazily through the air as it fermented outdoors, aging in thick, brown blocks on neighbors' walls.

I spent my afternoons with big brothers who were putting up tents and lighting ant hills on fire as they were learning to balance who they were before Korea with who they were becoming. Our yard buzzed with activity. The pop of Rick's air rifle. The crack of a baseball hitting Chris's leather glove. Mark's cheery chattering. The footsteps of Mr. No who tended the rose bushes, checked on the groaning furnace, and kept watch at night. I was in the middle of it all, a happy, social baby who was learning that a city was a tactile place, commuting to church was a contact sport, and shopping, cooking, and life happened in the open air. I was learning to expect hands pressed onto our backs in the thick crowds at the market and people pressed shoulder to shoulder on the city bus. I grew stout on rice gruel as I began to understand the world as a place of bus girls and street vendors, caretakers and outside men, old and new, wealth and poverty, concrete, dirt, and tile.

My parents came home one day from language school to find out I had spoken my first words, and that I had spoken them in Korean. I was acquiring Korean without effort as I acquired English without effort, like bilingual children so easily do. I was simultaneously acquiring different subject-verb-object orders and different verb conjugation systems. A transformation was underway. Mark was now *Maga*. Chris was *Curisu* and Ricky had become *Ricky*, the R turned into more of an L sound. Dad was my *appa* and Mom was *oma*. I was Elizabeth and *Lidgie*. We were still us, but we were becoming another us.

When November came, Mom traveled across the city to East Gate Market. She meandered through what seemed to her to be an endless number of stalls and floor levels to find a traditional first birthday *hanbok* for her baby girl, a style of dress with roots two thousand years old. With Korea's high infant mortality rates, a child reaching the age of one hundred days, let alone one year, was worthy of great celebration. The arms of my green *chogori* top were banded with bright colors of yellow, pink, purple, green, and red. Intricate embroidery of pheasants, chrysanthemums, and Chinese characters adorned the silk top and red *chima* skirt.

My parents had not come to Korea to stick to their own customs. They wanted to celebrate my birthday in the local way. They knew the importance of the birthday dress, but they had only heard a bit about the ceremony that should take place. They saw photos of ornately dressed children sitting in front of a low table full of seasonal fruits and stacks of colorful rice cakes. Various other items were placed on the table. A spool of thread, a paint brush, a pencil, a book, money, and a pair of scissors. They understood something about the family gathering to see which item the child reached for or picked up first, and that people believed this gesture foretold their child's future.

If the baby chose the stack of *won* bills, she would be wealthy. If she picked up a pencil, she would be a successful scholar. If she picked up the thread and needle, she would live a long life. Instead of choosing an item of destiny that day, I dug my fingers into pink chiffon birthday cake. My first birthday was some balance of who I was by birth and ancestry and who I was becoming because of my parents' answer to a call. Somewhere between ancient Confucian rites and Betty Crocker.

I learned many things that year I don't remember learning. A children's song about a mountain rabbit. Words of a language that would never sound foreign to me. That a person's life trajectory could be determined by reaching out for a thread instead of a pencil. The ways of women who held me close to their body-warmth as they made my family's first year in Korea possible. People we remained close to after we left that home. People who became dear to us within months, who we talked about for years. People we still talk about. Mr. No. Onni. Mrs. Kim.

I always understood I was a *miguksaram*. I knew I was not ethnically Korean. The children of Seoul, the ones I did not know, reminded me of this each day for sixteen years with their calls. "*Miguksaram! Miguksaram!*" they shouted, day in and day out. *Miguksaram* was merely a rank in my taxonomic category. Kingdom: Animalia. Phylum: Chordata. Species: Miguksaram.

We weren't immigrants. My parents didn't cross the seas for economic opportunity. We weren't refugees, forced away from our home country by war, famine, or persecution. We would never apply for Korean citizenship. Every time we arrived to Kimpo Airport we were asked, *What is the purpose of your visit? How long will you be staying?* We were officially foreigners. I was technically an alien.

We didn't have family to the north of the militarized border that separated one Korea into two. Mom didn't keep our ketchup and mayonnaise in earthen crocks, nor had my grandparents lived through a terrible war on their soil. My ancestors weren't buried under the sloped green mounds that dotted our hillsides, the ancient cemeteries that captured my heart. Only now do I see something ambiguous to our landing, an in-between place I would always occupy. But these distinctions didn't matter to me then.

From the moment my life in Korea started, one thousand things began to separate me from the people of my bloodline and the country of my passport. My umbilical cord of identity stretched out to the city and the people in front of me. To a young Korean woman I called older sister. To an American-Korean man named Horace Underwood. To a mountain we called Saddleback. To a wide river to our south that had witnessed centuries of change.

Closing one life door had opened up another. I was becoming part of a new family, not bound by blood or nationality, but created out of calling and circumstance, and the simple fact of what happens when a little girl's parents decide to make a home in a new land.

Nothing about that life or my identity felt particularly remarkable until I came to the U.S. Nothing about my place in-between cultures and communities, between fundamentally different ways of understanding the world, seemed like something I needed to reconcile until the day we left Korea behind. I only look back now and try to analyze this time, to pick it apart, to understand the people and places that were forming me, to remember the ways of those who were teaching me how to greet and grieve.

That September, as I began to hear the refrains of Korea, as I began to understand the words of my parents and the words of Mrs. Kim, I began to understand the world in some patchwork way, like a *pojagi* cloth with pieces of fabric that didn't seem to belong together, but somehow, when laid one next to the other, made a whole. Days and then months passed in Korea. Months, then years passed away from the U.S. The country of my passport, the home of my ancestors lay far over the horizon.

"*Arirang, Arirang,*" Koreans sang in melodic voices from picnic sites to national halls, calling the refrain of a national song of love and loss thousands of years old, "There, over there that mountain is Paektu Mountain, Where, even in the middle of winter days, flowers bloom." And these melodies, their haunting highs and lows, their cadence of joy and sorrow, and the people who sang them, began to take over my heart.

THE VAN LIEROP'S HOUSE

I was sixteen when I first lived in a house my parents owned. In the world of missions, houses were practicalities that came with assignments. Missionaries somehow managed to imprint firmly onto these places, making the possession of a deed seem so nonessential to feeling ownership of a place. The Kinslers and the Spencers, the Moffetts and Underwoods, and all of the many missionary families lived in Korea, and in these houses, as if they had lived there forever. Some of them had.

We lived in the Van Lierop's house while their family was away on furlough. That they would one day return was very clear as their belongings were stored in a locked second floor bedroom. We called it "the Van Lierop's House" while we lived in it and we called it that long after their family left Korea. A family name could be associated with a house forever, and a house left empty was fair game for the mission to loan out. Leave your house too long and somebody could very well be cooking in your kitchen and sleeping in your bed. Over the years, many families circulated through that drafty and wonderful old place. Years after the Van Lierops left Korea we would say, "Oh, the Ritchies are moving into the Van Lierop's house?"

We were entering into a world of mission tradition. We were joining our lives with so-called *oegukin* people, foreigners who had made a choice to leave the lives they were expected to live, and were living a life where expressions like "calling" and "God's will for your life" underpinned everything. While a number of these *oegukin* people had only lived in Korea for a few years, many of them had lived on the peninsula for decades. The word "foreigner" said nothing about how long someone had lived in Korea. Korea was no melting pot. This was no salad bowl. Although Seoul had its foreigner neighborhoods, the city was nothing like Niagara Falls, with its Italian, Polish, and African-American neighborhoods. Korean? Check yes or no. Anyone who looked "western" was called a *miguksaram*. I was an American baby coming of age in a nation of firm bloodlines and uncompromising homogeneity. But some missionaries were the third generation in their family to call Korea home, and they stopped by to offer welcome greetings and give my parents much-needed advice about grocery shopping and nearby services.

For my oldest brother, Rick, there was a new boundlessness to life. There were open hills, rice paddies, and dense neighborhoods to explore. He watched in fascination as people carried buckets of water home from city wells. He wrinkled his nose at the odor of sewage and fish. Seoul was like no place he had ever known. His new international school boasted a Quonset hut gymnasium made of galvanized steel, a soccer field, sports teams, and students and teachers from all over the world. His world had burst wide open. But he felt isolated and frustrated. He didn't speak the language of his new neighborhood playmates, the ones who came running to the house each day eager for his company. His small school and his foreign face made him feel like he was living in a fish bowl.

Each of my siblings, by the fate of our ages, carried some measure of the influence of the U.S., some balance of genetics and time spent in two countries. Who we were by personality would be shaped by the decisions my parents were beginning to make about how they wanted us to live in the world, and how they wanted us to live in Korea.

In the spring, sweet, chatty, tow-headed Maga left our communal nest. He took his four-year-old courage, held onto Mr. No's hand, and walked down the hill to Ewha Kindergarten. He was immersed into a school and with children whose language he did not speak, but would one day, in a few month's time, draw forth as if it was his native tongue. I know I missed Mark at home. He was good to me, patiently helping me put on my winter jacket, holding my hand as I learned to walk through the garden.

Sending an American boy to a Korean kindergarten was enough of an anomaly that it warranted an article in *The Korea Times*. The reporter said Mark beamed when asked about his school. They asked my parents how they felt. Mom's answer spoke volumes. "Mrs. Rice feels that he will 'gather much strength through being the minority for once.'" Mom believed a good life challenge could harden one's resolve. I guess Mark had it really easy in those first three years of his life.

The design of our borrowed home spoke to the way many missionaries lived in Korea. The bedrooms didn't have the traditional warm *ondol* floors found in almost every Korean home. The large living and dining room were designed for couches and stuffed chairs, furniture made for sitting off the floor, more appropriate to my birth place of Connecticut, perhaps, than Seoul. Our kitchen boasted a full-sized American range, but since it was fueled by kerosene, it blew up now and then, sending billows of black smoke throughout the house and blackening the walls.

After decades of use, these homes tended be a bit worse for wear with cracked plaster walls, not enough ventilation to combat the intense humidity of summer, and not enough insulation to stay warm in the cold of winter. But they were by and large comfortable places, and extravagantly-sized compared to most Korean homes. When Chris and I were visiting Korea a few years ago, we were talking about the missionary houses of Yonsei with a friend who went to the university some time after our family left Korea. Our friend remarked, "I always wondered who lived in those big houses behind campus." Chris and I laughed and said, "We did!"

I never thought much about what it took to make all of this mission life happen. In order to outfit a home for western-style living these household furnishings, American appliances, faucets, sinks, radiators, and door knobs, had to be shipped to Korea from the U.S. I am trying to imagine the long and complicated journey the radiators and porcelain sinks must have taken to get to the mission compounds in the early 1900s. In his book, *Living Dangerously in Korea,* Donald Clark described what it took to have a piece of toast for breakfast in the early to mid part of the 20th century. The toast, he said, was "made with bread from home-ground Korean wheat flour, baked in a Japanese oven, toasted in an American toaster, and spread with Australian butter and English marmalade."

Mom loved to shop the local market, where seasons determined what was available. Summer brought large Concord grapes (*podo*), green watermelons (*subak*), sweet peaches (*poksunga*), and the yellow-skinned, white fruit with an acquired taste known as *chamoe* which Chris once described, very accurately I felt, as a cross between a melon and a potato. Fall brought crunchy pears (*pae*), red apples (*sagwa*), and dark orange persimmons (*kam*). By late fall, *paechu* (nappa cabbages) were piled everywhere, tangerines were being harvested in the semi-tropics of Cheju Island, and everyone's winter *kimchi* was made and ready to store in the ground to last through the cold season. Late spring brought strawberries (*ttalgi*), various greens, and the bracken fern shoots known as *kosari*.

Namdaemun Market was the most fun place to shop, with thousands of tiny stalls and various levels of kitchen implements, foodstuffs, clothing, backpacks, shoes, and enough signage, bicycles, motorcycles, and people for a medium-sized city packed into a market with a footprint of about fifteen acres. The over five-hundred-year-old market was named for and situated next to South Gate, one of nine gates that once gave entrance into the old walled-in city of Seoul. Since the narrow market roads were not accessible to cars, goods were transported in and out by bicycle, *chigae*, and motorcycle. No price was set in stone, and bargaining was expected. In Seoul, shops of one type were often grouped together, so if you wanted souvenirs, you went to the souvenir district. If you wanted books, or pharmaceuticals, or human hair wigs, you would go to the neighborhood selling just those particular goods. Namdaemun was one of the places you could find a little bit of everything.

Since Koreans didn't distinguish breakfast food from lunch and dinner, and because my family was not prepared to dive into salty soup and rice before noon, Mom found relief from the few "German Bakeries," the middle-class shops selling respectable pastries and loaves of pre-sliced fresh bread. One store downtown sold import foods legally. I remember walking the aisles with Mom when I grew older. It was my first time in an indoor market in Korea. The red and white cans of Campbell's Soup, the boxes of Frosted Flakes, and the spaghetti noodles left me wide-eyed in wonder. I hoped Mom would accept the exorbitant pricing that priced many missionary families right out the door.

Mom learned from a few missionaries that we could acquire by "other means" some of the food my family missed. Each week, the man we lovingly called Meat Man Kim arrived on his bicycle to deliver red hamburger meat and long blocks of processed American cheese. Before I was old enough to understand the vast network of U.S. soldiers and various Korean middle men that made up Seoul's extensive black market of PX goods, I probed Mom as to how Meat Man Kim could buy this food when we couldn't. One day I asked her, in naive innocence, "Mom, where does Meat Man Kim buy the American cheese?"

She paused for a minute before she answered. "He bought it on the gray market, honey."

This was Mom's nice way of saying they were "illegal."

On weekends, Dad carried me on his shoulders to explore our neighborhood. In Sinchon, cozy *tabang* tea rooms sat next to cold noodle shops. Glass cutting stores shared walls with beauty parlors. Artificial limbs were displayed in store windows like fine goods for sale. Men, and sometimes oxen, pulled every possible cargo, from produce to empty oil drums to sacks of rice. Pedestrians weaved between bicycles, buses, taxis, and a moderate number of privately owned cars. Motorcycles jumped the curb to avoid traffic. Taxis made new lanes. Traffic laws were merely suggestive. People walked aggressively, trained from an early age to navigate thick crowds.

Market men carried impossible loads on a *chigae*, the wood and rope A-frame carrier that had served Korean farmers and merchants for generations. Women balanced large bundles on their heads as they carried babies on their backs. Office workers in western dress fought their way onto over-packed, lurching city buses, with young bus girls there to help push them in. Aged grandfathers sauntered narrow neighborhood lanes in loose, traditional white clothing, their hands clasped behind straight backs. Entrepreneurs appeared magically upon the arrival of heavy rains, lining up on city streets within minutes to sell disposable blue plastic umbrellas. Flat, puffed rice cakes came popping out of antiquated metal machines and silkworm larvae steamed in large tubs.

At the open market, makeshift tables were piled high with watermelons, crunchy red apples from Taegu City, and stacks of dried squid. Eggs were packaged in woven straw. Bicycles transported whole pigs and blocks of dripping ice through narrow market alleyways. Live sea creatures swam and squirmed in colorful plastic pans. Slabs of unrefrigerated meat hung from metal hooks. Pig heads were laid out unceremoniously in long rows on tables, staring blankly into the wet marketplace. Market ladies cooked cylindrical cigar-shaped rolls of doughy rice in a thick and spicy dark red sauce. No surface was left unused. When my father returned home from his first visit to the market, he came in the door and said, "Sue, don't go down there yet."

This was not Tops Market. These were not the tree-lined streets of Lewiston with their large oak trees and clearly displayed names, like Forest Road and Woodland Drive. With no street names, no reliable addresses to speak of, learning to navigate Seoul was calling for a new set of skills. Address numbers were given out chronologically, if they existed at all, so building 6 could be next to building 234. For my parents, there were districts to learn (*ku*), neighborhoods (*dong*), and provinces (*do*). As important as the dongs and kus were, it was just as important to distinguish one small alleyway from the next, to recognize one particular corner store from another.

Small, hand-drawn maps appeared in newspaper ads and on business cards, showing major markers, arrows pointing down this alley and up that street, the distance in meters to an unnamed road that led to the store or restaurant one hoped to find. Mom learned that a one block error in judgment could cause an afternoon of wandering. And my parents did wander. And they got lost. And they made language mistakes. And they went to the market with what little Korean they knew. And they started to make a life.

In 1968, attesting both to the rigor of Yonsei University's two-year language program, and to my father's determination to do things right, Dad won second place in a televised Korean speech contest. He later told me, in a hilarious and uncharacteristically catty way, that he would have won if it weren't for the brown nosey way the first place winner wore a traditional *hanbok* for his speech. Mom was one of a few "mission wives" to finish the full two years of language school. This was no small feat.

The U.S. Defense Language Institute classifies Korean, alongside Arabic, Chinese, and Japanese, as a Category 4 language, meaning sixty-three weeks of instruction are required to bring an English-speaking student to a "limited working level of proficiency in which she or he has sufficient capability to meet routine demands and limited job requirements." As a comparison, languages such as Spanish, French, and Italian are given twenty-five weeks.

My parents found it relatively easy to learn the phonetic lines and circles that made up the alphabet, and then sound out words on street signs and in the bulletin of Reverend Choi's church. Although Mrs. Choi did once catch Dad holding the church bulletin upside down. Though aspirated, Korean is not tonal. Learning a phonemic alphabet was easier than trying to decipher Chinese characters, although my parents had to learn hundreds of these, too, as they were still commonly used in newspapers, on train and bus schedules, and really everywhere.

Some sounds and aspirations required my parents to move their mouths and tongues in new ways. The alphabet was grouped into syllabic clusters, so what looked like a single character, like the word 한—(han) was actually made of up three letters, ㅎ (h), ㅏ(ah), and ㄴ (n). Seven levels of speech hierarchy reflected the formality of a situation and the relationship of speaker to listener. They ranged from *panmal*, "half-speech," used for children or between close friends, to the highest form, used for kings and queens. Eager not to offend, my parents bargained for socks in the language of nobles and spoke to children as if they were peers. Korean language used two separate counting systems, one for items and age, the other for dates, money, addresses, and more. For telling time, one system was used for the hour, the other for minutes.

One day, my parents were in the living room practicing Korean. They made a cassette tape of their conversation. The dialogue quickly dissolved into a ten minute argument about how to pronounce the phrase *"myot siyeyo"*—what time is it? The argument unsettled, they moved on. A year later they played the tape back and howled with laughter. Neither one of them was close to pronouncing the phrase correctly. One expat lady described her first experience trying to learn Korean thusly: "I just finished some thirty weeks of Korean language study—an experience during which I learned a great deal—even some Korean."

Words for family relationships reflected the importance of ranking in Korea's highly stratified society, a culture considered more Confucian than China, where these prescribed traditions came from. *Onni* was the older sister of a girl. *Nuna* was the older sister of a boy. The word changed again to refer to younger siblings. Adult first names were rarely used in public. Titles were critical. Dad was now called *moksanim*, honored minister. Mom, who had worked for ten years not to be defined by her role as "the minister's wife" in Dad's various church positions, was now called *samonim*, the honored wife of the honored minister.

People they met bowed to them. They bowed back, varying the depth of the bow according to the person's age and status. Social hierarchy was ingrained into the Korean psyche. Older men of position sauntered through the city with a stride of unhurried importance, walking in the knowledge of their firm place in society as a *yangban*—a member of the aristocratic scholarly class, a title given to them by birth. When Korean friends asked, "How old are you," or asked my father's Lunar Zodiac year, they did so not only out of curiosity, but to determine who was the oldest in the group.

I can't tell you that some of these ways felt like they were mine and some felt like they were not mine. It is all so much more complicated than that. I have bowed to people and I have loved *kimchi* for as long as I can remember. I never knew my father apart from his title of *Moksanim*. I don't recall a time I did not need sticky rice on a regular basis, nor do I recall a life without grilled cheese sandwiches and brownies, without a mother who made sesame glass noodles and a Korean maid who made apple pie. I also don't know why, within a few years, I found the odor of soy bean paste stew challenging to my early morning senses. Or why, two decades later, I craved that same stew in the morning as if my survival depended on eating it.

What I do know is that I was coming to understand the world from one of the most homogeneous and hierarchical cultures in the world, with one of the few peoples who could trace their continuous history on the same land going back thousands of years.

And what was strange and new to my parents in these customs, in this history, in this language, in this food, was the particular lens through which I began to look at the world.

THE WAR THAT
NEVER ENDED

If there ever was a house that could capture my identity, our red brick, east meets west home might have been it. Like the Van Lierop's house, the dining and living areas in our second house were laid out to accommodate couches and high dining tables. But the sliding rice paper doors that divided the living area from the bedrooms represented an important Korean delineation between public and private spaces. A large entryway was designated for shoe storage, a critical space in a country in which shoes were never worn inside the home. The bedrooms were made for sleeping on the floor.

To understand life in a traditional Korean home, one had to understand *ondol*. For centuries, heated underfloor passageways made the floor central to living, a place for sleeping, eating, gathering, and study. Because we were living in a modern home, the flame that warmed our floors during winter months was lit by oil, not by wood or rice paddy straw, as they were in rural homes. Nor were they heated by *yonton*, the ubiquitous, efficiently burning, paint-can-shaped coal briquettes citizens had turned to en masse during the meager years after the war, when much of the wood supply was depleted, accounting for South Korea's many treeless mountains.

A crack in an *ondol* floor could mean danger. An unsuspecting slumberer could be asphyxiated by carbon monoxide during the night without knowing it, and never wake up. Mom had a close call with *ondol* when she spent the night in an old mountaintop house in Pusan. She and my father had traveled south so Dad could perform the marriage ceremony for a friend. The owner of the house, worried her foreign visitor would be cold, shut the windows tight at night. Mom woke in the morning with an excruciating headache, and she was very sick for a couple of days.

If the sliding doors and *ondol*-floored bedrooms in our home were a sure sign we were living in Korea, the delicately balanced chrysanthemum arrangement on our dining room table was a testament to Mom's love of the arts and her penchant towards keeping up simultaneous hobbies. Mom was learning all she could about Korea. In the vast market halls above street level at Namdaemun we walked past stall after packed stall of traditional dresses of fine silk and multi-colored bolts of fabric stacked to the ceiling. She always took her time in the market. She talked with store-owners, felt the slick fabric of bright red and blue cushion covers, and asked about the intricate embroidery of phoenixes and dragons. She loved the practical patchwork beauty of *pojagi*, the square-hemmed cloth used by rich and by poor to carry, wrap, and store pretty much anything.

Mom's brush painting teacher, honored *Harabonim*, was famous in our family. He was so legendary that even though I was too young to remember him, I feel like I remember him. My family loved his traditional, old world presence in our home. Each week, he sauntered up the hill in a high horsehair hat, traditional white pants gathered at the ankles, and a deep green silk vest over a long-sleeved white shirt. After the proper greetings and bows were exchanged, he entered into the living room and laid out thin rice paper on the table, methodically dipping his horsehair brush into dark black ink to demonstrate the prescribed stroke of the plum blossom and bamboo shoot.

Harabonim once happened to come to our house on Halloween Day. Chris was dressed as Abraham Lincoln, wearing a foot high black hat made out of craft paper and a fake beard. Rick was dressed as Huck Finn, wearing short pants held up with suspenders, and holding a pipe in his mouth. Mark had an orange paper pumpkin over his head. I had my Korean dress on. One of Rick's friends asked, "Is *haraboji* dressed up for Halloween?" Everyone was confused. Mom had no idea how to begin to explain Halloween, so everyone posed for a picture together, a family classic.

Mom loved the arts and fine crafts of Korea. She loved to explore the old artists' neighborhood of Insadong, where homes once owned by bureaucrats and government officials had become side alley tea shops and stores selling horsehair brushes, antique lacquer chests, and stacks of rice paper. But she hadn't come all the way to Korea to serve as den mother to the Boy Scouts, take taekwondo classes, and brush paint. She was irritated the mission technically hired only my father, and my parents and other young missionary couples jokingly called their employment a "two-for-one deal." But Mom and Dad hadn't moved to South Korea for the salary, either. One doesn't become a missionary for the hefty paycheck.

Soon she began volunteering with a few Yonsei professors' wives at an organization for young women caught up in Seoul's many prostitution rings. She was beginning to do the social work that would come to define her, the work that would teach her, and thus me, about the tragic side of life for women in Korea. By 1968, Mom and Dad had worked hard to learn the language, navigate streets, and understand Korean customs. The reality was, we were two years into our life in Korea and they had barely scratched the surface.

In January, my parents heard unsettling news. A band of thirty-one North Korean guerrillas had infiltrated Seoul in an attempt to assassinate President Park and throw the country into chaos. They cut through a fence in an area of the DMZ defended by U.S. forces. During the cold of winter, they passed quietly along mountain passes and crawled through valley farmlands, carefully removing land mines along the way.

After three days, disguised in South Korean soldier uniforms and trained to speak in Seoul accents, they marched through a few military checkpoints into Seoul. They made it within a few hundred yards of the Blue House, the president's residence, which was much closer than one might imagine was possible given the size of South Korea's police force and its astounding level of military strength.

Close to the heart of the country's seat of power, they were con-
fronted by a suspicious district police chief. A firefight broke out
and the fighting spilled into the streets of downtown Seoul. One
grenade hit a crowded public bus. A school bus was reportedly
caught up in another crossfire, killing the women and children
aboard. A few men were said to be on the run in our neighborhood mountains. Three days later, a U.S. Navy intelligence vessel,
the USS Pueblo, was intercepted by a North Korean patrol vessel
in international waters. One U.S. soldier was killed and four were
seriously injured. After a firefight, its crew was taken prisoner.
South Korea was on high alert.

Mom called the U.S. Embassy to see what they advised. They
told her that if evacuation became necessary we should go downtown, to the embassy, to be airlifted from Seoul. Mom thought
downtown, with its important buildings and president's house
that was just nearly infiltrated, was about the worst place to be in
an emergency. Later that week she drove down the hill to run an
errand. As she reached the valley road, a soldier approached her
car and pointed a machine gun at her, pushing the barrel through
the window. Irate, he yelled at her in crude *panmal*, "Go home!"
When she told me the story a few years ago she seemed more upset
about his use of informal language than the machine gun in her
face. "It was so rude he talked to me like that."

My parents felt some comfort knowing we were living next to
the foreign school and close to people from the expat community.
Many of them had lived in Korea through times of great insecurity. But if war was to break out again, the families who worked
for us, like Mr. and Mrs. Lee, the caretakers of our second home,
had no choice but to run as far as they could only to be stopped by
national boundaries. We had a chance of getting to Japan, as some
missionaries had during the outbreak of the Korean War.

But it was much more complicated than just fleeing Seoul. We
lived on a narrow peninsula. Only a few bridges spanned the wide

river to the south. As anyone who lived through the Korean War knew, fleeing Seoul was like running sand through an hourglass. My parents felt great responsibility for the people in their employment, the people who took care of me during the day and kept our house in good order. They decided that if something did happen, we would evacuate with everybody.

Dad and Jerry Nash, our new neighbor and family friend, investigated back roads to find alternate ways out of the city. They found out the roads led to narrow alleys that led further in, dead-ending in dirt lanes and residential areas up in Seoul's hills. They built a wooden box to carry supplies on top of our Land Rover. Their carefully laid evacuation plan was to escape Seoul in one jeep with four Nashes, six Rices, and Mr. and Mrs. Lee and their two children, making fourteen people in all. Thankfully, for many reasons, we never had to employ that plan.

Over that week, some thirty South Koreans died. All but two guerrillas were killed in various skirmishes around the city. One man escaped back to North Korea, and one was captured. When asked about the mission, he said, "We came here to cut President Park Chung-hee's throat." The immediate danger of both incidents passed. In fact, the immediate danger of more than one hundred and eighty separate DMZ incidents passed that year. As they had long ago learned to do, the people of Seoul moved on with life. It was my family's first lesson in learning to do the same.

These early incidents, and the rumors my parents were hearing about growing demonstrations on college campuses all over the city, were their first lessons in the insecurity of that border, the tenuous state of South Korean democracy, and the reality of what people meant when they said, "The Korean War never ended." Dad never forgot seeing Onni's face drop when she heard the news of the infiltration. She knew too well what another war could mean for the people who lived on the Korean peninsula.

PUK AHYON-DONG

L ooking back, I can see why we loved our second Seoul house so much. We loved the view of Yonhi-dong's rustic, open hills. The convenience of living across the field from my brothers' school in a city that could be difficult to navigate could not be underestimated. In spite of the presence of the busy school and the many missionary homes and teachers' apartments surrounding us, there was a feeling of peace and quiet above the bustle of the valley road. SFS events and sports activities provided my family with a rich international community. Yonhi-dong was a friendly, residential neighborhood with plenty of shops and services. For my parents, there was just one problem with the house. It wasn't in a Korean neighborhood. Mom and Dad were restless people. They loved our expat community, they loved our new home, but they hadn't come to Korea to live like they had in the U.S.

My parents' approach to mission work was informed not only by their years crossing racial and socio-economic lines in Pittsburgh and Ohio, but also by the six months they spent at Stony Point Center, an arm of the Presbyterian Church Board of Foreign Missions. Stony Point served as an intensive training center for missionaries going into the world. It became known for its strong critique of historical ties of missions to colonialism. Stony Point later focused on the protection of human rights around the world, with many residents refugees who had fled violence and persecution for doing human rights work in their communities of origin. At Stony Point my parents were encouraged to integrate into their new communities and work with local people as peers. What they learned at Stony Point was, in part, what led us to move into our third home.

When I was three years old, my parents sold our couch, dining chairs, dining table, and western style beds, and replaced them with floor cushions, *yo* mattresses, thick *ibul* covers, and a low Korean dining table. We moved out of our nice house near the foreign school, against the wishes and better judgment of a number of long-term missionaries, who warned my parents of the risk of contracting diseases and feelings of isolation away from the expat community. After many months of long and difficult negotiations with mission elders, with my parents' hearts set on integrating into the community, we moved southeast to rent a house in a neighborhood called Puk Ahyon-dong.

One day, not long after we moved in, Rick and Dad watched as the family who lived across the street moved a western-style couch into their house. Rick was quiet for a minute, and then he said, "Dad, why can't we live like that?"

Rick knew about manses and temporary homes. He knew about moving across the world to answer a call and sitting on the floor for the sake of principle. One summer, while Dad was completing a ministerial internship in Pennsylvania, Rick lived with Mom and Dad in a choir loft cordoned off with curtains. Rick had lived in three different states and six different houses by the age of eleven. I'm not sure how happy he was about the move to Puk Ahyon-dong.

By all accounts, like our move to Korea, the move was seamless for me. Life can be uncomplicated when one is three years old and is not lacking for safety, security, and love. Toddlers have a way of not paying attention to national distinctions or moves. And, since little children usually befriend others not based on social class or nationality, my neighborhood welcoming committee was comprised of two siblings who lived in a shack down the road with their single father. Their circumstances, the loss of their mother, the paltry condition of their home, was the consequence of war. Without hesitation they welcomed me, a Korean-speaking *miguksaram* into their *konggi* jacks circle, where I learned to throw, scoop, and catch little lead-filled plastic balls with great skill.

At Nungan Nursery School down the road I called the butterfly to come fly with me, singing, *"Nabiya, nabiya!"* I formed my little hands into rock, paper, and scissors with new friends, calling out, *"Kawi! Bawi! Bo!"* I napped, made crafts and new friends, and learned to be an obedient, collectively-minded citizen.

My first life memory is set in this home. I'm sitting at a low dining table. The table is centered in a large room. My brothers are seated at the table, too. We're eating dinner on our own because our parents are out of the house for some reason, maybe for a meeting. Rick starts a food fight. Then Chris and Mark join in. It all feels very unsupervised. But I know Poe-bae's mother is in the kitchen, and I know that in spite of Rick's frequent shenanigans, we will be safe. In the moment I feel slightly anxious, like I'm not used to my parents being away at night, or I'm not used to eating alone with my brothers. In fact, my family was hardly ever alone.

Mrs. Kim was our new maid. She and her daughter, Poe-bae, lived with us during the week, and they ate and slept in a room just off the kitchen. While my brothers left for Seoul Foreign School in the morning with a few schoolbooks under their arms, Poe-bae's uniform and large middle-school briefcase made it look like she was headed to the office. Each night, after finishing dinner with my family in our living/dining room, I pattered over to Mrs. Kim and Poe-bae's room to eat a second dinner with them, which I believe accounted for my ample tummy girth and cemented my need for white rice and *kimchi* on a regular basis.

Not long after we arrived in Korea, my parents hired a woman to help our first Mrs. Kim with cleaning and laundry. The lady we called Cho-ssi was a sturdy washerwoman who lived by the rhythm of hard work. My parents never knew the circumstances of her husband's death or why she never had children. With three hundred thousand women widowed after the Korean War, her tragic situation was not uncommon.

My parents were surprised when Reverend Choi and his wife told them one day, after a few weeks of calling her "Cho-ssi," as if it was very polite thing to do, that this title was not that polite after all. They explained that the honorific "*ssi*" used with a last name could be considered discourteous. But Cho-ssi wouldn't have anything to do with a name change to Mrs. Cho, so she remained Cho-ssi and there were countless rules concerning titles and hierarchy for my parents to sort through.

Cho-ssi worked with so much vigor she broke a dish once a week. To clean the bathroom, she heaved water at the wall out of a plastic pan, in the same way our neighborhood storekeepers splashed water on the ground in front of their stores to clean and settle the dust and grime of Seoul city. That strategy worked well until we moved into a home that had a bathroom without tile walls, and Mom had to explain to Cho-ssi why she should not splash water on plaster.

Cho-ssi got down low to the floor to clean the sealed rice paper surface, swiftly squat-walking from room to room in her workaday skirt without rising up. It is easy, when remembering Cho-ssi, to understand how South Korea one day remade itself through the hard work of its people. Cho-ssi taught my family words we only realized years later came with a deep southern accent, after an amused waitress pointed this out to us in a Korean restaurant in New York City. We kept asking, "Really? It's *myolchi*? Not everyone pronounces dried anchovies as *maeduchi*? Really?"

Cho-ssi spoke frankly and openly. She didn't have the quiet reserve of someone like Choi Samonim, Reverend Choi's wife. But she also wasn't one to sit down and have a long chat like Ajumoni later would. Her work seemed more important to her than her social interactions. But she stopped to play badminton with me. She took time out of her workday to walk me, hand in hand, through our garden of forsythia and rose of Sharon bushes.

I loved her expressive country ways and her open heart. I loved the way her pitch varied when she talked, the way her *chogi* transformed into a deep and rough *chhhhooogi* to distinguish if a place was over there or waaay over there. Although Korea is a relatively small country, regional accents were quite varied. We had difficulty understanding some words spoken by people from nearby Taegu, let alone from the southern province of Kwang Ju, where Cho-ssi was from.

Cho-ssi was a Christian who believed in *kwisin*, restless spirits who had died a wrongful death. She mixed her traditional Korean shaman beliefs and her adherence to Confucian ancestor worship with her belief in *Yesunim*, Jesus. Like the people who went to Christian church each Sunday but still called the *mudang* shaman healer to their home when a family member grew sick. Like those who called themselves Methodists and Presbyterians who faithfully traveled to their hometown each fall to bow at the graves of their ancestors.

One day Cho-ssi spoke to my father in serious tones. "*Moksanim*," she said as she always began, addressing him by his formal title of minister, "because you are a minister, this house is not haunted."

Mom heard a rumor our house in Puk Ahyon-dong was a former dance hall. Needless to say, this was not equated with good house energy. But Cho-ssi was right. Our house had good energy. The *chi* flowed even when the water didn't, which was most of the day. It flowed even when the large four-foot-deep Japanese tub, the one that looked so luxurious to Mom at first, couldn't be filled more than a few inches with lukewarm water. The chi flowed even when winter came, and Mom watched Mrs. Kim light a flame torch, crouch down, and place it into the kitchen firebox so its heat could pass into the underfloor flues. This did not seem that safe to Mom. Our house may have had a good chance to set on fire. But those floors were toasty warm and the chi was flowing.

Long after we left Puk Ahyon-dong my family would call from passing buses and taxis, "There's the road to our old house!" We loved that house and neighborhood, with its steep, narrow road, mish-mash of poor and middle-class homes, local kindergartens, and corner stores.

My parents arrived to Korea with no actual work assignment. What they ended up doing was determined as much by their social nature as by their degrees, and as much by their desire to understand the complexity and nuance of Korean politics and society as it was by their best-laid plans. In fact, it seemed like the only aspect of my parents' lives not governed by strict mission protocol and a list of complex regulations was, strangely, their work assignment. This led me to believe that adults all over the world had flexible work schedules and careers, like entrepreneurs who owned their own company.

After two years of language school was over, Mom and Dad were invited by an older dean to teach English and start an ecumenical Christian group at Kyung Hee University. Their work started when a man showed up at our door and asked, "Rice Moksanim, would you and Samonim like to work at our school?" In Korea, personnel was personal.

My parents began daily one-hour bus treks across the city to Kyung Hee. Many Koreans saw the English language as a means towards helping the country advance and prosper, and my parents' students were, in large part, eager to learn. Soon, the members of the newly formed Christian group, the Hummingbirds, began to meet at our house. Then Mom and Dad started taking people in. One day, Mr. Pak was not just the nice student who came to meetings, but the nice student at the breakfast table trying to figure out what to do with the fried egg and bland piece of toast in front of him, and wondering where the soy bean paste soup had gone. One night, after Mr. Pak went to sleep, Rick played a cassette tape of his voice saying, "Mister Paaaaaak . . . Mister Paaaaaak," in ghostly tones.

Mom and Dad's work at Kyung Hee University had an unforeseen effect that would have far-reaching consequences. By working with college-aged people early on, they were spending time with the group who had the most freedom to protest. Since high school students were under their parents' and school's strict control, they had little time to demonstrate. Beyond college, people were under pressure to find work and start a family. College students had a bit of freedom, and they took many risks over the years for democracy. The student movement in Korea had a long history, with many college campuses serving as centers for anti-government activism.

One day, Dad watched from his classroom window as army tanks rolled onto campus. The next week he witnessed a violent street protest involving students and police. A few students told him President Park and his party were trying to amend the constitution to allow him to run for a third term. They were angry about the brutal police response to protest. A number of them expressed anti-American sentiments. "Why," they asked Dad, "isn't the U.S. government doing anything? Doesn't the U.S. believe in democracy?"

On another day my parents passed an active demonstration at the front gate of Yonsei. They were shocked to see a USAID logo imprinted onto the side of the riot police tanks. They learned that under its aid program, the U.S. was supplying riot control material, such as tear gas and vehicles, to the Korean army. My parents joined the "Group of 50," a loose organization of foreigners concerned about what they were hearing. The group drafted a response to President Park's constitutional amendment. They drew up a petition calling on the U.S. Government to withdraw its support for Park. They drew attention to the USAID logos. Several members met with the U.S. ambassador.

Others traveled to Kimpo Airport to approach Vice President Hubert Humphrey when he arrived for a state visit. Holding me in his arms, in a move that seems hardly believable in today's high security atmosphere, Dad and his colleagues walked out onto the tarmac to greet Humphrey as he de-boarded the plane at Kimpo. In a photo taken that day, the U.S. vice president holds me, laughing, having just been approached by a group of *concerned expats*. My parents' mission work was merging into two categories: official and unofficial.

Thin lines of distinction separated my parents' work life from our home life. I think this is what they wanted in moving overseas. I think this was the life they were seeking. I was carried out to airports to speak with U.S. officials. I roamed freely in and out of house meetings. I sat on the laps of college students, and clapped along with high school students from Toksu Church who came to study the Bible while they practiced English. I was a missionary kid of social activist parents in a collectivist country. I was stifled by fellowship and overwhelmed by a lack of privacy. And I loved it. I was growing to understand work as life and life as work, and as far as I knew, everything was meant to blend together. I had no reason to believe this cross-cultural, communal, and highly purposeful way of living in the world was different from how most people lived. I thought ours was a very normal life. And perhaps it was.

Mom and Dad were always chatting with store owners, taxi drivers, and umbrella sellers. They were genuinely curious about almost anyone who crossed our path. Dad went into ministry because he wanted to work with people. He was good at it. He made everyone, from the youngest to the oldest, feel seen and heard. He made me feel seen and heard. Mom went into social work for similar reasons, but she was more of a compassionate, solution-oriented networker with a heart for justice. Both of them were wired to connect deeply to their community. They didn't just want to gather with people. They weren't just social. They sought *fellowship*. They didn't just invite people over for dinner. They had *gatherings*. Meetings broke into small groups. Throw out twenty cushions, buy a few jugs of purple grape juice, cut a tray of fruit, and call it a meeting. Ministers and missionaries, and by proxy, their children, are often steeping in fellowship. A friend of the family who is married to a minister once said, "Liz, we're circus people." I was four years old, coming of age in a Korean-style, western-influenced fellowship center on a hilly neighborhood in western Seoul.

On one hand, my parents' social nature was not all that surprising. My grandparents were active members of their community. They served on hospital boards, attended Country Club gatherings, and kept up memberships in various regional clubs. But my grandparents were social people who needed *privacy*. Social people who were happy to have doors to close at the end of the day. People who needed a *reasonable amount* of togetherness. A Korean friend once told me the closest equivalent to the concept of privacy in Korean meant something negative, more akin to exclusion or seclusion, which explained a lot about Korea.

The level and type of fellowship in our home was best expressed in the number and variety of shoes in the entryway. Irish Nuns, my parents' classmates from language school, celebrated St. Patrick's Day with us. Their sensible walking shoes were made of leather good enough to last, but not so good as to seem extravagant. Reverend Choi's shoes were made of fine leather, elegantly styled for a man of his *yangban* and *moksa* status. Missionary families, the Strawns and the Nashes, spent long afternoons with us, their shoes practical and comfortable, big and little, made for feet getting used to miles of walking, in a city in which a private car ride was more rare than a bus trip or a long stroll.

We went on outings with college student groups and enjoyed after church lunches with the Choi family in fancy downtown restaurants. We gathered formally and informally with missionaries of all denominations. We took trips outside of Seoul to visit the Nashes, our family friends, when they moved north to minister to U.S. soldiers stationed at an army base. One weekend, we embarked on what turned out to be an epic ten-hour picnic with friends from Toksu Church. The trip included a jostling, rambling, three-hour journey to the site, during which Dad saw a sign that read, "DMZ – Keep Out." All of these relationships, varied piles of shoes, and picnic excursions had evolved naturally by moving to Korea.

I was in my forties when I first learned our two years in Puk Ahyon-dong were not easy for my parents. I was skipping down the road with playmates and playing badminton with Cho-ssi, but the chi was not always flowing for Mom and Dad. After we moved in, our next door neighbor became angry at them. Rick was lobbing fruit and rocks onto her sons in the house below us, playing out skirmishes that had begun on the main road. Mark told me that one day Rick stood up on our courtyard wall and threw *Monopoly* money into the air like confetti, shouting, "Cash! Cash!" while children came running. Although my parents were beginning to speak Korean well, they were still far from fluency.

If only we would have explained to our neighbors that Rick was an equal opportunity pest. One day, when he was three years old, Rick locked Mom out of the house when she went outside to hang laundry, then giggled with delight as she tried in vain to get back in. He jabbed and prodded Chris for years. I think the teachers of Ewha Kindergarten would have run screaming down the road if they had seen, instead of sweet *Maga*, a four year-old version of Rick coming in the door with his devilish grin, looking for a way to upset the *sagwa* cart.

But there was more to the neighborhood trouble than Rick's mischievous nature. He wasn't doing well in school. He struggled to learn Korean. The neighborhood boys annoyed him. My parents learned that not everyone in the neighborhood was cheering our arrival. Compound life didn't take people out of Korea, but it did put up more walls. In Puk Ahyon-dong, those walls came tumbling down. My parents learned that moving across the world or even across the city can be difficult. They learned that sometimes children don't want to move because of integration or calling or any other reason, really. There would be hard lessons ahead about what can happen to children when a family crosses national and cultural lines. But by persisting, by simply deciding to stick it out, my parents also found out that children can find a way to work things out, suspicious neighbors can become friends, and a friendly chat with the man who runs the corner store down the street can be the best part of a long day.

The two years in Puk Ahyon-dong solidified something in me at a deeper level. Something Onni and Mrs. Kim had started. I learned to bow to people who came into our home. I learned houses could hold restless spirits and shoes were for outside. I learned a distinct rhythm of entering in and leaving a house, the cadence of shuffling slippers on a rice paper floor, the easy steps of a rubber-shoed walk through a courtyard. I was learning American ways in Korea and I was learning Korean ways in our American home.

When Korean friends came over I beheld a cultural dance choreographed long ago. Our guests paused at the front door to remove their shoes. They moved inward, then paused again before fully entering in. They stat down on the floor, but they didn't move quickly. They crossed their legs carefully onto a floor cushion and, once settled, sat up straight. When my parents offered food or drink, they refused the offer three times, and then said yes. Mom carried a plate of carefully cut apple and pear slices from the kitchen. Our guests thanked her as they lifted a small fork, stabbed an apple wedge, moved it to their mouth, and then crunched the well-selected fruit. These gestures and rites of belonging were as instinctual to the people around me as breathing.

What happened in our home when non-Korean friends came over was a different dance, choreographed in places far away, the movements adapted to a new country. My parents called friends by their first names, even older friends. They didn't bow to one another. These friends leaned back against the wall after dinner was finished, casually stretching their numb legs out in front of them as they laughed and talked freely. But then many of them broke into perfect Korean when needed. And Mom was Sue, and Dad was Randy, and another night Dad was *Moksanim* and Mom was *Lidgie omoni,* and I was learning to shift, to adjust, to understand how to eat fruit, talk, what to call people, and how to sit, whether Reverend Choi was with us or Helen Nash was there.

Maybe I was learning to love Korea because of the way my parents were choosing to live there. Or maybe this is just what we do as children, no matter who our parents are or why we find ourselves in a place. We send out roots. We set our compass point. We look around us, and if we are secure and loved, and maybe even if we are insecure and unloved, we grow attached to places. We begin to love the stores and the fruit and the people right in front of us. And in doing this, we become who we are. It doesn't do any good to tell a child, "All of this doesn't really belong to you." It doesn't do any good to say, "You are from somewhere else." This was the country my parents had chosen for me. This was my home.

I don't think it was just these trappings, these ways we lived at home and who we spent time with that made a difference in how I began to feel about my identity and how I began to understand the world. But they mattered. It matters how we live in a house, in a city, in a country, and in the world. It matters that we stop everything to take our shoes off at the door or that we don't. It matters that we sit on the floor, close to the earth, or up off the ground. It matters how we learn to eat, how we learn to greet people, how we gather with them, and how we learn to depart from them. It matters who comes to our door and who enters in. It all matters.

What I grew to believe during these years about my family and myself was based on a mythology. I thought we had always been in Korea. I thought we were home. I intellectually knew we came from somewhere else, but I didn't feel it to be so. I believed not only that my family loved Korea, but that we *belonged* there. I saw us as part of Korea, like the yellow forsythia that bloomed in our courtyard. Like Puk Ahyon-dong. Like Cho-ssi.

I felt magic when each person came in through our gate, sat around our low dining table, and sang in our living room. I felt the joy of human fellowship in those floor-cushion gatherings and endless countryside picnics, the sense I had even at the age of two, and three, and four, that people wanted to be close to one another and spend time together.

There is a particular body warmth created while sitting knee to knee in a floor circle. There is an intimacy to sitting around in stocking feet. I was growing up in a world of washerwomen and shared purpose, blurred cultural lines and unexpected loyalties.

When I think of our two years in Puk Ahyon-dong, when I try and measure the influence of that time and place and weigh the impact of my parents' choice to cross cultural lines and go against the wishes of a strict mission protocol, I am left with a strong image that has nothing to do with heavy topics like integration and acculturation.

A woman rings the bell. She ducks her head and passes in through our front gate, allowing the high stack of egg cartons balanced on her head unhindered passage. She walks confidently through the courtyard on strong, thin legs, and settles herself in the entryway. I'm happy to see her because her arrival is always special, even though she comes to us on a weekly basis for a most ordinary task.

We called her *Kyeran Ajumoni*, the Egg Lady, and she had delivered eggs to us since we first moved to Korea. She would do so until the week we left, years later. She somehow knew when we moved, and where we moved to, never missing a week between. I almost expected her to show up at our house in the U.S. when we went there on furlough, believing in the Egg Lady's resolve to deliver eggs to us no matter where we were. Believing in her perseverance and her strong legs, knowing they could take her across continents to feed her family if need be.

When the Egg Lady reached the entryway, she let out a sigh and lowered her load to the floor with a laugh and words of greeting. She squatted down, untied a large *pojagi* cloth, and removed the top level of eggs to the floor. She greeted Mom and began a gossip session with Mrs. Kim. After some talk, after enough stories were exchanged, she passed over the eggs and received the *won* bills passed to her, tucking them into her long workaday skirt, into a hidden pouch carrying her hopes and dreams. And while there was no hurry in her movements, there was determination in her steps as she left us to deliver eggs to another foreigner's home, and then another, until her eggs were gone.

The Egg Lady was just one of so many people of industry and hope who formed my little circle of life in Puk Ahyon-dong. Another widow showing me what stubborn perseverance looked like. A woman who laughed freely, even though, I presume, had shed many tears. Kyeran Ajumoni and Cho-ssi, Puk Ahyon-dong and Nungan Kindergarten were teaching me I was part of a complex web of human frailty and strength, part of a human family who needed one another, and part of a humble peninsula of egg ladies and washerwoman that felt to me like the center of the world.

WEEPING UPON PLACES

*"The lesson to draw from this, of course,
is that when you move from one country to another,
you have to accept that there are some things that are better
and some things that are worse,
and there is nothing you can do about it."*

— BILL BRYSON, *I'M A STRANGER HERE MYSELF*

"In the year 1782, while I lay in barracks at Tin mouth in the north of England, a recruit who had lately joined the regiment was returned in sick list. He had only been a few months a soldier; was young, handsome, and well-made for the service; but a melancholy hung over his countenance, and wanness preyed on his cheeks. He complained of a universal weakness, but no fixed pain; a noise in his ears, and giddiness of his head . . . As there were little obvious symptoms of fever, I did not well know what to make of the case.

Some weeks passed with little alteration, excepting that he was evidently become more meager. He scarcely took any nourishment. He became indolent. He was put on a course of strengthening medicine. All proved ineffectual. He had now been in the hospital three months, and was quite emaciated, and like one in the last stage of consumption. On making my morning visit, and inquiring, as usual, of his rest at the nurse, she happened to mention the strong notions he had got in his head, she said, of home, and of his friends. What he was able to speak was constantly on this topic. This I had never heard of before. He had talked in the same style, it seems, less or more, ever since he came into the hospital.

I went immediately up to him, and introduced the subject; and from the alacrity with which he resumed it I found it a theme which much affected him. He asked me, with earnestness, if I would let him go home. I pointed out to him how unfit he was, from his weakness to undertake such a journey till once he was better; but promised him, assuredly, without farther hesitation, that as soon as he was able he should have six weeks to go home. He revived at the very thought of it. His appetite soon mended; and I saw in less than a week, evident signs of recovery."

—ROBERT HAMILTON
"History of a remarkable case of nostalgia affecting a native of Wales and occurring in Britain."
Edinburgh Medical Communications.

Seattle, 1995

My homesickness had turned into an illness. I was living under a heavy fog of grief. Almost ten years had passed since I had seen Ajumoni. Ten years had passed since I set my feet on Korean soil.

I walked past blooming rhododendron bushes, and under the dense green foliage of linden trees. The florae of the Northwest was beautiful, but I was longing to see bamboo groves. I wanted to walk through gnarled pine trees. On a quest for some semblance of home, I made my way to the Japanese Garden.

As I neared the gate, I noticed two women squat-walking along a grassy median, harvesting a roadside plant. Compared to the orderly, minimalist garden I was about to enter, with its obsessively-raked gravel grounds and geometrically arranged rocks, the movements of these women were coarse and practical. I recognized the way they talked as they pulled at the plants, the way they cut swiftly across the roots. I knew each shift of weight, each bodily adjustment.

Engrossed in their task, they didn't notice me. What was there to notice? I didn't wear my history on my face. But I was drawn to them with the weight of a heavy magnet. I approached and greeted them, and asked them if they were Korean. They looked up, the sun blinding their eyes, confused to see a *miguksaram* speaking their language in a Seattle park.

"*Ottoke hangukmal arayo?*" They asked, their eyes big with wonder. How do you know Korean?

In Korean, I begin the explanation I had perfected from explaining my story so often. "I lived in South Korea for sixteen years, from 1966 to 1982. My family went to Korea when I was nine months old. My parents were missionaries. My mom was a social worker and my dad was a minister."

"*Ah, kuraeyo?*" Is that right? The younger woman replied. "*Hangukmal chalhaeyo!*" You speak Korean well! Koreans give language compliments easily. I knew not to be overly flattered.

"I don't speak very well," I replied in the modest way you're supposed to reply to this statement. Besides, it was true. A furlough at the age of five and years of international school after that took away my easy kindergarten fluency. But I could get by.

I squatted down with them and we continued to chat. I joined in, helping them harvest plants as we moved across the grass. I didn't know the name of the plant, but I suspected I had eaten it as a side dish garnished with sesame oil and sesame seeds in one of Korea's mountain towns, where people ate every green, nut, and bracken that could be eaten without harm.

They told me they were mother and daughter. They had lived in the U.S. for less than five years. When they said this, I immediately imagined the scene at Kimpo Airport the day they left Korea. I imagined the loved ones they had likely left behind, parents, siblings, maybe aunts and uncles, too. Did their shoulders shake with grief that day? Did their family pat at their arms and pull at them, saying, "Don't go?" Or was there relief in their departure? Then I thought of my own leave-taking from Korea, how I didn't know I needed to grieve, how I didn't understand what leaving meant.

I told them my *kohyang*, my hometown, was Seoul. They giggled when I said this, because *kohyang* is a very Korean concept. It's funny for a Korean who doesn't know me to hear *kohyang* come out of my mouth in relationship to Korea. *Kohyang* isn't just the place one is born and raised. It's the place where the bodies and the spirits of revered ancestors reside. When a Korean person leaves their hometown, they are considered to be leaving their ancestors behind.

I told them more about my time in Korea—our neighborhood, the location of my international school. They nodded knowingly. My old neighborhood is a well-known area of the city.

"Ah, you lived in the West District," the younger woman said.

Subarus and Volkswagens passed us as I handed plants to the younger woman. She took the greens from me and stuffed them cheerily into a plastic bag with the others, then quickly cut more with the dexterity of culling for a lifetime. I was longing for my tongue, for my body, to move in a Korean way. I was longing to have a conversation with any Korean. I ached for the Korean part of me to be seen, to emerge from inside of me where she sat alone, with a homesick heart. For just a brief moment, with two complete strangers, I was back in my own skin.

I wanted to tell them the first language that came from my tongue was theirs. I wanted to explain my bond to them, to say I woke up to life on the same streets they did, shopped from the same stationery stores, and grew up under the same divided sky. But I knew this was impossible to explain. And so, after a few more minutes, I began to rise up. I had already stayed too long and my squatting skills were rusty.

I couldn't make this moment last forever. I couldn't expect these women, or the proprietors of the Korean grocery store, or the waitress at the Korean restaurant across the city, to understand the grief I carried inside of me for their country, my country. I couldn't offer everything up to these strangers. My sorrow was not theirs to take or to carry.

I spoke a proper Korean good-bye. I told them I was so happy to meet them. As I began to leave, I heard the mother say something to her daughter.

"What did she say?" I asked.

The younger of the two replied in simple English. "She says she thinks you are lonely."

The words fell like a heavy stone.

I entered the garden and sat on a wooden bench that overlooked a quiet pond. A few koi fish jumped to the surface, breaking the calm of the water below me. The world was still and quiet. Everything was moving slowly. A stranger, if they had passed, would have noticed nothing out of ordinary about a woman sitting on a bench in a Seattle park. But I was broken in two. Thirty years had passed since my parents first set their feet upon Korean soil and carried me into my Korean childhood. And I was still weeping upon that place.

FURLOUGH

Korean Missionary Comes Home

By VIRGINIA HOWARD
Gazette Correspondent

BACK FROM KOREA — The Rev. Ransom Rice Jr. of Youngstown, and his family recently returned after four years in Korea where the Rev. Mr. Rice served as a pastor at a university, left, daughter Elizabeth, a son, Christopher; Mr. and Mrs. Rice and son Ricky. Elizabeth and her mother are wearing native Korean garments. Another son, Mark, 8, was not home

My big brothers are excited. They are marching around the house, chanting, "We are going to the States! We are going to the States!" Because we receive a box of Christmas presents from our thoughtful relatives each year, I know the States is the place where the best toys and candies come from. I know going to the States means we're getting on a plane and traveling for a long time, Mom and Dad will give us Dramamine for the flight, and we will see our grandparents. I trust in my big brothers. I follow their lead. I'm excited because they are excited, and so I march around the house announcing, to whomever is within hearing distance, "I'm going to the States to see my grandparents!"

I had no idea what "the States" was. The nearby countries of Japan and China felt far away. Because of heavy rains, bad roads, and overflowing streams, it once took us twelve hours to drive to our vacation cottage at Taechon Beach, less than one hundred miles from Seoul. The DMZ was thirty miles from us and it felt a world away. A country seven thousand miles from me was pretty much on another planet.

To place a phone call to the U.S., Dad traveled across town to the telephone office to set up an appointed time to make the call. When the time came, we gathered in the living room around our black rotary phone, whispering in hushed tones as we watched Dad dial a long series of numbers. Making an international call was a momentous occasion, worthy of appointment-making and gasps.

On a good day, the connection traveled through the thick phone cord and entered into the wall. Outside the house, a phone line weaved through an impossibly-tangled web of lines just above the streets of Puk Ahyon-dong. At some point, the line left our neighborhood, traveled through the city and then the country-side, and reached the shoreline. It then left the peninsula, running underneath the sea towards the American continent. Once the dialing ended, we waited in anticipation for the cheery, somehow American-sounding, "bring-bring!" and then hopefully the crack-ling "Hello?" of a grandparent's voice.

While making an international call was exciting, trying to carry on a decent conversation was hopeless. Mom swore she could hear the sloshing of waves while she talked. Every sentence spoken and every sound made echoed back to us. From an early age, I became much too aware of the sound of my laugh. Until I was five, the cable that ran under the ocean and that inelegant conversation was my tie to the U.S.A., a long umbilical cord to people and a life we had left behind.

If making an international phone call and going to Seoul Station to take the train was exciting, going to Kimpo Airport was like entering a space portal to another dimension. Planes took off there! People flew to exotic lands! A trip to Kimpo for Koreans often meant they were emigrating, or leaving for a very long time. An arrival often meant a person was returning after years away. This simple fact made Kimpo into a hall of hopes and dreams, a terminal of great joy and great sorrow.

Groups of family members of all ages arrived dressed in their fin-est clothing. They gathered in masses around departing and arriv-ing loved ones. Not really comfortable huggers, their sadness or elation was more often expressed through vigorous arm tugs, wails of *aigo*, and falling tears quickly wiped away with cloth handker-chiefs. For me, Kimpo had its own excitement and its own emo-tional toll. If everything went smoothly, I would wake up on the other side of the world. It was called furlough. For missionary kids, furlough came every four to five years and it meant life was going to turn upside down, unravel, and reveal itself in new and puzzling ways.

I'm not sure how long it was after we arrived in the U.S. for our first furlough that we drove to my grandparents' house, but what happened there formed my first memory of my passport country. At the threshold of Ransom and Viola Rice's home, in the open, shoeless entryway of their lovely white colonial along Forest Road, I did what I had always done. I took my shoes off at the door. Nothing extraordinary, really. Yet this instinctive gesture launched my grandfather into a fit of laughter from which it took him a minute to recover.

For a few seconds time passed slowly, as if I was suspended in place and time. I was ageless, five and fifty. I was thinking, with the wisdom of fifty years, how strange it was that my grandfather thought this was funny. Then I began to feel the self-consciousness of a five-year-old. I had done something wrong. Ill-fitting. Out of step. I was embarrassed. Without saying a word, I slowly put my shoes back on, taking care to do so very quietly. I never made that mistake again. In a way, that experience set the tone for the year.

A week later, I stopped speaking Korean. I refused to speak it for the rest of the year. I defiantly told my parents I didn't need to speak Korean. To children, a language is not a hobby to prac-tice here or there. Bilingual children generally know when to use which language, with whom to use the language, and when the language is no longer useful. In Lewiston, New York, Korean was not useful. My parents later reminded me of this, like it had really bothered them. "You spoke Korean so well, Lizzy! You and Mark used to translate for us in Puk Ahyon-dong. When we went to the States you refused to speak it!" When they said this I felt like I lost something I could never get back. During that year, Korean became my second language, and I would never speak it so easily again. Furlough had so many unforeseen consequences.

A couple of months later, or so it seems, because a child's mem-ory comes in bits and pieces, I walked into the lobby of a large brick school. I felt like I was watching myself from above. The lobby seemed to stretch out the further I went in. Dad's cousin, Velma, was a teacher at the school, and she led me in that first day. I remember holding her hand tightly and staying closely to her side. I liked Velma. She was funny, and she laughed a lot like we did. Although I didn't know her well, I was getting to know her, and she was the only familiar person to me in that place. Beyond that large lobby I remember nothing else about that school or anyone in it.

After those two vivid memories I just remember being in the U.S., as if we had been there for awhile. It wasn't not home and it wasn't home. It was the U.S. I was still with Dad and Mom, Rick, Chris, and Mark. I was still playing Candyland, so in a way, I was okay and everything was the same. But then again, nothing was the same at all.

"Korean Missionary Comes Home" was the title of the story in the *Niagara Gazette*, the newspaper serving the area. In the photo accompanying the article, five of the six of us are sitting on the couch of our newly rented ranch home in Youngstown, in a neighborhood of houses originally built for plant workers. Mom and I are wearing *hanbok* dresses. Except for Mom, no one is smiling. Not only are we not smiling, we have the somber faces of traditional Korean family portraits. I don't think it's an exaggeration to say that Rick, Chris and I look morose. My family laughed all the time. We were prone to start giggling during funerals and otherwise somber affairs. Mom was the worst, her shoulders shaking at the slightest provocation or absurdity, the risk of a belly laugh so close.

Maybe I was sad because I had just lost a game of *Candyland*. Or maybe it was because I had just graduated from Nungan Kindergarten and I wasn't around my classmates anymore, or because we had just said good-bye to Cho-ssi and Poe-bae and now I was sitting on a couch in a ranch house in Youngstown, New York and a lady I didn't know was taking a picture of me.

The earth's atmosphere and a fourteen-hour flight was never an adequate acclimation zone between Korea and the U.S. I was too recently running streets hazy with bus exhaust and teeming with life. I had just left a house with an open flame that lit up the kitchen and warmed the floor as the floor warmed my body and my heart. I stepped away from that cozy, high-sensory life of fellowship, with Cho-ssi in the courtyard and Poe-bae coming home from school, and stepped into a postcard of colonial homes, relatives I did not know, privacy, and clear escarpment vistas. My last name was painted on signs that hung from downtown office buildings. Our family homes sat high up on the escarpment. My relatives lived lives many people might aspire to. Niagara Falls was just down the road. Does anything say American grandeur quite like Niagara Falls? Could any town or life contrast more to industrializing, developing Seoul than Lewiston did?

In my parents' hometown, a wide, well-paved road led from a quaint, quintessentially American main street, called Main Street, up to Lewiston Heights, where the air blew fresh and clean. I loved Seoul with all my heart, but after a few visits to Lewiston even my beloved Yonhi-dong began to look a little overrun in comparison. Lewiston Heights was the neighborhood where my grandparents lived. Most of my aunts, uncles, and cousins lived in Lewiston and Niagara Falls, too. It appeared everyone but the six of us lived in the U.S. But I couldn't figure out which seemed stranger—staying in the same place forever or moving thousands of miles away.

"That's where Aunt Mary grew up, Lizzy." Dad said as we drove past a large, dark brick, two-story home. "Her father was a doctor. That's Uncle Short and Auntie Babe's house. This is your great grandmother's old place."

I looked out of the car window and saw a large white Victorian house set on a double corner lot. It was twice as big as any home I had ever seen. When Dad told us our great-grandmother had servants, this sounded different than Cho-ssi worrying about restless spirits as she vigorously cleaned tables with a damp rag. We drove to the nearby city of Niagara Falls, where my parents pointed out more family property.

"That's where Vi lived before she met Rans. There's Rice Insurance, Lizzy."

Then Mom stopped the car in front of a charming two-story brick house. "This is the house where we lived until I turned sixteen," she said as she wiped a small tear away. "Bumpa designed it. I loved that house."

She said that every time we passed her old house on Deveaux Street. It seemed like my parents loved their hometown. In many ways it seemed like they cherished their childhoods. Who wouldn't?

On Sundays, we rode in our well-maintained, borrowed car along the wide Niagara River. We passed the Yacht Club where Uncle Jim and our cousins sailed. We passed more large homes with even more expansive lawns. I smelled no odors except for the smell of freshly cut grass. No one was cooking food or selling anything along the streets. No taxis or buses were on these roads, only other well-maintained private cars that traveled at designated speeds to enclosed supermarkets and church services that began, and ended, spot on time.

White-steepled First Presbyterian Church came with ancestral history and an efficient and quiet furnace humming quietly somewhere far from view. During cold winter months, it was hard not to think about how chilly everyone probably was at Toksu Church, where I once was so cold I melted my parka from sitting too close to the large, central coal stove, causing a strange chemical odor to spread through the worshipful sanctuary.

Both grandparents' houses smelled of some magical mix of port wine, gin, and historical books. Hard-back tomes about the history of Niagara Falls lined den shelves. Majestic, well-framed prints of Niagara Falls adorned the walls, each offering a different view of the Falls, Devil's Hole, or Goat Island. I was fascinated by my relatives and their homes and lives. Not around them enough to make them real, I made them out to be larger than life, like characters in a movie.

My graceful, white-haired grandmother, Vi, felt familiar to me, like she was a part of me and I was a part of her, as if she carried the easy warmth of Poe-bae's mother, Dad's nostalgic heart, and Cho-ssi's ready laughter. Vi kept toys for her grandchildren in a corner living room cabinet. I was happy to sit in that corner for hours, spellbound by the antique stereoscope viewer and the black and white photographic cards showing scenes of 1940s Americans visiting the Falls. These were scenes as exotic as the ones in the pages of *National Geographic*.

My grandfather, Rans, was gregariously gruff. He was a popular man, a pillar of his community. He was all chin-up and don't air your dirty laundry. He was an unfamiliar type of person to me in the emotional and physical distance he kept, even in his moments of friendliness. I could not reach across the distance that stood between us.

Mimi and Bumpa, Mom's parents, called us the "Korean grandchildren." Their two-story, white and gray home had a perfect view of the Country Club's 14th green. Their large, stately, living room was not a place to run and play, but a space to sit quietly and watch adults sip tea from matching cups and saucers. I preferred the casual comfort of the large den, where every surface was covered with Mimi's collection of green glass banker's lamps, hand-forged copper pots, and old cameras. Mimi's abstract oil paintings, Bumpa's hilarious understated quips, and his basement darkroom were clues to the eccentric, non-conventional side to the Belden family.

That year we turned many times down Forest Road and up Fort Gray Drive. We passed acres of green grass, large trees, stone mansions, and more relatives' homes. And I knew that in some way, what I was seeing through the window was a part of me. We passed the neatly raked sand pits of the club, and I knew that those sand pits and long greenways were in some way a part of me, too. These well-groomed neighborhoods, the sweeping view of the Niagara Gorge, and even the quiet power of the hulking hydroelectric station was my birthright. The United States was a place of freedom, ingenuity, and possibility. I loved that view. I loved those beautiful old homes. But it almost felt too big to take in. I felt small in that universe. I was unsure and unsteady. I was an outsider looking in.

I did not ask, "Mom and Dad, what made you leave this life?" But the question lay just underneath the surface of each interaction. My relatives' lives had nothing to do with mission work. My grandparents valued success in business, American patriotism, community service, and good citizenship. For the most part, the Beldens and the Rices lived in the same houses, along the same circles, got the same haircuts, and shopped at the same department stores, year after year. It was as if my parents had chosen a life not only different from, but the opposite of how they had been raised. They had walked away from something significant. And by doing that, they had fundamentally and irrevocably changed my life.

That year my parents spoke at churches to raise support for and awareness of their work. My brothers and I slid into pews and doodled in church bulletins like the professionals we were. We whispered inside jokes as parishioners looked at us with nice smiles as if we had done something *interesting*. We were the family who lived in the *Orient*. Sometimes our family picture was on the church bulletin board with a pin and a string pointing from us to Korea. My brothers and I found it so funny that somebody deemed our life bulletin board-worthy.

One day, before speaking at a local church, Dad donned a traditional *hanbok* to add a bit of dramatic flourish to his presentation and teach people about Korean customs. The outfit included *paji*, the roomy white pants that gathered at the ankle, *chogori*, the wide-armed top that tied in front, and *komusin*, white rubber shoes. As Dad descended the stairs my grandfather took a long, blank look at him and said, "Well, what do we have here?"

Mom spoke to a women's group about her work with single mothers and the difficult life of Seoul's factory workers. At the close of the session a lady raised her hand and asked, "Did you have electricity in your home?" Years later, Mom told me Mimi said she was proud of her that day. Mimi wasn't easy. Mimi didn't understand why we were in Korea. It meant a lot to Mom that Mimi said that.

As a child, and even as a teenager, I didn't often think about what had made my parents leave their hometown and then, ten years later, leave their country. Of course we were living in Korea. Where else would we be? I couldn't imagine for one minute Dad negotiating an insurance deal or picture Mom spending her days playing bridge with the Tatler ladies. But when Dad came down the stairs in a *hanbok* that day, the irrationality of what they had done from the viewpoint of Lewiston was stark and clear. In Lewiston, it seemed that faith in God was integral to life, but something to hold close to the heart. It was certainly not something to announce from the mountain top or get all crazy about and have it lead you to another continent.

Lewiston may have felt removed from what Mom and Dad had become. But it was still a fundamental part of who they were. I could picture my parents growing up in Niagara Falls and Lewiston. They hadn't left thirty plus years of life behind them in their move overseas. I could easily see Mom running along Deveaux Street and "playing tourist" with her friends at the Falls, the same friends she kept in touch with forever. I could picture Dad running through the "second woods" with his Rice cousins. Lewiston explained Mom's love of matching tea sets and her insistence we dine at a table free of soda cans and Tupperware. Lewiston explained the great joy Dad took in eating liverwurst sandwiches slathered with Nance's mustard. The U.S. explained Dad's easy going, egalitarian manner, Mom's belief in women's equality, and her love of peanut butter. While enjoying a meaty lasagna in a corner booth of the cozy, dimly lit restaurant called The Coat of Arms, I begin to understand why my family loved Seoul's La Cantina Restaurant so much.

I loved the things that made Mom and Dad who they were. I loved their skill at white short sports like tennis and badminton. I loved the pleasure they took in a long canoe ride on an Adirondack lake, how skillfully Dad raked a yard, how breezily Mom skied down the rustic, snowy slopes outside of Seoul. I loved how they passed the joy of those things on to us. But I knew my parents more for who they had become than for who they once were.

When I saw them sitting across the dinner table at the Country Club, I thought of them sitting at our low table in Puk Ahyon-dong. When I saw them standing next to my smartly dressed grandparents, I thought of them sitting on floor cushions with our missionary friends. Dad was a great golfer, but it seemed funny when he took a swing, like he was being someone he wasn't anymore, like he had left that Randy behind.

Other than public talks, my parents didn't talk about Korea with our family. Lewiston was not generally a place to have long, intimate talks with people. There was little context for dramatic life change, except perhaps in explaining a mission to strangers. My parents were too thoughtful to complicate a nice lunch at the Red Coach Inn with talk of human rights abuses and the plight of single mothers. I think Mom felt bad turning the nice missionary talk at the church, the one expected to be about Bible work, into a talk about politics and Korean student demonstrations for democracy.

I think my parents understood the futility of trying to make people understand our life, or to understand why they wanted to return to Korea. But there was something in the silence that spoke volumes to me. It seemed like anything uncomfortable or difficult shouldn't be given too much air time. Like race problems. Or single mothers. Or serious illness. Or questioning the actions of your own country. Strangely, I think there was something about us living in Korea that fell into that category.

Not talking about Korea made me feel like my grandparents wanted us to put Korea behind us, as if living in the States was what mattered. As if we had been "somewhere very interesting, dear" but now it was time to get back to real life. It made me wonder if my grandparents thought Mom and Dad had done something wrong in taking us to South Korea.

In one way, I shared so much with my relatives. My easy laughter came from them. My love of the arts, the outdoors, picnics, camping, eating good food, drinking good drinks, and canoeing on clear lakes came from them. But in other, fundamental ways, our lives were so different.

It would take years for me to feel comfortable in my parents' hometown, for me to feel a connection to my relatives and not just what made me different from them. I had to accept I got the names of the local stores wrong or misquoted one of Bumpa's famous quips. I'm still not one hundred percent sure the custard stand is called Hubbard's or Hibbard's. We can't make a place a home. We can't force a feeling of belonging. We can't make a national anthem stir our heart. We aren't close to people just because they are related to us. We have to earn these things. We have to build relationships and ties piece by piece, moment by moment. Belonging is not just a matter of genetics and passports. Belonging takes time.

It was Sunny and Dwight Strawn who cheered me on as I first crawled across their warm floor. Mrs. Kim was there the day I took my first steps. It was John Sibley, family friend and rural doctor, who gave Mom needed advice when I held a fever for too long. It was the Chois of Toksu Church who met us at the airport, making the long trip across the city just to welcome us into their country. Who kindly saw my parents through the hurdles of acculturation, and said to them, on our first Christmas far away from family, "Yes, we will join you for dinner. That would make us very happy." This is how people become family.

My relatives were always there for us in the way they could be. Over the years, they sent us much-needed items from the U.S. They helped us out during furlough. They did so many things for my parents in those years that I never knew they were doing concerning bank accounts and furniture storage, finding rental houses and acquiring the temporary use of a car when needed.

Decades later, I sat with my aunt in the kitchen of her three story Tudor home. I looked around at the family portraits and the framed Niagara Falls prints. I caught the whiff of old hard-backed books and the bottle of port in the liquor cabinet. And I knew I had an attachment to those people and places, too. I had come to a place where I could appreciate what I shared with my relatives instead of only feeling what made us different. I laughed with my cousins about family idiosyncrasies, our Rice heads held back in easy laughter, our Belden hands holding our stomachs. I grew to understand how similar we were in some fundamental ways, no matter where we lived, and that what was different about us would just always be so.

I took the time to visit my grandparents' graves whenever I could, to thank them for instilling in my parents some unique and life-changing mix of curiosity, kindness, and life spirit that had taken us to Korea. And I learned to accept I would never get some things back. I never knew my grandparents like a granddaughter should.

In the late 1960s, each set of grandparents came to visit us in Seoul. Their feet fell on Korean soil with mine. Rans looked up at the brightly-colored eaves of the long halls of Kyung Bok Palace. He saw our home on the hill and our foreign school, and he saw that we were healthy and happy. And I think he realized, in some way, that we were home. I think he understood in a small way on that trip, in a way he could not understand before, why his son had chosen this place so far away, this life so different from his.

My dear grandmother, Viola, held me in Korea. She ran barefoot in our campground river, walked arm in arm with our college student friends, and looked out across the rustic, open hills that formed the backdrop of my childhood. And I like to think that in some way she found comfort in that view, too, like she found in the escarpment views of Lewiston Heights. At least for these moments, my two opposing worlds, so distant from one another in miles and in spirit, came together. This will always mean something to me. For when we choose one life we have to let go of another. After we left Lewiston that year, I never saw my grandmother again.

On one January evening, two years later, a feeling of sadness hung in the living room air. It was not a normal feeling in our normally cheerful Yonhi-dong home. The moment stood out like only few can in a childhood, clear and vivid. Dad asked us to gather together. My brothers and I looked at one another nervously through awkward grins. What was going on?

Dad told us, quietly and carefully, that our grandmother had passed away. I was confused and unsettled by the news. I knew my father was with Vi a few months before. I thought she was doing better, that her breast cancer was being treated successfully. But now she was gone.

I was too young to fully understand death, but I knew in that moment that our connection to the U.S., usually so tenuous, was real. It was a stark reminder of who we were and where we came from. We didn't go to the U.S. for my grandmother's funeral. Dad had just returned, and the States was too far away and too expensive to return to.

The pain in losing a beloved mother and grandmother is universal, as is the pain of not getting to say good-bye. For my father, there was also pain in knowing that in that moment, when he should have been close, he was thousands of miles away. Thousands of miles away from a mother who once nursed his ailing, asthmatic young body back to health. Thousands of miles away from the woman who gave him his gentle, nostalgic heart. Where he was meant to be, but still, too far away. And I was too far away from her, too. From my dear grandmother who I knew, who I still feel, always loved me. That evening my father sat down in his upstairs study with a heavy heart, full of grief and thankfulness, and wrote the following entry into his journal.

Viola Proudfoot Rice died in the body, put on a new body, and went ahead of us. She went home. Jesus met her, and she is looking at the face of God. It is arranged that we will soon be seeing her again. Thank you, Father, for the gift of my mother. My parents visited Korea for several weeks in the summer of 1968. They loved the land and the people they met, and they were much loved in return. Mother, with beautiful silver hair, was buried in her blue Korean dress.

AJUMONI

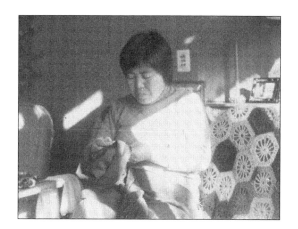

W
e are accustomed to jet lag. So we are not surprised when we are awake in the middle of the night, lights on, roaming around the house like a family of nocturnal possums. Over the years we hold on to the belief that we can beat jet lag, that next time we will sleep on the way, or not sleep on the way, or take a sleeping pill, or stay awake longer. Nothing ever works, but we never give up this fantasy, confidently discussing a new strategy each time we cross the world.

Jet lag was not the only reminder of how far we had traveled. One day I was drinking Shirley Temples with Mimi and Bumpa and shopping for Prell shampoo with Mom at Jay's Drug Store. The next day I was dodging motorcycles and avoiding the corner where the silkworm larvae man set up his cart. The U.S. was almost forgotten in the transition as life slipped easily back into routine.

Our new house in Yonhi-dong belonged to a Yonsei University professor, but it didn't matter to me that, once again, we didn't own it. The persimmon tree, the two gingkos, and the *ondol* bedrooms quickly became home. We were just over the hill from SFS, still on the foothills of Saddleback, and only a short walk from the Van Lierop's house.

Not long after we returned, Mom and Dad received a call from a staff member at Mark's former kindergarten. One of their workers had died suddenly, and his wife needed to find work to keep her children. The tragic loss of her husband brought Kim Kap-gil into our lives. We called her *Ajumoni*, a word that roughly meant 'auntie.' But we turned a generic title into a beloved name.

Ajumoni was in her thirties when she came to us. She grew up in the port city of Incheon, twenty-five miles west of Seoul. She was living with her three children in a small apartment not far from

Toksu Church. The tragedy of her husband's loss was still fresh. Neighbors and family members had been urging her to give up her children, insisting this to her on a regular basis. If she could just find a work, she thought, she could raise them on her own.

Ajumoni stood less than five feet tall and had a full, cheerful face. I remember the first time I saw her in our home, but past that moment I don't remember a time she felt new to us. I remember a time without her, but I don't remember that time as long. Ajumoni, a keen observer of personal traits, quickly declared each of us a *chaengi* of some sort, a professional, a lover of.

"*Lidgie cheese chaengi!*" she said from a mock serious face as I cut an orange square from a block of black market cheese. "*Curisu uyu chaengi!*" she announced as Chris poured a glass of milk.

We couldn't get away with just liking something a lot. We were *chaengis*. She was using the word so often I started calling her *chaengi chaengi*.

Ajumoni declared dairy a tasteless food. Other than eggs, she had never seen so much dairy until she came to work for us—the cartons of milk from Yonsei's dairy school, the PX cheese, the yogurt Mom made by keeping a culture going in the back of the refrigerator. She told me one day, rather matter-of-factly, that Korean people thought Americans smelled like cheese. She turned up her nose when she said this, and I thought this sounded worse than smelling like *kimchi*. Who wanted to smell like a dairy product? At least when you smelled like garlic-laden, fermented *kimchi* you knew you had really done something.

From the frank feelings Koreans had about dairy products to the difficult years of Japanese colonization, I learned a lot from Ajumoni. I was still recovering my Korean language after a year of furlough, so Ajumoni spoke to me simply and threw in the few English words she knew. She was very proud of her Konglish.

Ajumoni spent her childhood living under the Japanese colonial government. Like all people her age, she was given a Japanese name and forced to speak Japanese at school during a time when teaching Korean history and language was not allowed. Ajumoni talked about incidents with the Japanese as though they had occurred the week before, as though the scars had not even begun to heal.

"*Ajumoni, ilbon mal arayo?*" I asked her one day. Ajumoni, do you speak Japanese?

She scrunched up her face into a scowl and nodded, forcing out a couple words as she chopped vegetables. "*Konnichiwa.*" She paused, then cut some more. "*Arigato.*"

She exaggerated the Japanese pitch when she spoke, moving her head side to side in a different way than when she spoke Korean, as if the very act of speaking Japanese conjured up days of a systematic campaign of cultural assimilation she would rather forget. By the 1970s, the Japanese were more than twenty years gone. Seoul's street signs were no longer written in Kanji as they had once been. But the lasting legacy of *Ilbon* in the shape of empty palaces, imposing neoclassical government buildings, and a maid's bitter resentment still remained.

Sunday school lessons about forgiving my enemies and turning the other cheek could not stop me from feeling bitterness at how Koreans were treated by the Japanese. Japan was the rich nation to the east who arrogantly called our East Sea, the Sea of Japan. Their pricey, Swiss-styled Ghana chocolate bars and electronics sold in fancy downtown stores were only more evidence of their greed. My bitterness did not stop me, however, from thoroughly enjoying those Ghana bars or hoping to receive one of those electronics as a Christmas present. My indignity had its practical limits.

Much of the evidence of forty years of colonization lay beneath Seoul's veneer. Sometimes, the evidence was right in front of us, in glaring view. Seoul's main boulevard ran from south to north, ending at the main gate into Kyung Bok Palace, the home of Korea's last serving monarchs. The site for the palace, and the city, was said to be chosen by a geomancer monk in the 1300s in accordance with Korean beliefs in the flow of energy. The long hall, the many residences and government buildings, were nestled between the mountains to the north and the mountains and river to the south, allowing, it was said, *chi* to flow into the capital.

During colonization, Kyung Bok Kung, so important to Koreans as a symbol of their monarchy, was shadowed by a massive, imposing five-story granite Japanese colonial headquarters built inside the grounds of the palace. Imagine if the British Parliament Building was erected in front of the White House. It was said that with this one move, the flow of the Korean national spirit was choked off. Though the copperplate-domed building gave a certain grandeur to downtown, the placement of the building was said to be an open wound to Korean people.

Mom and Dad never made snap judgments about people. A few times they spoke of the difficulty in navigating Korean protocol. Dad talked about the intricacies of serving on the boards of churches and other organizations. One time he told me, in his usual understated way, that Korean churches did have a tendency to be a little bit factional, which I think was a bit like saying Seattle is a little bit rainy. Once in a while, my parents talked about the complexity of the conditional favor concept called *putak*, leading me to understand the fine gifts they sometimes received were not always given without expecting something in return.

But when it came down to it, Mom and Dad seemed to take each person on their own merit, whether they came from New York or Kyoto, whether they were Christian or Buddhist, American or Korean, or anything else. Mom thought so highly of her Japanese pen pal from high school. We visited Shigeyoshi and his family on our way to Korea. They were so nice to us, writing letters throughout the years and sending delicate Japanese gifts. They gave me a beautiful kimono. It's hard to be angry with somebody who gives you a beautiful kimono. Ajumoni applied her views about Japan sweepingly. I suspect she would have found something suspicious about kindly Shigeyoshi, and his cute daughter, Keiko, if she had met them. Her feelings were in some ways refreshingly uncomplicated. She had a lot to be angry about.

Forget Mom's social work training about learning to understand the world from another person's point of view. If I complained to Mom about someone's behavior, she would pause and say, "Honey, he isn't well." This simple assessment did remarkably explain a lot about the world and people. But the analysis was so unsatisfying, shutting down my righteous indignation with four simple words.

I carried Ajumoni's anger about Japan as I carried an understanding that not all Japanese people were to blame for what had happened between the two countries. It was illogical for me to feel resentment towards Nobie, one of more than a few Japanese classmates at school. What had Nobie ever done?

Ajumoni regarded the people that came into our home as fair game for scrutiny. She was suspicious of some and she loved others. "*Jennie chakhaeyo,*" she always said with approval when I told her Jennie was coming over to spend the night. Jennie is goodhearted. When I grew older she confided in me her opinion of a dear friend of my parents. "Oh, he's a fake." She said bluntly. "He was only nice to me when your parents were home."

At Christmastime, my parents gave Ajumoni a cash bonus, as was customary, and we put together a package of gifts for her family. I loved to help gather together little presents, like packages of *ramyun* noodles, that I knew she liked, and candy and gifts for her children. We usually dropped the gifts off at her small, modest apartment. These were the few times I saw how Ajumoni and her family lived. The rooms were small but tidy, the kitchen and bathroom rudimentary. We were crossing a threshold that stood between our families. Ajumoni knew my home life intimately but I didn't know hers hardly at all.

Even at a young age I felt some strangeness in this, some imbalance. I was happy when we gave Ajumoni her Christmas package.

I wanted her to like it. I hoped she was happy. I hoped she knew how much we loved her.

Sometimes, Ajumoni and I watched soap operas together in the afternoon. She would keep her eyes on the TV as she lightly dusted around the telephone, lifting framed photos of smiling American grandparents, and cleaning under painted wedding ducks. She usually paused for a dramatic scene.

"Ajumoni, why is the mother crying?" I asked, and it seemed like I had to ask again and again, because there always seemed to be some distraught *omoni* crying in a modest *ondol* room.

Ajumoni explained why it was this time dear mother was crying "*aigo, aigo*," the great expression of lament, grief, and disappointment. There was so much anguish in each episode. One horrible heartache and tragedy followed another. Didn't anything good ever happen to these poor people?

One day I asked Ajumoni about her husband's death. She described a complicated series of events I only understood a part of. Tears fell as she began to speak, and I remember the story like this.

"Before I met my husband he came from the north for school, before Korea was divided. Only he and his brother were in the south. He never saw his family again. He lost his brother, an army pilot, in the war. His sorrow made him drink too much. He was sick, but we didn't know why. One day he had a stroke."

She made a face as she said "stroke," her mouth turned down on one side in a tragic-comic gesture. A few weeks later she showed me a photo of her husband. His face was thoughtful and strong, and his high cheekbones were prominent, like Myong-ju's. When I grew older, I understood why the light in Myong-ju's face was always dimmed by a sadness deep in her eyes.

Ajumoni's husband didn't look like someone who should be dead. His death changed her life. It changed our lives, too. It brought her to us. We were two families bonded and bound by fate, by the circumstance of crossing a border, a calling to leave one's country for another, a moment where a blood clot interrupts flow to the brain and a young father loses his life. Another moment to grieve on one Seoul day.

One day, a year or so after Ajumoni came to work for us, I called to her cheerily from another room, using the same words she always used to call me to come. "*Ajumoni, iriwa!*"

I had unknowingly used *panmal*. Because of a year of furlough, I hadn't properly transitioned from speaking as a toddler to speaking as a young girl. As soon as the words left my mouth, Mom marched into the room. Mom never marched into a room or did anything suddenly.

She said firmly, in a way she never spoke to me or really to anybody, "Never use that language with Ajumoni, Lizzy. She is your elder. Speak to her respectfully. You need to say, '*Iri oseyo.*'"

I was mortified. I looked over and saw Ajumoni making an embarrassed, sorry face. She smiled and said, "*Kwaenchanhayo, Samonim. Lidgie mollassoyo.*" It's ok, *Samonim*, Lidgie didn't know. But I felt terrible about what I had done. I made sure to never make that mistake again. I didn't need only Koreans in my life to remind me to be a good Korean. I had Mom and Dad, too.

My parents' friends and colleagues had long ago entered into our home and lives. But Ajumoni was different. She was the seventh member of family. I knew she belonged to Myong-ju, Un-ju, and Sang-yongi. I knew she worked with us so she could put them through school and give them a good life. But, in some way, they were all part of our family. Our lives were bound together.

Time passed easily with Ajumoni. No subject was deemed too difficult to talk about. Few topics seemed off limits. The expression of the pain of her losses, her husband's death, the early loss of her mother brought her no embarrassment. Her emotions were not swept under a rug. Everything was out in the open, to be mourned again, as many times as it took. There was no shame in her lament.

But she didn't seem to wallow in her sorrow, either. She would finish telling me a terribly tragic story and then, in the next moment, crack up laughing about something. Some afternoons, Mark arrived home from school to find Ajumoni napping in his room. Cozily spread out on his *yo* and laying underneath his *ibul,* only her head was visible. She became very comfortable with us.

When Ajumoni sat next to me, she almost always reached a hand out to rest it on my arm or knee. Our relationship was easy from the first day. We enjoyed each other's company. I was close to Mom, too, but Mom pushed me to be a better person. Mom wanted me to get out into the world and do things I didn't want to do, like take piano lessons and wear dresses to church. Like a true grandmother, Ajumoni didn't ask anything of me. We came from radically different ancestry, but in some ways our families were alike. We were cut off from our relatives. Ajumoni, the only child of her parents, was raised by a distant step-mother. Her family had just a few extended family members. I still believe we were meant to find each other.

Ajumoni was there when Rick began to have problems. She was there when he left us at the age of fifteen to finish school in the States. She was there when Chris, Mark and I ran into the kitchen in panic after we set a patch of our lawn into a bright, fiery blaze. For years after that she told the story with tears of laughter in her eyes. She was there when Dad was arrested by the Korean CIA, and she was there as I grew from a child into a young woman.

Ajumoni loved our persimmon tree as much as I did. Sometimes she stopped to take in the long view from our house on the hill. This is how people become family. By sharing vistas. By plucking *kam* from the same tree. By simply being there for the events, big and small, cheery and difficult, that make up a life. It was the loss of Ajumoni I would feel most deeply after I left Korea. Living a life without her in it broke my heart in two. I couldn't just walk away from her.

88   *Elizabeth Rice*

It was my parents calling to go to Korea. In doing so, they gave me a Korean heart. They gave me a Korean grandmother. It would one day be my calling to find Ajumoni again, to complete the circle.

FINDING KIM KAP-GIL

Seoul, 1986

I walk into a Yonhi-dong neighborhood office. I'm carrying a piece of a paper with an address written on it. I wait a few minutes and then sit down across a plain desk from a low-level bureaucrat. I want to see if he can help me find someone dear to me, someone who used to live at the address written on the piece of paper I'm holding. Half an hour later, I leave with some hope. "Maybe," I think to myself, "I will find Ajumoni today."

Four years had passed since my family left Korea. Four years had passed since I had any contact with Ajumoni. Between my junior and senior year of college, I enrolled in Yonsei's summer college program for international students. I returned without my family because I needed to go home. I needed to try and find Ajumoni. It was difficult, almost impossible, to keep in touch with her after we left, to send letters to homes without addresses, to keep track of when she moved. I wasn't even sure she was alive.

I walked up a steep road, passing small shops and concrete middle class homes. I climbed up further still, passing more houses as the peak of the mountain came into view. Near the top, I arrived at a complex of short apartment buildings. The paint was peeling. The buildings looked like the cheaply built "citizens apartments" constructed in the 1970s to replace bulldozed shantytowns, the ones made with low-grade materials, the concrete poured dangerously thin in exchange for generous bribes.

I checked the piece of paper and confirmed the information. Shipom Apartments. No. 209. I followed a small set of tiled stairs to the second floor and knocked on a thick metal door. Every sound seemed to amplify. Time stopped. I heard shuffling from the other side of the door, and then an uneasy voice called out, "*Yoboseyo?*"

I recognized the voice immediately.

"Ajumoni?" I called hesitantly and hopefully through the door, my heart pounding in my chest.

The reply came immediately. "Lidgie!!?"

The door swung open with a flurry of bumps and bangs. Ajumoni grabbed onto me, her short arms circling my waist. We jumped up and down and wept. After a few moments of *aigos*, as we were still wiping away tears, we sat down on her living room floor. She took my hands into hers and began to pat at my arm and ask me one thousand questions. The words were coming out of both of us so quickly. There was too much to say, too many years to explain, too much time to make up.

"How is *Moksanim*? Is he healthy? How is *Samonim*? *Aigo*, this can't be a picture of Ricky, Curisu and Maga! Ricky gentleman!"

We talked about Myong-ju and Un-ju, about their beauty parlor business, and her son Sang-yongi's college. Their family was living together in one apartment to save money for a bigger place. Neither of her daughters had married. This was considered bad luck. People think there is something wrong with a woman who doesn't marry. It's seen as pitiable. Ajumoni made out to be upset about this, but then she added, cheerfully. "Well, we have each other!" I thought of her husband's death and its lasting effect on the family.

When I looked up I saw the photo of her husband that always hung high on her bedroom wall. His handsome face will always be imprinted deep into my memory bank, in the place where my most important memories are kept.

"*Nappun saram*," she said with a scowl and a hint at humor. Bad person. "How could he die and leave me with three young children?"

Ajumoni shuffled into the kitchen in her loose, comfortable *ajumma* pants. She removed a green zucchini and a block of firm white *tubu* from the refrigerator. She cut the zucchini into thin rounds, sliced the soy blocks into squares, dipped them in egg wash, and placed them carefully into an oiled frying pan. When she walked away, I picked up the spatula and flipped the food. The oil sizzled. Were Ajumoni and I ever apart? Was I really gone from Korea for four years? It felt like I had never left. Coming back was that easy, like slipping in between my old *ibul* and *yo*.

Ajumoni unfolded a dining table from the corner of the room and poured soy sauce and vinegar into a small dish. As we sat down to eat, she lowered her head and made the sign of the cross over her chest. She whispered a quiet prayer of thanks, and I heard her say the word "*hananim*." One God. A word I knew so well, spoken from the mouth of Choi Moksanim and from the mouth of my father. A word, like so many words, I had not heard for too long.

I put my head down and sent out my own invocation. I thanked the God to whom my parents always looked to in faith. I thanked the mountain and river spirits of old Korea, the ones who had protected me for sixteen years. I feared they had forgotten me. In this moment, I felt them watching over us, laughing as Ajumoni and I stuffed fried *tubu* and *hobak* into our mouths. I was sitting on a rice paper floor in a dilapidated apartment building and I was happier than I had been in four years.

I wanted to understand things I couldn't understand as a little girl. I wanted to know about Ajumoni's childhood, to understand just how she came to us, and learn what happened to her after we left Korea. That summer, Ajumoni relayed stories of crossing rivers during the Korean War, of being raised by a distant stepmother. I learned more about what happened in the months before Rick left, stories of his late night arrivals from rice wine bars, stories that sometimes Ajumoni knew better than any of us. She talked about all of this with candor, more freely than I could talk about that time with Mom and Dad, as if Ajumoni and I shared a feeling that talking about something painful or difficult didn't dishonor anybody, but maybe needed to be said. Whatever story she told about Rick, good or bad, she always ended by patting her heart and saying, "Ricky has a good heart. One time Ricky brought me Pond's Cream from the U.S." She has never stopped talking about that Pond's Cream.

Once a week that summer I walked from my Yonsei dorm to Ajumoni's apartment to spend time with my Korean family. With the social barriers between us gone, with the maturity of age, I came to know Myong-ju and Un-ju in a new way. We shared our impressions of one another as children. We reminisced about the days they used to come by our house in the afternoons in their stiff black school uniforms. They told me what they knew and remembered about their father's death. One night, after we talked for a while, I said something that had been on my heart all summer.

"Myong-ju and Un-ju," I said, "I know when your mother was with me in the afternoons, she was not with you." I told them I was sorry. I spoke the Korean word intentionally. *Mianhamnida.*

Myong-ju nodded quietly and said, "Yes Lidgie, that was not easy."

One evening, towards the end of the summer, I told them how much I had missed Korea. I told them I had been very sad in the U.S. As I spoke, they listened closely. They nodded silently. I wasn't sure what they were thinking. After I finished talking, everyone was quiet for a moment. Then Myong-ju said, in a soft voice, "Lidgie, we did not know you felt this way." She pointed to her heart. "Lidgie," she said, "you are half Korean."

And I sighed. And I stopped talking for a moment. Because it had been too long since somebody had really seen me.

Inches and Li

When first grade began, and for the next eleven years, I was immersed in the tightly contained community known as Seoul Foreign School, the place we called SFS. I dove right in, and for years I didn't look back.

SFS, founded in 1912, was one of the oldest international schools in the world. By the 1960s, it served as Seoul's academic center for all non-U.S. military foreigner children, including business, missionary, and diplomat kids. Classes were taught in English and the curriculum was based on the one used in the U.S. In the 1970s, a new gym was constructed with beautiful light maple flooring. Huge red lettering across the top of the wall at the back of the gym announced, proudly, WELCOME TO CRUSADER COUNTRY. Before the new gym was constructed, our beloved Quonset hut facility hosted sports teams from U.S. Army schools in Seoul, Taegu, and Pusan, and the Christian boarding school in Taejon.

My new classmates, Jennie Rader and Debbie Patten, were like me in a few important ways that made it so we would always be close. We were the youngest members of our families. Jennie's parents came to South Korea in 1962, three years before she was born, when her oldest sister Edie was two and her brother, J.P., was a baby. The Pattens also came to Korea in 1962, when Becky was two, Rachel was one, and Naomi was three months from being born. Debbie was one of the last mission kids to be born in Severance Hospital downtown, before the facility moved to the campus of Yonsei. I had to laugh a few years ago when a friend told me she wasn't sure she wanted to take a three hour flight with her new baby. I thought of these Pattens and Raders and Rices, and I wondered, "What were they thinking?"

The Pattens lived on the campus of a small seminary in northern Seoul. The Raders lived in one of the Salvation Army houses in a neighborhood across the city. Since Jennie and I insisted on weekly sleepovers, her parents became like second parents to me and mine to her. Mrs. Rader championed issues of women's equality. In the late 1970s, she successfully petitioned for a change to the Salvation Army uniform for Corp women, who were still wearing a Victorian bonnet-type hat with ties. I admired Mrs. Rader for the way she stood up for women, like Mom did.

Unlike my family, with no hint of missionary in our lineage, one of Jennie's ancestors was an influential evangelist. An aunt and uncle of hers were missionaries in Zambia. When I heard this I realized that some of my friends had relatives who understood and possibly even embraced their parents' choice to live in Korea. This seemed very convenient.

While our families didn't have anything close to the longevity in Korea of families like the Moffetts and the Underwoods, whose ancestors came in the late 1800s, or even the families like the Wilsons and the Grubbs, who came in the 1950s, we had enough years to make it feel like we were old-timers in the SFS and mission community by the time I started first grade. Rick had to forge his own path at SFS. He had to get used to riding in a Land Rover to school and learn how to navigate an insular international community in which no one knew him. By the time I began first grade, I showed up and slipped in easily as the last in a legacy, more than happy with the insularity. I had it easy moving to Korea and I had it easy transitioning into SFS.

My classmates at SFS were Dorows from Minnesota and Matthews from Iowa. They were daughters and sons of ambassadors from all over the world. Over thirty different countries were represented at our school. The four Patten girls came from Oregon loggers. The Rader family came from Kentucky. The Neils were from Australia. The Basingers were from Iowa. But then again, most of my friends didn't really come from those places at all. Many of them had long been riding around in jeeps, donning Korean first birthday dresses, learning Kenyan songs, attending mission meetings, living on company compounds or deep in the well of cross-cultural relationships and fellowship. I was part of an extensive, established, diverse, and dynamic community of people who had lived all over the world.

My identity story seemed straightforward compared to some of my friends. Kimberly Wood, daughter of Salvation Army missionaries from England, spent the first five years of her life in Kenya, years five through eight in England, and years eight through seventeen in Korea. My tennis teammate, Ingeborg Loon, lived in Zambia, Korea, and Holland before she turned eighteen. Wolfgang Herschler, who I believe was the son of the German ambassador, was one of the few of us who held tightly and proudly to his national heritage. Wolfgang wore leather lederhosen breeches to school once a week as if this was a very fitting and reasonable thing to do in Seoul.

At Nungan Kindergarten in Puk Ahyon-dong I had been part of a community of children who only knew Korea as home. My blonde hair may have stood out on the pages of my kindergarten year book, but I don't remember feeling I belonged to that school any less than my classmates did. I had lived in Korea for too long and had too many Korean playmates to feel I was in any way an anomaly in my Korean school. At Seoul Foreign, I was part of a community of children who did not know how to live in the countries of our passports, and I slipped comfortably into that identity, too.

We were like sea creatures moving to land when we visited our "home" countries. We were more comfortable in the countries stamped into the visa pages of our passports. We occupied some indefinable in-between place. Many of us instinctively changed our behavior, body language, and spoken language depending if we were in the halls of SFS or talking with the proprietor of the local store. But we didn't recognize our strangeness. There were enough of us to give us the impression we were normal children.

Passports in our expat community spoke more about where our parents or grandparents had once lived or were born. We categorized ourselves not as much by nationality, ethnicity, or social class, but by the (non-military) expat trinity of missionary, business family, and diplomat. The father of one friend worked on the design and construction of new power plants. Another worked for Northern Telecom, modernizing South Korea's telephone network. Another was a civil engineer working on water supply and sewage treatment systems.

Most of my Korean-American friends came from business families who had lived a significant number of their years in the U.S. These Rhees, Kims, and Lees, with their Korean-speaking homes and years in U.S. somehow managed to be both more American and more Korean than I was. Then there were the inter-cultural missionary couples like the Paks, the Matthews, and the Kinslers, whose children were part of our international community but also had the added identity intricacy of having one Korean parent and one American parent.

On the foothills of Ansan, I mastered the purple cards in the SRA Reading Laboratory Kit, my mind beginning to love the English language. I read voraciously, falling asleep each night to *The Lion, the Witch, and the Wardrobe* and *A Wrinkle in Time*. I loved to spiral a football and kick a soccer ball. My first grade teacher, Mrs. Smithers, taught me how to fill pine cones with peanut butter for the songbirds.

I was thirty miles from the North Korean border singing "King of the Road" with my guitar-strumming teacher from the U.S. Mark took on the role of Little John in *Peter Pan* and Chris captained the basketball team as Korean soldiers patrolled the skies for signs of invasion. In a land measured in kilometers and *li*, we learned to measure in inches and miles. In a country where temperature was measured in Celsius, we learned to measure it in Fahrenheit. In fifth grade, my charismatic teacher, Mr. Debelak, shepherded us through a breathtaking celebration of the U.S. bicentennial with reenactments of Declaration of Independence signings and a lesson plan that seemed to go on for months, as if we were living in Pennsylvania, as if we were not attending a school in East Asia with students from over thirty nationalities represented. That I was two hundred fifty miles from Communist China did not stop me from learning about liberty and the pursuit of happiness, nor did it stop Jennie from dressing up as Betsy Ross.

The missionaries who founded SFS, as well as the people who ran our school, respected Korea. They felt it was important we understand the country we were living in. I learned how to use an abacus, although never coming close to the speed or skill of the owner of our corner store. I learned that King Sejong invented the Korean alphabet in the 1500s so common people could learn to read and write. I learned that the influence of Confucianism came from China, which explained a series of behaviors I had never questioned before. This was why we bowed to people and why my brothers were numbered, one, two, and three. This was why my parents were honored with titles. I had Confucius to blame and thank for all of this.

We learned about the bravery and wits of Yi Sun-sin, the navy Admiral who defeated the powerful Japanese navy in an epic 1500s battle. Admiral Yi's bronze statue struck an imposing posture in downtown Seoul, a long sword held firmly his right hand, a replica of one of his famous *kobukson* iron turtle boats beneath him. Generations of us took Korean language classes from Mrs. Hahm. We learned about the great dynasties, the Paekje, the Silla, and the Chosun. We watched black belts perform taekwondo demonstrations at school assemblies, snapping thick wooden blocks in two with high feet kicks.

Something was happening as I transitioned into the all-consuming, English-language based international school life of SFS. My Korean nursery school classmates moved on with their lives, too. I was too caught up in school assemblies and sleepovers to wonder where these old friends of mine were. Our furlough in 1970 meant I hadn't seen them for a year. Were they attending the large public school down the road? Were they amongst the multitudes of students I saw letting out of school each day, the girls passing me arm in arm, the boys walking hand in hand, arms slung over shoulders? Did they learn math in the same way I did? From what perspective did we each learn about the history of the world? What were we each taught about the causes of the Korean War?

I was still eating red bean paste ice cream bars, snacking on shrimp chips, and shopping at Midopa Department Store during Christmas. I still lived under the same dictator and beneath the same divided sky. My old classmates and I lived in the same world but we lived in different worlds. Our schools didn't even have the same vacation times. Now, other than Korean-American friends at school, my close relationships with Koreans were almost exclusively with adults. Maybe this was in part why my relationship with Ajumoni was so important to me, beyond the other obvious reason, the absence of my grandparents from my daily life.

One day, Mark and I heard a disturbance coming from the middle school over the wall behind our house. When we peered curiously out of an upstairs window, we saw a student standing with a teacher in the schoolyard. The teacher was holding a yardstick. He was yelling at the student, his red, angry face an inch away.

"*Yah, oecure?!*" Hey you, why'd you do that!

A few seconds later the teacher raised the stick into the air and cuffed the student on the leg. Another day we saw a teacher shouting at a group of boys as they took punishment for some act of disobedience. The boys were jumping around the schoolyard on their haunches, their hands clasped on top of their heads.

This was not the "talk it out" society I inhabited. These were not the ideals espoused in Parent Effectiveness Training, the lessons Mom was learning in social work classes that detailed ways to communicate effectively with children and resolve family conflicts *so everybody wins*. My siblings and I were being taught to think for ourselves. We, the daughters of oil executives and missionaries, the sons of German and Canadian ambassadors, were learning about equality and unalienable rights. Mrs. Smithers never used shame or humiliation as a means to mold me into a better citizen. Kathy Smithers looked like Mary Tyler Moore and she had her personality, too. Kathy Smithers could turn the world on with her smile. As I watched these incidents of corporal punishment unfold from my comfortable perch, I wondered, *what happened to the kindly Korean nursery school teachers who cheerfully marched Mark and I around the schoolyard singing songs about mountain rabbits?*

SFS was a bastion of individuality compared to the Korean middle school over the wall. We didn't have to wear uniforms. The boys of SFS were not required to have regulated brush cuts. Classmates returning from furlough and the embassy kids newly arrived from Europe brought western trends with them. In the early 1970s, a couple years after the hippie movement peaked in the States, Rick and his long-haired friends began to lurk around the halls of SFS in bell bottom jeans, green army surplus jackets, and big black boots, à la Janis Joplin and Jimi Hendrix.

Each year, a few missionary kids returned from furloughs spent in exotic places like *California* and *Michigan*. They were easy to spot with their new haircuts and Levi's 501 jeans. I swear they smelled like McDonald's cheeseburgers. These were the signs someone had been *away*. But if they were from one of the families who had lived in Korea for what seemed like forever, they quickly drifted back into the fold, missionary bowl cuts and hand-me-down jeans intact.

A year in the U.S. changed people. Access to American shampoo and Lucky Charms changed people. Eating at Burger King and
Kentucky Fried Chicken changed people. But Korea changed them
right back. I can only tell you with about twenty percent accuracy
which state my American friends came from. I did not associate the
Matthews family with Iowa. I associated them with Chung-dong.

It would have been impossible not to understand I was a
miguksaram in homogeneous Korea, where being Korean meant
one thing. Being ethnically Korean. Even foreigners who had
lived in Korea for twenty, thirty, even sixty years were asked, on
a regular basis, "Where are you from? No, where are you *really*
from?" But I knew what people were asking. What is your ethnicity. Where are your people from. Where did you live before
you came here. The answer, for me, was always the same. "*Nanun
miguksaram imnida.*" I am an American. But even I knew I was not
the most American American.

The *real Americans* lived in the U.S. If they lived in Korea, they
lived on one of the walled-off U.S. military bases. They shopped
from the base PX, drank Dr. Pepper casually, with great regularity, and dried off in their large houses with adequately-sized, fluffy,
machine-dried towels. Real Americans celebrated July 4th with
fireworks bursting in the air over Dragon Mountain with the same
ancestral fervor Koreans celebrated the Chusok Harvest Festival.
Real Americans went to Seoul American School, used dollars on
base, ate french fries at their movie theater, and were represented
by imposing school mascots like Falcons and Eagles.

I was different. I was a *Crusader*, proud to be part of a long-
standing institution of people who loved and respected Korea. But
let's be honest. I was part of a school whose mascot was a Roman
Catholic warrior recovering Holy Land from the Muslims. I felt
terrible when I learned my beloved school was built on a former Korean gravesite. I felt even worse when I learned some mission workers were instructed to use the back door when entering

compound homes. My parents once heard a Korean theologian talk about growing up next to a mission compound he was not allowed to enter. This couldn't be true! But it was.

There was a message sent in all that made up SFS and our mission community, too. We might not have been Seoul American School, a school and a student body that in truth I knew very little about. A people I quickly and easily stereotyped. I might not have been raised on what I saw as the enclave that was a U.S. military base. But our foreign curriculum of inches and Fahrenheit, our sports leagues with basketball, football, and tennis teams, our textbooks from the U.S., could not be called integration by any stretch of the imagination.

Many missionaries had integrated deep into Korean society. A few, like our dear friends the Strawns, sent their children to Korean elementary and middle school. These were the people who inspired my parents to leave the cozy cocoon of the compound and the SFS hill and rent a house in a Korean neighborhood. So many missionaries had given their lives to Korea. They started needed schools. They provided medical care when there was little. They helped people at the lowest levels of society. But if I looked at all of this honestly, the world of Korean missions also included a lot of walled-in compounds and institutions made "for us." I knew that when the Strawn girls came over to our house in their school uniforms that they knew Korea at a level I didn't know anymore.

So these are the questions I ask myself now. Did a genetic love of grilled cheese sandwiches make me an American? Did a learned love of *kimchi* make me Korean? Did learning about Paul Revere make me into an American any more than learning about Admiral Yi made me a Korean? I know I was not cut from the exact same cloth as my Korean nursery school classmates, although I unconsciously felt like I was a part of that nursery school when I went to it. I know going to SFS changed me. It made me into an international school kid. It separated me culturally and physically from the children I once played with in Puk Ahyon-dong, the friends I once ran with on the old mountain path near the Van Lierop's house, and the children of the school guards, my best friends when I was three and we lived on the SFS hill. I was an immigrant but not an immigrant. Korean but not Korean. American but not American. I shared fundamental values and an insider's knowledge of Seoul with my former nursery school friends, knowledge I could never share with my own cousins. In many ways I was more similar to Ajumoni than I was to my grandparents. So who was I? And who was I not?

Not long ago, a writing teacher asked me, after I explained to her that I felt Korean in many ways, "But Liz, didn't you look in the mirror when you were little and know you weren't Korean?"

I had to stop for a minute. I had never been asked this question before. I realized she was equating feeling Korean with ethnicity. She saw my skin, hair, and eye color and she couldn't put it together. Here I was in Minneapolis, a city full of immigrants and refugees from places like Mexico, Somalia, and Laos, people called Americans, talking to a writing teacher who must have known that the book of identity was not always identifiable by the cover. Was it the novelty of hearing a person of European decent say she belonged to an Asian place? If I had a Korean passport would that have made a difference? What if I had an accent when I spoke English?

Though South Koreans hold tightly to the idea of a *hanguksaram* as an ethnic Korean, most people in the U.S. don't equate being American with ethnicity anymore. Americans, for the most part, at least accept the concept of Chinese-Americans and Mexican-Americans and Korean-Americans. Recently a new friend looked at me and said, in reference to my mixed-up identity, "Well, those blue eyes don't lie." But sometimes I think my blue eyes do lie. Or maybe they are telling half-truths. I was never confused about my ethnicity. But I never thought I wasn't from Korea.

I know I can't measure how Korean or how American I am. I can't quantify my identity by calculating how much of my school day was this or that, which church we attended, or whether we lived on a mission compound or in a regular neighborhood. I can't find who I am on some scale of selfhood. None of us is a recipe made up of a simple list of ingredients.

All I know is that the memories I carried with me from Boston to Seattle, from Oklahoma to Vermont were not just of Girl Scout hikes and tennis tournaments on Yongsan Army Base. They were not only of school dances and watching *Daniel Boone* with Dad. I would later look upon a box of Choco Pie cookies with the love that only a child can have for a fake, marshmallow-filled, waxy chocolate snack. I would remember the particular slope of Nam Mountain, the turn of the Han River as it met southern Seoul, and how wide it felt when I stood, so small, at its sandy shores.

I would one day ache to see the morning light fall on Saddleback, to hear the sound of cicadas breathing through the searing humidity of a July Yonhi-dong day, to hear the call of the taffy man, and the shuffling of Ajumoni's slippers against the floor. These were the places that rooted me, the slope-shapes and insect calls that told me who I was. This was the geography and these were the people who announced, as one great chorus, no matter what school I went to, no matter what kind of house we lived in, no matter whether I learned to measure in *li* or in kilometers or in feet, *This is where you come from. This is your country. This is where you belong.*

UNDER THE DIVIDED SKY

"Korea is one . . .through these years
under the divided sky and land,
tree rings of the people's suffering were etched
and a whole new generation of people grew up.
But who is to say he can slice a stream of water into two?
Who is to say he can split the sky in two?"

—PYONGYANG TIMES, JULY 15, 1972

Rick loved to hike. From the time we arrived in Seoul he ventured up into our neighborhood hills alone, walking for hours on the narrow pathways that snaked between houses and corner stores. He entered deep into labyrinths of busy open markets and crested serene mountaintops. Rick would ride any bus, to any part of Seoul, walk into any market, and explore any neighborhood. Sometimes he stopped to offer to help people carry water up the hill from public wells. Rick was often gone for hours. Mom would say upon his return, "Rick, you need to tell me when and where you go!" Rick would point out and up and say, "Mom, see that mountain? I went there! See that mountain? I went there, too!"

For a few years, Rick climbed to the top of Saddleback every Saturday. He marched past middle-class homes, past our neighborhood Buddhist Temple, continuing up beyond the concrete army outpost near the top. Sometimes he cooked bacon near the summit. He loved Korea's mountain culture, and he was always highly entertained when climbers yelled a hearty "*yaaa-hhho*" as they reached the summit.

We loved to climb Saddleback. During our first year in Korea, Dad once woke up at six o'clock to hike up our neighborhood hill. He discovered, much to his surprise, that most of the people he met were coming at him from the opposite direction, on their way back home, exercise taken, morning cooking fires lit, and rice pots perking away. Dad had found a people who could out-Vermont an ancestral Vermonter.

Rick's favorite activity was strapping an army surplus rucksack to his back to forage in the nearby woods for war relics. One of the long term missionaries, whose family had lived in Korea for generations, told my parents one day that Rick really shouldn't be digging around in the woods. He said some areas could still contain live grenades. But Rick foraged on. In the first few inches of topsoil he found spent bullets of all sizes, clips for M1 rifles, jagged pieces of exploded mortar rounds, and metal canteens. In the small stalls in the back corners of South Gate Market, he found C-rations, helmets, tents, and old army boots. Rick's room was a war museum, and Saddleback was a 1950s battleground, a site of one of the war's bloodiest battles. Korea's tragic history was always close at hand, even on a leisurely elementary school hike up our neighborhood mountain.

Rick was old enough when we arrived in Korea to feel the culture shock of landing at an airport surrounded by rice paddy fields and farmhouses, to a country of squat toilets, honey bucket trucks, and ancient palaces. He was old enough to understand the earth-shaking transition that had taken place as his peaceful life in the quaint town of Fairfield, Connecticut ended and his new life in a somehow simultaneously frenetic and bucolic ancient Asian city began. But he was our Huck Finn, and he relished an adventure. He loved how we used buses and taxis instead of a private car. He loved riding to school in a Land Rover on our west district's bumpy roads. He also understood we had moved to a tenuous place, to a nation whose peace was held together by a thread.

I can't tell you when I learned about the war Koreans called *Yuk-ee-oh*, 6-25, for the June 1950 day it broke out. I don't remember a time I didn't know about our divided peninsula and its divided people. I was in elementary school when I first saw pictures of the war. These were haunting images, with ditches packed high with civilian bodies, hillsides laid bare with artillery fire, and valleys crawling with armed soldiers and large tanks. Roads and bridges swarmed with people on a long march, fleeing advancing armies. People carried their most important worldly possessions. They pulled overflowing carts. They balanced sacks on their backs. Parents carried children. Children carried younger children.

I came to understand more about the background of the Korean War as I grew older, blending different perspectives about who was to blame for the terrible things that had happened and who was to thank for the good that came. To understand the three-year battle, one had to at least go back to the beginning of the 20th century, although the causes of Korean historical events often seemed rooted in centuries old history and mired in the complex, age-old dynamics of Northeast Asia.

In the early 1900s, the Chosun Dynasty was dismantled by the Japanese, bringing an end to feudal life and almost two thousand years of kingdoms and dynasties. The colonial Japanese government ruled with a heavy hand for the next thirty-five years. During World War II, Roosevelt, Churchill, and Chiang Kai-shek agreed that if Japan lost, they would have to relinquish all countries they had conquered by force. With Japan on the verge of surrender, Soviet forces advanced into Korea. Anxious the Soviets would continue into the entire peninsula, two U.S. officers were given the task to define a temporary American occupation zone in the southern part of Korea. In a period of thirty minutes, using a *National Geographic* map as reference, they drew a line down the approximate middle of the peninsula at the 38th parallel. The border meandered from west to east, from Kyonggi Bay to the East Sea. It cut through the middle of some villages.

Soviet troops settled in to temporarily occupy the northern region of Korea. U.S. and U.N. troops established themselves in the south to do the same. Even while many Koreans demanded immediate independence, the divide was put in place as a provisional arrangement, until Korea was deemed ready for self-rule. When the Japanese flag was finally run down from its position at the Government Building in Seoul after almost forty years, the Stars and Stripes, not the *taeguki*, was raised in its place. Over the coming years, separate governments were organized, joint elections never happened, and one nation separated into two antagonistic entities with deeply diverging ideologies and influences. Sixty years later, the country of Korea is still divided at the exact same location.

Hearing North Korea's version of the breakout of war and comparing it to South Korea's version was like hearing different takes on a couple's horrific breakup. The other person was always to blame. North Korea called it the Fatherland Liberation War. They said they attacked the south to unify Korea, to take it back from the "Yankee Imperialists." The South said the North attacked unprovoked.

Personal war stories didn't come readily from missionaries or Korean friends, but when they came, they were heartbreaking. It was impossible to get a consistent official version of war events, to pull apart the atrocities and acts of heroism committed by people on all sides, to understand why three of the world's superpowers had committed so much firepower and lives to one small peninsula.

My high school textbook, written in the U.S., placed the war within the context of the Cold War. Some Korean scholars pointed to historical and political divisions already in place within Korea as another cause of the War, which was a quagmire of history whose proportions I knew I could never fully understand. Since my parents looked upon events like wars and cultures with complexity and nuance, I grew up believing no version held the complete story. People lived on both sides of that border. People who shared the same history and carried the same bloodline. I did not learn to call one side "evil" and one side "good."

Between 1950 and 1953, hundreds of thousands of Chinese and North Korean forces, backed by Soviet Union firepower, and hundreds of thousands of South Korean and United Nations forces, predominately from the U.S., steamrolled up and down the peninsula three to four times, depending on the location.

In a peninsula the size of Virginia, in a country of bitter cold winters and hot, humid summers, soldiers fought through cities and villages, battling from mountain valley to mountain peak. They fought from the perimeter of the southern city of Pusan to the border of China.

Up to one million civilians fled south alongside U.N. troops retreating approaching communist forces. People from the north left ancestral homes and family members, believing they would return after the fighting ended. Millions of family members were separated as a result. Although precise numbers vary widely depending on the source, an estimated 1.5 million Korean civilians died during the war. Military deaths are estimated between eight hundred thousand and 1.2 million. As much as 80 percent of industrial and public facilities and 50 percent of the country's housing was destroyed. The peninsula was practically leveled. This was loss at catastrophic proportions. When a worker with the International Refugee Organization saw what had happened first hand, he said, "I have never seen destruction and human suffering on so large a scale as in Korea."

After three years of intense fighting up and down the peninsula, a temporary truce brought the battle to an end, and Korea remained split in two. In 1953 the Korean Armistice Agreement ended "all acts of armed force" until both sides were able to find a "final peaceful settlement." That truce and the ironically named demilitarized zone held the two Koreas apart.

The demilitarized zone was, and is, one of the most highly militarized borders in the world. The two-and-a-half-mile deep, sixty-mile-wide no-man's land was laden with land mines and lined with immense military firepower. The southern edge of the zone was a little over thirty miles from Seoul. The threat of another war, and the close proximity of that border, was like growing up with an active volcano in the distance. It was a lot closer than it seemed. It smoked, it simmered, and on most days I didn't give it much thought. But deep down I knew it might one day blow a hole into the sky.

A few incidents during our first years in Korea were a lesson for my family in understanding what people meant when they said, "the Korean War never ended." There was the incident in 1968, when specially-trained North Korean soldiers cut through a fence at the DMZ and crept into South Korea. I was too young then to understand that the president was nearly beheaded, soldiers were battling in the nearby hills, or to worry about packing into a jeep with my family, the Nashes, and the Lees to make our hurried way south. I wasn't old enough to worry I might watch my country fade from view through the windows of a U.S. Army helicopter.

By the time I was in elementary school I was accustomed to the forbidden fortresses of U.S. might in South Korea. Yongsan Garrison, the 600-acre U.S. base in southern Seoul, served as the headquarters for military forces in Korea. The high concrete walls of Yongsan were topped with barbed-wire, the concrete studded with broken glass. Only Koreans who worked on the base and Americans who carried a U.S. military ID were allowed regular entry. In the 1970s, over forty thousand U.S. soldiers were stationed in forty plus bases all over South Korea. The Falcons of Seoul American School were our main rivals in our league of international and Department of Defense school teams.

I was on Yongsan a few times during each year of high school for school sports events. I couldn't believe my eyes when I saw a snack bar selling hamburgers and french fries and a movie theater showing the latest films from the U.S. Mom managed to get onto Yongsan more frequently, in the way she always seemed to manage these things. Military police guarding the gate let her in the first time to borrow books from Yongsan Library. Each time after that she explained, in her nice Sue Rice voice, that she needed to return books she had borrowed. This continued for years.

As my Girl Scout troop clambered up Saddleback Mountain, young soldiers with machine guns and serious faces peered out at us from small concrete outposts as we earned hiking badges and settled onto sit-upons. These young guardians, part of South Korea's conscripted army, were posted along every mountain peak. They were huddled in sandy bunkers near our cabin at Taechon Beach. They stood outside government buildings and guarded old palaces. Sometimes it seemed like they were everywhere. I understood that a wrong move, like staying on the streets after Seoul's midnight curfew, or entering into one of these outposts without asking, could result in a machine gun in the face. I knew I had some special dispensation as a foreigner, and as a child, but in the case of national security, I knew it was not limitless.

The general public, from store clerks to taxi drivers, seemed to appreciate the U.S. and its role in the Korean War. Every now and then Ajumoni would say, in English, "America number one!" while giving a thumbs up. The general perception of U.S. citizens during the 1960s and '70s can perhaps best be illustrated by the reception President Lyndon B. Johnson received when he came to Seoul in 1966. He arrived to the sound of hundreds of exuberant *hanbok* clad children singing "Arirang," Korea's national folk song. A massive banner with the images of the U.S. and Korean president hung outside the airport. As Johnson stood listening to the chorus, a fleet of army jets flew over, the jet exhaust red, white and blue. The *Stars and Stripes*, the U.S. Armed Forces newspaper, said LBJ got a "rip-roaring Texas style welcome." Schools were closed for the historic day. An estimated two million people stood along the streets, twenty to thirty deep, to greet the motorcade. People waved American flags on roads strewn with chrysanthemums and confetti. Throngs broke down metal fences and climbed rooftops to see the American president. Dad, who hoped to get a glimpse of the motorcade, couldn't get more than ten feet through the thick crowd.

"Here in Korea," Johnson said in a speech he gave outside of City Hall, "our fighting men stand with your own along the Demilitarized Zone, and we shall come once again to your defense if aggression—God forbid—should occur here again . . . More than 54,000 Americans died in the bitter 1950-53 battle to save this mountainous peninsula country from communist invaders from the north. Today South Korea has around 45,000 soldiers helping the allied cause in South Vietnam . . .To an American, the free soil of Korea is hallowed ground."

I don't know what a three-year-old comprehends when she hears adults talking about guerrillas running through the nearby hills. I'm not even sure I can tell you what a five or six-year-old understands about borderlines and separated families, or about the geopolitical motivations that cause one nation to fight another. But I always knew the DMZ was more than a border or a political limit. The place we called Panmunjom was a reminder of what could happen in life, a sixteen-year lesson about unhealed scars and broken places, teaching me the world was not always peaceful or fair, even to those who had done nothing wrong.

The incidents that occurred along that line of division would be a long lesson about the futility of concepts like fairness, or thinking people got what they deserved, or expecting everything to work out like I thought it should work out. I don't remember a time I didn't know this story of heartbreaking separation. I don't remember a time I didn't understand life as some delicate balance between complete safety and utter peril. And I don't remember ever feeling safer anywhere else than I felt in South Korea.

The country of my passport and the country of my heart had a complicated relationship, entangled in the events of a devastating war, the heavy presence of U.S. troops on the strategic East Asian peninsula, and the commitment of President Park to send troops to Vietnam in exchange for a huge influx of U.S. money for development. A series of incidents along that border stayed with me long after I left Korea. When I grew older, when I came to understand more, I began to question whether my passport country was really deserving of all that praise, complicating my national identity even more.

THE BEHEADING HILL

I could not pass Choldusan, the "Beheading Hill," without imagining the horrible fate of the thousands of Catholics whose lives were violently taken in Korea in the 19th century. The martyrs' monument on a rocky prominence overlooking the Han River was always a reminder that people who tried to spread Christianity in the past centuries not only faced persecution. They lost their heads. They got tossed off of cliffs.

Westerners called Korea the "Hermit Kingdom" in the 19th century, due to the isolationist policies of the Chosun Dynasty. Until the late 1800s, foreigners were forbidden to reside within Seoul's walls. The Russian Legation, built in 1890, and Seoul Anglican Cathedral, built in the 1920s, were just two of many buildings and embassies that gave evidence to the fact South Korea had since opened up to the world. By the 1970s, many foreigners lived all over the country.

Each year, missionary families arrived from near and far to attend the annual Presbyterian Mission Meeting. These were jolly affairs for a social kid like me, with skits and pot luck dinners of *pulgogi*, jello salad, peach pie, and tuna casserole. I looked forward to reuniting with my country cousins, the missionary kids I knew from shared summer vacations at Taechon Beach, who lived in smaller cities like Taejon, Kwang Ju, and in remote villages and island outposts. The feeling of joyful fellowship amongst the adults can perhaps best be attributed to what scholar Donald Clark so aptly referred to in his book about Korean mission history as the "exhilaration of shared purpose." For missionary kids, our joy can perhaps best be attributed to the "exhilaration of shared identity."

There were various theories as to why Koreans had taken to Christianity in such big numbers. Some said it was because the first missionaries to Korea were Koreans themselves, returned from China, where Christianity had already begun to spread. Others said it was because missionaries to Korea stressed the doctrine of individual worth before God, regardless of social status, making Christianity a call to butchers, the poor, women, prostitutes, people with leprosy, and laborers, those who had faced generations of class persecution with no way to rise up out of those lives.

Others pointed to the similarities between Christianity's monotheism and the ancient Korean belief in *hananim*, one God. Many scholars spoke of a religious vacuum in Korea. As Buddhism came out of favor, Koreans lived more by the philosophy and tenets of state-sponsored Confucianism in the 1800s, than by any specific religion. Scholar and missionary Samuel Moffett put it like this: "Like Confucianism, Christianity taught righteousness and revered learning. Like Buddhism, it sought purity and promised a future life. And like the shamanists, Christians believed in answered prayer and miracles."

In the 1900s, missionaries founded schools, hospitals, and colleges, including Yonsei University and Ewha, the first college for women. Other missionaries ran rehabilitation centers for those disabled during the Korean War. Others started programs for war widows, orphans, the blind, and the deaf. Some were involved with church planting and evangelism, translating scripture from English into Korean. In the 1950s, missionaries started community health projects providing low-cost health care to isolated and poverty-stricken islands. In the 1960s, a few began organizing and addressing the myriad of problems faced by industrial workers in burgeoning factories. From the 1960s and into the 1980s, the number of Protestants in Korea grew faster than any other nation.

I was less than a year old when I first entered into the comfortable, time-worn living room of Horace G. Underwood II, the president of Yonsei and the grandson of one of Korea's first Protestant missionaries. These old mission houses were fascinating places, full of books grown yellow with age, maple tables hewn by Pennsylvania craftsmen, antique rice chests, dark Korean cabinets, and three-paneled screens gifted by former Korean kings and queens. The Underwood family, the Moffetts, the Clarks, the Appenzellers, and a number of other families were intricately tied with Korea.

In one way, I saw these people to be similar to my Yankee grandparents in dress and manner, with their no-nonsense, New England ways. But these families had deep roots in Korea. Horace Grant Underwood was integral in starting Yonsei University. He was a scholar in Korean history and cultural heritage and introduced much of that history to the outside world. Sam Moffett grew up in a house in Pyong Yang that shared a wall with a house built during the biblical time of David. The first of the famed Underwood family to come to Korea were once on such familiar terms with the royal family that their young son recalled sitting on Queen Min's knee.

But Queen Min was long dead at the hands of Japanese assassins by the time we came, and like the wild tigers and boars the Underwoods once hunted in Korea's remote mountains, the pioneering missionary era had long since passed. The era of settling in had passed, too. Missionaries, hundreds of them from dozens of denominations, were hunkered in. They were heading universities, schools, and social programs their ancestors had founded. The Seoul tombstone of one of Korea's earliest missionaries was inscribed, in *hangul*, "I would rather be buried in Korea than in Westminster Abbey."

Outside of our own mission, my friends included children of Nazarenes, Seventh Day Adventists, Oriental Mission Society, Methodists, Lutherans, Southern Presbyterians, Salvation Army Corporals, and Southern Baptists. As my family arrived to our annual mission meeting in our Nissan Bluebird after a breezy twenty-minute drive across the city, tiny, sixty-year-old Lilian Ross traveled by bus from her southern province home hours away. She was born in Korea, and lived with Korean people in a Korean style home. She wore a simple Korean country dress, her white hair pulled back in a bun. She had lived in Korea over sixty years by the time we arrived. A Korean friend once asked Dad, "Are you sure she isn't Korean?" I really wasn't.

Knowing someone like Lillian Ross was like knowing someone not from the last century, but from two centuries before. When she was growing up nobles were carried around in palanquins and the scholarly class wore horse hair hats. She wasn't the only child of missionaries to stay in Korea the rest of her life. These people called "foreigners" had seen the country through colonization, war, and division. People like Lillian Ross made our years in Korea look like a blip in time. Though I didn't know her well, I felt tied to her, as I did to people like Horace Underwood, as if they were related to me.

I looked up to the long term missionaries not only because they were my aunts and uncles. I admired them for their fortitude and dedication. For their practical, nose to the grindstone way of getting things done. For building our sweet summer beach vacation community with not only tennis courts and a long, forest green clapboard lodge overlooking the sea, but with a library stocked with crossword puzzles and classics like *The Wonderful Wizard of Oz* and the entire Hardy Boys and Nancy Drew series. I loved them for building a bakery at the beach. Who has the foresight to add a bakery with freshly baked cinnamon rolls, sliced bread, and chocolate pie to a remote Asian vacation place? This is brilliance!

But maybe I loved them the most for the way they told Korean folk tales, for the way Mrs. Moore taught us about the constellations in the Korean sky, and the way Mrs. Moffett was a scholar of shaman women, the *mudang* whose connection to the spirit world held so much fascination for me.

I idolized the pioneering missionaries who came during the time of dynasties. Their one to three month passages made by passenger and freighter ship made our fourteen-hour Japan Airlines trip look like a commuter flight. I respected them for taking on hardship for a cause bigger than themselves. For their perseverance in the face of adversity. Having been taught from an early age to respect austerity, the harder the trip to Korea sounded, the more admirable these people were.

Upon their arrival, they found rudimentary roads, barely heated homes, and little in the way of indoor plumbing. Some of them lost children to disease. I placed those who refused to bow at Shinto shrines during Japanese colonization on an even higher pedestal. When I heard they refused to do this in part because of their Christian beliefs rather than because of their loyalty to Korea, I questioned the source. I reserved my highest admiration for those who stayed during the Korean War, when all non-essential foreign personnel were advised to evacuate.

Missionaries didn't talk about this history very often. Once in a while, I would hear an understated story of an attempted evacuation from Seoul, or hear a missionary kid from the generation before me talk about playing in a bombed-out government building in the weeks after the war ended.

I differentiated our missionaries from the ones I heard my parents talk about, the ones who had disallowed Hawaiians from speaking their own language, who tried to 'civilize the savages' in the Americas, who decimated those populations and their cultures. I came to believe, through a combination of fact, naiveté, positive thinking, and misinformation, that almost all of our missionaries were different.

Every summer, my family piled into our Jeep and then, into our station wagon, to head into the countryside for vacation. My brothers settled into the banquet seating in back to happily ride sideways through Korea. For the first few summers we took our vacations at the YMCA camp outside of Seoul, where my parents raised the sooty kerosene lantern of assimilation as they washed pots and pans in the river and ate from a pot of rice cooked by the campground staff. My parents explored different vacation options outside of leaving the country, which turned out to be not only unaffordable but highly impractical for a family of six on a missionary salary.

The third summer we joined missionaries from all over South Korea at our vacation area of rustic cottages known as Taechon Beach. We took in the annual musical, swam in the Yellow Sea, participated in the annual Rook tournament, and gave one hundred percent of ourselves to shell collecting contests. Apparently, there was only so much of a moral stand my parents could take in the name of integration when soaked to the bone with four small children in a jerry-rigged military tent during the intense rainy season called *changma*.

When the train pulled out of Seoul Station, we left the pollution and the crowds of the city behind us. Just minutes outside Seoul, rice paddies and farmlands intermingled with clusters of old farmhouses. These farmlands led to more mountains and valleys, through small villages caught in time, where people lived out a long-standing rhythm of planting and harvesting that connected them directly to the land and to their ancestors. In less than a half hour, I was looking out onto terraced rice paddies, mud houses, and village gates guarded by spirit totem poles. As grandmothers walked along the high paths that surrounded flooded fields, I snacked on dried cuttlefish and seaweed-wrapped *kimpap* rice rolls. The country air, tinted with the smell of night soil and wood fires, drifted in through the open window. We shared the train car with chain-smoking grandfathers and middle-aged ladies carrying sacks of produce.

Our trips to Taechon represented a compromise my parents made in attempting to integrate into Korean life. But they awakened something in me that Seoul could never do. At Taechon, I fell in love with fireflies, kerosene appliances, and the red glow of a toxic green mosquito coil. I fell in love with the salty smell of the sea, the white cranes who landed on rice paddy fields, and the purple starfish that scattered across Taechon's fine sand. Those thatched countryside roofs were so beautiful and bucolic from a distance. I loved the sun-browned faces and the country twang of the ladies who sold fruit and vegetables by the entrance to our cottages, and the fisherman who came to our cabin to sell Mom crab from his bamboo basket. I loved old Korea. And I grew to love the extensive community of missionaries who came to Taechon from all over the country.

Back in Seoul, setting aside denominational and theological distinctions for the sake of community, missionaries from all denominations worshipped together at Seoul Union Church. In a much more well-heated space than Toksu Church, we listened to our missionary fathers give sermons and our friends' parents sing in the choir. We could expect anything from Mr. Rader's thoughtful and alliterated Salvation Army messages about God's eternal love and Christmas trees "tangled in tinsel" to Reverend Stanley's ecumenical call for us to be better people. We attended Toksu Church regularly in the first years, but for me and my brothers, the draw to attend a church with our friends was strong. No matter how many years we attended Toksu Church, my family was treated like special guests. We were too often asked to get up and sing. We are not a "get up and sing in front of people" kind of family. Add the long length of services and sermons to the mix, and I can see why Mom and Dad started taking us to Seoul Union Church more often.

With many of the same people we just swam with at Taechon Beach, we sang songs about Christian soldiers going off to war. We raised rousing choruses of "How Great Thou Art." We sang, "When peace like a river, attendeth my way, When sorrows like sea billows roll, Whatever my lot, Thou hast taught me to say, It

is well, it is well with my soul." And I thought of the missionaries who had lost children to disease, and those who had dedi-
cated their lives to war widows. And I thought of how, in spite of
Korea's hardship, in spite of the great war, some missionaries had
stayed. And not only had they stayed, they hunkered down. They
shipped furniture, pianos, books, and appliances to Korea. They
planted rose gardens. They raised their children. And then, and
this next part feels like a bit of a departure from "sorrows like sea
billows rolling," they constructed brick homes with porches, radiators, western bathrooms, and spacious living and sleeping rooms.
They put up walls around compounds, built servant homes, and
poured concrete for tennis courts.

The beach community I loved, the green clapboard lodge overlooking the Yellow Sea, the tennis courts where historic tournaments played out, year after year; our rustic, numbered cabins
with their wooden shutters and Coleman lanterns; the city mission
compounds, our foreign church and school; the social club with
its pool and bowling hall, was all part of a story. An industrious
people of faith had come along before us and set up a convenient
and wonderful world. My international school had been around
for sixty years when I started first grade.

As Seoul Union Church came to a close, a precise hour after it
began, we said the Lord's Prayer in unison, placed *won* bills in the
offering plate, and heard a strong-voiced, raised-arm Benediction:
The Lord bless thee, and keep thee: The Lord make his face shine upon
thee, and be gracious unto thee: The Lord lift up his countenance
upon thee, and give thee peace. And we would all go out into the
world and end up at the Seoul Civilian Club. The Lord's face was
indeed shining upon us. We were sufferin' for Jesus over plates of
meat loaf made from U.S. army import beef and mashed potatoes
blended with American butter. Seoul Civilian Club was on the
American Corps of Engineers base in an East Seoul neighborhood
of modest homes and small businesses. Unlike the U.S. army bases,

the Civilian Club was open to any U.S. citizen. It also had one of the few restaurants that served proper steaks and mashed potatoes. We flocked there after church, missionary families seated at fancy, white-linen clothed tables, gleefully waiting for meaty cheeseburgers and cokes served on ice.

In spite of the longevity and these long-standing traditions and institutions, the adults never described their move to Korea as an immigration. That the work required ten, twenty, fifty, sixty years, or even a lifetime, still didn't make anyone call it immigration. That these people had shipped all of their earthly belongings in huge containers across the seas did not make anyone call it an immigration, either. But when does a mission become a life? When does a mission field become, simply, home? Does shipping a piano and a fake Christmas tree across the seas, maybe, just maybe, seal the deal?

On one hand, I had this extraordinary example of committing to a place for a lifetime, for generations. I grew up thinking missionaries were an integral part of Korea's modern history and South Korea's foundation. I believed there was no other place we should all be. I paid no attention to the clues hinting at another reality. Friends whose great grandparents were born in Korea but still held U.S. passports. Houses whose furniture spoke to another way of life. My own family, living in Korea as if it was home, but storing the possessions we did not bring with us at Charlie Kuhns' warehouse in Niagara Falls. Never quite understanding what it meant that my parents were serving "terms." (My life was governed by a term?) I was coming of age in a country I would one day likely leave, part of a community that was as rooted and permanent as it was a temporary construct of a particular time and place. But I didn't reflect for one minute on the mixed messages and inconsistencies built into the design of my life.

I've heard people say children are lucky to grow up overseas. I've read many essays touting the benefits of cross-cultural childhoods.

We're so adaptable! We make friends easily! We traveled the world! I know what they're trying to say. I wouldn't change my childhood for anything. I was given so many blessings as a young girl. I have no idea who I would be without Korea. But sometimes, I wonder if the people writing these things are trying to cover over a deep well of sadness. Sometimes I wonder if this wonderful world I grew up thinking belonged to me really wasn't mine after all. Sometimes I wonder if my childhood was in some ways a heartbreaking setup.

I Call Their Names Quietly in My Heart

"I cannot see nor touch you, my dear baby,
so I call your name quietly in my heart.
Although you are not here with me now,
I miss you very much, my beautiful flower.
You will always be loved in my heart."

—I Wish for You a Beautiful Life: Letters from the Korean
Birth Mothers of Ae Ran Won to Their Children

Books on sociology and the status of women in Korea lined the bookshelves in Dad's study, the large upstairs space he liked to call his Upper Room. They sat next to Korean hymnals, a book written by American feminists called *Our Bodies, Ourselves*, a Sears catalog, stacks of *Mad* magazines, and scholarly titles about the history of the Christian church. I never once thought a book celebrating the female body and one describing the impact of church planting might not belong together.

It was easy to pick out the books that belonged to my father, our poet and theologian, the books that belonged to my feminist-leaning, social worker mother, and the slightly raunchy political satire magazines that belonged to Rick.

One book on the shelf drew me in even more than the Sears catalog and its boys in Green Bay Packer pajamas, its large white American appliances, and its Mrs. Beasley dolls. The book depicted vivid paintings by a Christian activist. The painter was in trouble with the government. When he was taken in for questioning, they threatened to cut off his fingers. The paintings were considered dangerous material, the artist's take on society's injustices seen as a threat to national security.

In one painting, well-fed children of different races sit around a dining table. Underneath the table, emaciated children are eating their scraps. In another, a rich man is inside a house, laughing and drinking. He's seated at a table full of food, being entertained by a group of women. Outside the home, a servant is shooing poor children away. In another, a man is relaxing in a large, tile bathtub. Several faucets are spewing hot water. Outside the window, ten modestly dressed people crowd around a single faucet, fighting over one drip.

One painting, though, haunted me, and I never forgot the image. A rail-thin boy in torn clothing is begging at a rich person's home. His ribs are visible under taut skin. His bony hand holds out an empty pail to a large woman, twice as large as any Korean woman I had ever seen. She's sitting cross-legged on a mat. Folds of weight heave under a dress of new and opulent material. She's holding a large bowl of sparkling white rice and is shoving a big wad of it into her mouth. The lessons told in these paintings expressed the way my parents understood the world. There were haves and there were have-nots, and the actions of those of us who were given more than others were often the reason for this discrepancy.

House of Grace was Mom's official workplace. The organization was started in the early 1960s by Mrs. Van Lierop to reach out to women and girls caught up in prostitution, who were working in the many brothels surrounding U.S. army bases and in downtown Seoul. The program provided housing and scholarship money so the women could obtain a certificate in work such as barbering, tailoring, and nurse's aide work. The agency later expanded their mission to work with unwed pregnant woman. The programs were housed in three humble homes not far from where we lived.

With little opportunities in rural areas, many young girls were moving to the cities to find work. Some were sent to the capital by their families. Free public education was only provided through elementary school. Beyond that, many families couldn't afford to educate their children. Some parents would or could only pay for advanced education for their sons. After arriving in the city, country girls worked as bus girls, as waitresses in small restaurants, or in large factories. Others were lured into brothels by men waiting at Seoul Station, promising good jobs in restaurants or businesses that didn't exist.

The need for a place like House of Grace was not just due to poverty and urban migration. Traditionally, the family system placed women at the bottom of the rung. Women were judged by their value in providing sons to the family, serving husbands, and in-laws. Poor girls were particularly vulnerable. Most of the young women at House of Grace had only a primary education. About half of them came from broken homes or homes where one or both parents were deceased. The Korean War left a legacy of disruption in family life.

Unmarried mothers were shunned no matter the reason for their pregnancy. Women who kept their babies had trouble finding employment. Their children were often ridiculed at school. With no legal birth father, the babies were not written into the family registry, a document central to family life in a nation obsessed by bloodlines. The shame of single motherhood was like a deadly virus that could pass through families and linger for generations. Even the Korean word for shame, *changpi*, sounded so heartbreakingly terrible to me when it was spoken. This was not just guilt. This was *changpi*. This was collective shame of epic proportions, shame you might not ever recover from.

I was not happy when Mom carried a two-year-old girl into the living room one day and announced she was staying with us for a short time. I held onto my place as the youngest and the only girl, and I was not about to give up my position easily, even for an orphan who was only going to be with us for a few weeks awaiting a foster home. I was used to college students living with us, maids living with us, and student groups coming into our home. I had grown to expect a life where work and home were never separated. That toddler simply crossed the line.

But I was happy to share Mom with House of Grace. I was proud of Mom when she became the organization's second director, and I was proud of her when she stepped down to make way for the organization's first Korean director, to serve in a capacity of advisor. Mom was too busy getting things done to care about titles and positions.

Sometimes Mom took me with her to work to share a simple lunch with the staff and the young women. To some degree, I understood why the women were living there. But I was too naive to imagine the moments of horror or to completely understand the narrow societal thinking that got them to this place. Mom was careful about what she shared with me, but she didn't shield me from real life, either. She imparted a sense of non-judgment to me, a feeling that if my circumstances were different I might be in these girls' shoes. She reserved her judgment for the broken society and the brothel owners. Her attitude to this and to most other societal problems were lessons for me in learning to take care when trying to understand where the blame for social ills should be placed. Mom hoped the program would expand to include women who wanted to keep their babies, not just those who were going to relinquish them upon delivery.

I remember passing down the narrow hallway of the old home. I peered with curiosity into the modest rooms that lined the hall. I remember a few young girls sitting together on the floor, and how they looked like they weren't much older than I was. They giggled when I appeared, covering their mouths in modesty. A chasm of nationality and circumstance hung in the air between us. Just an outfit or two of simple clothing hung in the closet. Their bump of pregnancy was their mark of *changpi*, and in those moments I knew that there were some experiences I could never fully understand.

International adoptions began in haste after the Korean War, when over one hundred thousand children were left homeless or parentless. Grinding poverty kept orphanages full. Many intact families couldn't provide enough food for one more mouth and domestic adoption outside of the family was not deemed acceptable practice. In 1966, the year I flew as an infant to Korea, almost five hundred children were adopted into families of Americans and Europeans. By the mid-1970s, over five thousand Korean children were adopted internationally each year. Over sixty-four thousand children were adopted during the sixteen years we lived in Korea. Over a third of them were born to single mothers.

Mom took me with her once to one of Holt's orphanages just outside of Seoul. This particular organization was a home for so-called "unadoptable children," those with some kind of special need or physical flaw. The visit left a big impression on me. Some children had cleft palates. Others had large birthmarks covering an arm or face. Others walked with the tell-tale limp of polio. The bright white skin and fair hair of the albino children stood out glaringly. I stood behind Mom, trying to hide my shock. The children shrieked with laughter when Mom greeted them in Korean.

Mom was a networker, a Chemistry-minded social worker, a fixer of machines and problems, a woman who came through, head down, whether your piano was out of tune or you needed a home. Mom later worked with Catholic Social Ministries in the U.S., conducting home studies for families trying to adopt internationally. She saw adopted children living happy lives. She saw others having great difficulty. Mom helped me understand each story was singular. In the straightforward way she approached these things, she taught me there wasn't always a simple fairy book ending like the adoption brochures told about, and there wasn't always a tragic ending, either. Adoptions were stories of human loss and they were stories of human resilience and hope. I grew up with the understanding that some birth mothers and adoptees carried the pain of separation with them their entire lives. I did not grow up under the assumption that they were leaving for a better life when they went to the States.

When I was in middle school, Mom began to provide assistance to a group of biracial teens. The U.S. government was allowing them to emigrate if they could prove their father was a U.S. soldier. She brought a few of the young women into our lives as they began to prepare for a life away from Korea. I remember feeling worried about Hyun-joo, the teenager who came over to spend time with us. Would she be able to find a home in the vast place called the United States, in a country that even I had come to learn could be hard to wrap small arms around? Would she be happy away from her country? I also knew that for some bi-racial teens, a ticket to the U.S. meant leaving behind a life of discrimination. I knew that Hyun-joo felt like an outsider in Korea. She was a reject in her homeland due to the simple fact of her kinky hair and darker skin.

Through the years Mom learned more about women's rights from attending classes at Ewha University and serving under women at the forefront of the women's movement. Mom told me about the courage of Lee Tae-young, Korea's first woman lawyer, who started the first legal aid center for women. She taught me about Lee Hyo-jae, professor of sociology at Ewha University, a key figure in raising awareness of discrimination against women. I looked up to these women who were defying convention and expectation. Women who took on issues people barely talked about, barely even acknowledged the existence of.

I talked to a Korean man once when I was older. He calmly explained how Korean belief dictated men were *yin*, sky and warmth, and women were *yang*, dirt and cold. He told me men were considered far superior to women, and how much better it was to have a son than a daughter. I wasn't surprised to hear this. I knew how women were looked upon in Korea. Although many of the Korean men we knew behaved outside the norm, I saw many women prepare meals as their husbands sat at the dining table waiting to be served. I heard stories about newly married friends working to the bone in their in-laws' homes. I knew how valued my three brothers were to some of our friends. Patriarchy permeated Korean society.

One day I told Ajumoni a friend of the family had a baby girl. She said, matter-of-factly, "Oh good! She can help with the housework!" More than once, Korean friends of Mr. Patten, who had four girls, looked at him in pity and said, "So many girls!" People were always praising Dad, sometimes for things I knew Mom did. "*Moksanim* is so wonderful!" It drove me crazy.

But even knowing all of this, everything that man said went against what I knew in my heart to be true. I watched women carry buckets of water and move heavy stones. I witnessed mothers and grandmothers bend into rice paddy fields and pull carts of produce piled into the sky. I watched the Egg Lady put her son through college with a simple business of delivering eggs to foreigners. I witnessed Ajumoni raise her children on her own, without a husband, in a society that said a fatherless child was considered less than.

I saw Confucianism as a force for good. It bound us together. We were brothers and sisters. I was a *haksaeng*, a student. The adults in my city were my *ajumonis* and *ajossis*. When I used these titles, I felt that the flower lady, the shoe repair man, and the bus girl were not strangers, but my aunts and uncles, my sisters and brothers, part of my extended Seoul family. In the following years, because of my parents' unofficial and official work, because of the crushing poverty that played out on the streets and in the hillsides of Seoul, I was not naive to suffering. Grandmothers came to our front gate to beg for rice. Men, their legs bluntly cut off at the knees, dragged themselves through South Gate Market, singing for change. Almost every underpass was lined by at least one to two beggars. The men called rag pickers sorted through the trash bins outside our gate, using tongs to pick through food waste, empty tin cans, and discarded papers. We found nothing but spent ashes in the bin after they left. Some days I wondered when I might see one of Dad's old sermons or my math homework on the paper bags used at the corner store, the small sacks made of homework pages and discarded letters, not bleached white, but glued together to carry candies and cookies while telling the history of a nation.

Somehow, even having seen all of these things, I still believed the Confucian-based values I had learned from the time I was a little girl were the underpinning of all that was good. I believed in the spoken and silent gestures that connected me to people of my city. These titles and customs created order. They told me who was teacher, first born, youngest, and oldest. They told me where I stood. I felt security knowing I was part of a singular, definable culture. I did not yet understand how the hierarchy, the titles, the levels of speech, were also used to keep people down, take away human dignity, and stamp out any deviation from the norm.

One day, during a summer spent in Korea between my junior and senior year of college, I sat in a class of mostly Korean-American students at Yonsei University. I was enrolled in one of Yonsei's summer programs for international students. In sociology class, a few Korean-Americans who had grown up in the U.S. began criticizing Korean customs and culture, laying heavily into all they felt was wrong about Korea. What I had always taken for granted as good, they saw as narrow-minded. What I saw as communal, they saw as oppressive. What they saw as a lack of freedom, I saw as order. My first reaction was surprise. I had no idea people felt this way.

My next response was to feel my classmates should open their hearts and minds to the possible reasons behind what they saw. I spoke up. I found myself in the strange position of defending Korea to ethnic Koreans. I was defending Korean ways as if they were my own. Were they looking through more of an American lens than I was?

As the summer went on, I began to understand something. I had a patriotic love of Korea that was sometimes blind to and too forgiving of Korea's faults. For a long time I thought Korean women kept their last names after marriage because they were liberated, not imagining it might be because they were not deemed worthy of the last name of their husband. But it wasn't only that I had a child's love of her homeland. As the child of Americans, my experience in Korea *was* different. I didn't have Korean parents or relatives. I would never be fully subject to the expectations of a nation or a Korean family. I would never have the pressure to marry someone my parents insisted on or who was found, God forbid, by a matchmaker. I was not expected to grow up to serve a husband or a mother-in-law like many Korean women had to. My parents never gave me a sense that my gender should have any role to play in my life decisions. Taxi drivers praised me when I spoke Korean. My poor Korean-American friends, the ones who never learned Korean, endured twenty-minute shaming sessions just to get from Yonsei to downtown Seoul. One friend started telling taxi drivers she was from Japan.

I knew Korea's societal expectations intimately. With so many Koreans in our life, having lived in Korea so long, I followed these practices closely. I used a higher form of language when required. I gave up my bus seat for elders. I held people's bags on the bus when they had to stand. I took children onto my lap. I carried an instinctive feeling that my actions didn't just reflect on me, they reflected on my parents, too. One of Mom's Korean friends who lived in the U.S. once told her, "I wish my daughter was a good Korean daughter like Lidgie is."

But I wasn't strictly subject to Korean protocol like Koreans were. I came to understand that summer at Yonsei that I needed to look at my story in an honest way. My nostalgia and mixed-up influences complicated the picture even more. In the U.S., I longed for the warmth of Korean togetherness, the closeness that could deliver the deepest love and smother you in the same instant. I missed the distinct rhythm of Korean rituals. I missed holidays celebrated by the moon's cycle. I missed eating honey and sesame-seed filled New Year's rice cakes. I missed bowing to people. I missed stifling communalism. But the same culture that bound me so tightly to it also sent its own babies away. The same place that opened its arms so wide to my family rejected many of their own who deviated from the norm. Korea could be a rigid and unforgiving place. Societal expectations and group shame were heavy burdens to carry. It was so hard for me to look on Korea as an outsider. But it was also impossible for me to see it as a true insider. I could never be truly objective or subjective.

Many years later, while I was completing a masters program in teaching, I taught a history class in a high school in Concord, Massachusetts. We were discussing the bombing of Nagasaki and Hiroshima. One student in particular kept defending the bombings no matter what anyone said. As I listened, I wondered how she could push aside any sense of sorrow for the innocent people killed by that act. I wondered how it was possible for someone to take one side with so much certainty.

The next week my mentor teacher pulled me aside before class. "I'm really glad you're going to teach today's lesson about the Korean War, Liz. Maybe you can explain why so many atrocities were committed by Koreans on Koreans. I can't believe the kind of things they did to one another."

I didn't know what to say. Since class was starting, I mumbled something about atrocities being committed on all sides, and I continued down the hall. Later that evening, while stewing at home, I crafted a series of witty retorts about how I would be really happy to do that if he could then follow my little wrap-up with an explanation of the genocide of Native Americans, centuries of institutionalized slavery, and the atrocities committed by U.S. soldiers around the world. And anyway, who can explain atrocities?

I think we all carry an instinctive feeling about who we belong to and who we will defend. At least most of us, when pressed, have some central place deep within that tells us, if it came down to it, which side we would choose. We value what we have been taught to value. We defend the people we understand. We defend the people who understand us. Which lives matter?

It's more difficult to make quick judgments when we love and know people on different sides of a river. It's much harder to talk about good and evil countries when you hear not only about atrocities committed by North Koreans against South Koreans, but also about atrocities perpetrated by Americans in that same war. It's impossible to only celebrate adoption programs when you understand the complicated stories, the impact of a war of proxy, and the prejudiced system that led to many of those adoptions. It's impossible to only criticize adoption programs when you've witnessed the resolve of the social worker friends of your mother who have defied their families' wishes for them to be housewives, and who are instead working with people society has deemed the "bad girls."

In my Korea, women were warm like the sun that set on the Yellow Sea. They were strong and sturdy like the bamboo that grew even during the bitter cold of winter. I grew up in the bosom of one of the most intensely Confucian and patriarchal societies in the world, feeling in my heart that it was the women who were the strongest of all. Women who had the courage to address society's deepest injustices. Women who looked away the moment their baby was taken away from them, and then tried to carry on with life. Mothers and sisters who marched up to riot police and shook their fists in defiance and anger. Ajumoni, determined to raise her children on her own, even when others told her to give them away. And my own mother, a woman of enduring life spirit and ready compassion who taught me how important it was, when we see an injustice, to simply do something about it. These weren't perfect people. They weren't saints. They were just extraordinary, ordinary women who persevered in the face of insurmountable obstacles. They were not weak. They were of infinite courage. I still call their names quietly in my heart. *Cho-ssi. Ajumoni. Kyeran Ajumoni. Song Hae Omoni. Sue Rice. Faye Moon.*

Axe Murders,
Self-Immolations,
and Assassinations

Every few weeks, our Girl Scout troop gathered in the open concept area between the fifth and sixth grade classrooms to make sit-upons, earn badges, and pledge to be honest and fair and help where we were needed. Each meeting began with the Girl Scout Promise.

On my honor, I will try:
To serve God and my country,
To help people at all times,
And to live by the Girl Scout Law.

I was fully on board with the Girl Scouts, especially since Mom said I could buy a Girl Scout knife. But there was just one problem. I wasn't sure which country we were referring to. But I had a strong feeling we were talking about the U.S.

Citing the Girl Scout Promise was similar to reciting the Nicene Creed at church. I chose not to dwell on the many questions it brought up, such as: Just who were the Nicenes? Why did they need a creed? And why are we saying it now? *Do* I believe in the holy catholic church? I don't even know what that means. And does it make sense to promise to serve a country I have lived in for one year?

The words to the U.S. Pledge of Allegiance felt even more misplaced in Seoul, even further removed from what was happening across the city at the Blue House. One nation? Indivisible? With liberty and justice for all? Where was that happening?

Park Chung-hee was the only president I had ever known. Since his eighteen-year rule practically defined South Korea's formation after 1961, it was hard not to feel some begrudging respect for the stern-faced man who looked down at me from the government portrait that hung on our police station wall, year after year. As the U.S. transformed under the distinctly different leadership styles and philosophies of Kennedy, Johnson, Nixon, and Ford, we had Park. I took his presidency for granted, as if he and his official photo would always be there. Apparently that was his plan, too.

Despite coming to power in a military coup, Park was popular with the U.S. government for politically stabilizing South Korea. In 1967, the U.S. ambassador to South Korea said Park was "the prototype for the new political figure" in Korea because he had been exposed to the "ways and ideas of the outside world." Many Koreans and long-term missionaries championed him as an industrializer who was moving South Korea into a new, modern era. His ambitious economic programs and anti-communist, pro-capitalist views made him a friend to the U.S.

In August of 1974, my family was glued to MBC News. Reporters were speaking in mournful voices. We learned that while President Park was giving a formal speech at the National Theater in celebration of Korea's independence from Japan, a man in the audience, a Japanese-born Korean, pulled out a gun and took a shot. He missed the president and hit the president's wife, killing her with a misfire. I remember the day when thousands of citizens lined the main boulevard downtown as the motorcade carrying the first lady's body passed through the heart of the city.

Unlike her husband, Yuk Young-soo exuded a down-to-earth kindness. Though she came from a wealthy background, she seemed able to cut through the thick barriers of social class. Newspaper articles talked about her visiting elders and orphans. In photos, she seemed at ease with everyone from village farmers to uniformed soldiers. She engaged with the poor and the sick. She worked on behalf of women's rights, mentally challenged kids, and leprosy patients. She was highly revered, and I really admired her.

Not long after she died, I carefully placed a series of stamps memorializing her into my stamp book.

One year after the first lady was killed, another incident shocked me out of my international school complacency. In the months before I turned eleven, a group of U.S. soldiers were dispatched on a routine detail to prune a large tree that blocked the sightline from the United Nations Command checkpoint at the DMZ into North Korea. Considered a provocation, the soldiers were attacked by a group of North Korean soldiers. A few U.S. soldiers were hacked to death. The nation was on high alert.

A photo captured the moment. One group of soldiers was running frantically away from another group, who were wielding axes. Two ladders were leaning nonchalantly against a tree as if someone was about to pick fruit. The photos were blurry, so I couldn't tell who was hacking and who was running from getting hacked. But the incident taxed my young brain. Actually, I was horrified. A person could be hacked to death with an axe? Over the trimming of a tree?

Korean media didn't shy away from graphic detail. I was still thinking from time to time about Chun Tae-il, the seventeen-year-old who set himself on fire in protest at the Peace Market, in frustration that his efforts to make conditions better for fellow sweatshop workers were going nowhere. He was said to have chanted as he went down in flames, "Observe the Labor Standard Act! We are not machinery!" His story was famous in Korea. The English word they used was for his action was "self-immolated." This sounded like a terrible way to die. Self-immolation. Axe murders. Militarized borders. Assassinated first ladies. Chanting for justice as you go down in flames. Our peaceful Land of the Morning Calm could be so intense.

Three days after the axe murders, in an maneuver called Operation Paul Bunyan, two eight-men teams of military engineers were sent in to cut down the tree. In a show of strength, two security platoons, one South Korean Special Forces team, and a U.S. infantry company of over twenty helicopters was sent in as backup. A number of Air Force jets and a U.S. aircraft carrier were deployed. The task force included over eight hundred men. U.N. forces were put on battle alert.

United Nations Command notified North Korea minutes before their arrival that their work party was there "in order to peacefully finish the work left unfinished." Over one hundred heavily armed North Korean troops arrived to the scene. They set up machine gun positions and watched as the tree was taken down. Just a stump was left standing. Later that day, United Nations Command received a message from Kim Il-sung, the leader of North Korea, expressing regret for the axe incident without taking full responsibility for it. Another incident had passed without war. Again, the nation asked, *Where is the tipping point?*

The government regularly warned us of the threat that could come from the North. Three-wheeled government trucks passed slowly and methodically through the neighborhood, the men sitting in the front seat calling out serious warnings in deep-throated voices, cautioning us about diligence and safety through cheap microphones. On most days this roving reminder was like background noise, unless a voice sounded more frantic than authoritarian, and then we knew to begin to worry.

I only knew shadow stories about North Korea—rumors of what life was like in a place of mass rallies, work camps, cooperative farms, and a man the people worshipped, called the Dear Leader. I knew South Koreans were supposed to hate North Korea, to think of it as a bad place with bad people, in spite of the fact that so many people had relatives there.

My parents told me the people in the north were Koreans, too, and that many of them had family in the south. They said they hoped one day the two Koreas could be one again. They said some of our friends came from North Korea. Syngman Rhee, their boss who lived in New York City, hadn't seen his siblings or parents for twenty years.

I couldn't hate North Korea. I couldn't hate a country in which our friends' relatives lived, a country Ajumoni's husband's family once came from. But I knew not to talk about North Korea in public. I knew not to pull out a camera and start snapping pictures. Seoul was a city on high alert. Pictures could get into communist hands. While pictures of palace rooms were fine, mountain pictures were questionable. I did not even think of taking pictures from airplane windows. A photo could fall into the wrong hands. And someday, because of my snapshot, a city might get bombed. I never once thought it might be appropriate to ask Ajumoni over a bowl of spicy noodles, "So, Ajumoni, what do you think about the president?"

By middle school I was a well-trained citizen of Seoul. When sirens blew shrill on the fifteenth of each month, I ducked inside the lobby of whatever building was closest to me to wait out the monthly air drill. I stood quietly passing time with whoever else happened to be on that same street corner at the moment the drill commenced. I stood with ladies carrying bags of produce and men yawning and smoking cigarettes. I stood with stooped, wrinkled grandmothers. I stood with young children who looked at me and said, "Hello! What time is it?" and giggled. This was apparently what one needed to do when a tense enemy border was thirty miles away and dangerous commies were over that border. I was standing in the lobby of a five-story office building. We were yawning, carrying fruit, smoking cigarettes, and ready for war.

A strict midnight curfew kept Seoul dark and quiet at night. The government said a dark city was a safe city. A scurry of activity began as 11 pm approached. Citizens competed like musical chairs for empty taxis. People squeezed into cabs with strangers if the driver deemed their destinations were close enough. Others sprinted for the last buses, the ones that carried procrastinators, late night workers, and red-faced, inebriated men home.

One day I asked Dad about the thick black pen lines blotting out an article in *Time* magazine. Dad said the government didn't want people to know certain truths. He told me this was called 'censorship.' I wondered in what grim, windowless building workers were covering up paragraphs about demonstrations, military dictatorships, and opposition leader Kim Dae-jung. When the workers went home each night after a long day of stifling the truth, did they whisper their secrets to their families? How many college tuitions, mortgages, and apartment rentals were paid with these salaries? What did they say if asked, "What work do you do?" And did the government know the censorship only made me want to read those articles more?

In one way, President Park's ambitious development plans were working. South Korea was industrializing at an astounding pace. Sand-suckers stood in the middle of the Han River, preparing dikes for a new 700-acre island city. Work was underway on another bridge to span the Han River. Jackhammers cracked into the ground in every corner of the city. The New Village Movement sought to inspire citizens to modernize remote country villages mired in poverty. Saemaul Undong came with government money, uniforms, hats and pins, and theme songs. People chanted, "Mansei!," the old battle cry, "May Korea live ten thousand years!" The government encouraged full participation based on concepts of diligence and self-help. The songs were sung so energetically that I wanted to sing along, to get up, to not be idle one more minute. I will clean my room! I will walk Sport around the yard! I will finish my homework!

Senior citizens swept the streets of our neighborhood in smart uniforms, sweeping up candy wrappers and plastic yogurt cups with brooms made out of sticks and straw. Neighborhoods of dilapidated one-story homes we had passed for years were being bulldozed, transformed seemingly overnight into clusters of cheaply made concrete apartments and office buildings. One year, on the way to Taechon, we were shocked to see that almost all of the thatched roofs had been replaced with orange tile, which from the comfort of a Nissan Bluebird felt like such a loss for Korea.

Pictures of President Park appeared on the front page of the newspaper each week, standing next to new oil refineries, watching as country people tried out new farm machinery, holding ribbon cutting scissors to dedicate one of many new factories. A century of growth was being compressed into a single generation. The collective loss of the prior decades was poured into concrete and mixed into steel. It was as if in taking down the past it could be forgotten. Forget historical preservation. South Korea pushed forward at any cost, even at the price of human life.

The world applauded President Park and his "Miracle on the Han River." But my parents said this miracle was happening on the backs of ordinary people.

The Peace Market, Pyonghwa Sijang, was made up of a series of long city blocks of six-story cement buildings. It served as Seoul's main center for wholesale textile and apparel goods. The market was established after the end of the Korean War next to Cheonggyecheon Stream, near the neighborhood of stilted shacks occupied by displaced families. By the time I remember, the shacks were torn down and the stream was cemented over by a road, with an elevated roadway constructed above street level. Pyonghwa Sijang was the workplace of Chun Tae-il. It didn't seem very peaceful in the Peace Market.

One day, when Mom and I were visiting the market, we turned into one of the inner buildings and Mom led us up a narrow set of stairs. I don't remember why we went there that day, but I remember a set of dilapidated wooden stairs and taking them one at a time, slowly but steadily, as I followed my determined mother deep into another level of Seoul.

The top step opened into a low-ceilinged room lit by one bare bulb. The space felt tight. The air smelled stale, of people who had been sitting for too long in a room without adequate ventilation. The smell of textile goods was strong. Dozens of young women were hunched over antiquated sewing machines. As we entered, a few of them looked up at us and then quickly returned to their work. The atmosphere grew tense. Mom spoke a few words with a man who seemed like he was in charge. After that we didn't stay long.

As we left, weaving our way out of the tangle of the marketplace, Mom told me she and her friend Linda Jones were trying to help factory and garment workers get better conditions. She told me young women were suffering severe eyestrain working on assembly-lines, looking through microscopes to solder computer chips onto motherboards for electronic and computer firms like Motorola and Control Data, while making eight times less than their U.S. counterparts.

Not long before that day, unbeknownst to me, Mom had visited one of these sweatshops with a Fulbright scholar to interview workers about their conditions. Since she couldn't afford an inconspicuous transistor recorder, Mom and her colleague carried a recording device the size of a large movie camera into the small space. The story was later broadcast on National Public Radio in the U.S., the country in which many of the garments made in the Peace Market ended up. Not long ago, I asked Mom if she remembered why we went to the Peace Market that particular day. She paused, thought for a minute, and said, "I probably wanted you to see where your clothes were made."

Opposition to President Park was relatively quiet after the unrest following the change to the constitution in the late 1960s. In the early 1970s, tensions escalated again. Park narrowly defeated opposition leader Kim Dae-jung and began a third term as president amid charges of voter fraud. The next month, Kim Dae-jung was run over by a truck and permanently injured. Not long after the election, President Park declared a state of emergency. He imposed martial law, suspended the constitution, dissolved the National Assembly, closed universities, prohibited all political activity, and began strict censorship of the press. My parents were hearing accounts of arrests of academics, laborers, journalists, and clergy who worked with labor unions.

I don't remember a childhood time without days, weeks, and months marked and punctuated by cycles of curfews and air raid drills, demos and army maneuvers, as if they were regular seasons. The fact that we lived under a military dictatorship or under martial law never hit me over the head. It was more of a quiet tap on the shoulder. Sure, the presidential picture on the wall of every public facility never changed. Yes, army trucks passed through the city and countryside with regularity. Soldiers were stationed in bunkers near our cabin at Taechon Beach. And there was that threatening country to our North. But none of this was new or surprising. What was surprising was to realize this was not true in every country. Presidents changed? Army convoys weren't rolling through U.S. towns on a regular basis? Not every vacation cottage was surrounded by bunkers and patrolled by soldiers with automatic rifles and submachine guns?

Sinchon, the hub of our West District, was full of life. Handmade furniture stores of the 1960s had become flower shops and pop music stores. Well-stocked stationery emporiums carried an endless variety of quality pens and paper. At night, rock and roll beats pumped out of bars with names like Harlem. The main road of Sinchon dead-ended at the front gate of Yonsei campus. During the 1970s, Yonsei became a hub of student anti-government demonstrations.

For a few years, the protests happened almost every week. In a strange way, they became commonplace. But we never knew when a routine demonstration might escalate into a violent encounter.

When riot police were deployed we tried to avoid the front gate of Yonsei altogether. But this was nearly impossible. Our house was just down the road. Because of this, I witnessed many demonstrations throughout these years, and I was caught more than once within breathing distance of thick clouds of pepper gas and within sight of Molotov and rock-throwing students.

Mom told us to refer to the riots as "protests" or "demonstrations." She said we should call the activists "protesters," not "dissidents." She wanted to make sure we got these things right. She felt strongly that definitions and labels mattered. I heard her correct Dad sometimes. "Honey, don't call them that."

Mom might have been the one to teach me the politically correct way to refer to demonstrations, but it was Korea that was teaching me how to live quite normally in the midst of unrest and unpredictability. Sometimes protests ignited at our neighborhood campus. President Park was using arrest and torture to clamp down on freedom. The country I called home was rumbling for democracy and restless for change. My parents' involvement in the struggle for human rights would be one of my childhood's most profound lessons.

THE MONDAY NIGHT GROUP

In the early 1970s, a new group of people started meeting in our living room. These weren't the hymn-singing Ecumenical Christian Fellowship students Dad worked with, like Lee Jae-sun, who taught me how to play guitar by instructing me to "Grab C!!" Or Song Ki-hyun, who gave me my Korean name, and then, when she asked me to give her an English name, I inexplicably named her John. These weren't the graceful, tough as nails social workers who met with Mom about new program possibilities at House of Grace. This new group added their shoes to the entry-way pile, just like everybody else did. They sat on our floor cushions and couches, just like everyone else. These were the members of the Monday Night Group, and their presence in our home and lives was an indication that my parents' work as missionaries had taken a turn.

I knew many of the members of the group from our mission community, but they were coming together in a new way. Mr. Matthews, the father of Mark's best friend, Paul, was a Methodist missionary from small town Iowa who came to Korea in the 1950s to do relief work with rural farmers at a time when the country had one of the lowest per capita incomes in the world. Mr. Matthews had the look, demeanor, and dry comic timing of the comedian Walter Matthau. When the Monday Night Group tried to come up with a name, he said he was going to propose Christian Radical Action Program, until he realized the acronym was CRAP.

A number of the men in the Monday Night Group sported facial hair in various states of length and upkeep. Some of them lit up cigarettes when they left our house. Dad's look, that had once announced, "I'm a strong, handsome, fresh-faced young minister from the U.S.A.," now said, "I am a conscientized *moksa*." One of Dad's ECF students later told me they thought Dad looked like Moses.

Mom and her cronies, as she called them, Faye Moon, Louise Durst, and Linda Jones, wore loose, comfortable pants and sported short, practical haircuts that said, "I am woman, hear me roar." Some evenings the four of them went out for a dinner of fried chicken and beer, which was close to a subversive act for a woman of the missionary community.

Jean and Bill Basinger were a nurse and rehabilitation counselor who moved from Iowa to Japan in 1968, arriving with four young children to work with mentally and physically handicapped children and adults. In 1973, after six years in Japan, Mr. Basinger was asked by leaders of Korea's rehabilitation programs to join in their work. As a veteran of the Korean War, he felt some responsibility for the U.S. role in the division of the country, and for the devastation caused by the war. Working in Korea was a way to give back.

Mrs. Basinger worked as a nurse with an NGO providing basic health services to low-income families who were living high up in the hills of Yonhi-dong. Their ready compassion, mellow nature, and open-mindedness was a part of who the Basingers were as much as working with the disenfranchised was a part of who they were. The Basinger children quickly became a part of the fabric of SFS, somehow leading me to believe that they had lived in Korea as long as we had. The Basingers met with the Monday Night Group one week after their arrival to Seoul.

Father Jim Sinnott was a Maryknoll priest who came to South Korea in 1960 to serve a small island parish. He arrived steeped in 1950s anti-communism. Over time, he awakened to the reality of Park's dictatorship. He was greatly inspired by Cardinal Kim, Korean Catholics' highest church leader, who was outspoken in his opposition to South Korea's military regime. Cardinal Kim once addressed a group of western missionaries saying, "You missionaries can help our Korean Catholics overcome one great defect in their training. They do not realize the dignity of each person in this world. If an army climbed the hill to break the stained glass windows and destroy the cathedral, Catholics would throw their bodies down and die to protect the house of God. But today fellow Koreans are being deprived of their basic dignity, falsely imprisoned, tortured for their beliefs, and our Catholics do not react. You westerners must teach them to care for others who are in danger of oppression, as well."

By the mid-1970s, this not-so-politically-active Father Sinnott was being dragged away from anti-government protests by police and traveling to the U.S. to give talks like, "Does President Park Chung-hee have the U.S. in his pocket?" He earned his nickname, the Rat Priest, from pasting photos of the Chief of National Police, the Prime Minister, and the next head of the Korean CIA onto the heads of the pictures of rats on Rat Catching Day posters plastered around Seoul.

Robert, pronounced with a French flair as *"Robair,"* was a priest with Paris Foreign Missions. Robert spoke with great gravity in a thick French accent. His voice was easy to pick out as I passed by the living room. He cleared his throat dramatically, announcing in conspiratorial tones, "I have important information to tell you." Dad said Robert read notes from BBC and Voice of America broadcasts he had scribbled onto his hand.

South Korea was turning a small group of otherwise respectable, kindly people from places like Saskatoon, Saskatchewan, Lewiston, New York, and Wapello, Iowa into quiet rabble-rousers. Not all of the Monday Night Group members had been, at heart and in practice, political before South Korea. These were humble kind of people who came up with the name "The Monday Night Group." Their self-deprecating humor made any chance at self-righteousness impossible. They had unglamorous skills, like fact-sheet writing. They delivered underwear to prisoners. But they had a heart for social justice, a keen eye for the truth, and they made an impact on the democracy movement in South Korea.

Faye Moon met her husband, Reverend Stephen Moon (Moon Tong-hwan), at Hartford seminary. Rev. Moon was a highly respected theologian completing a doctoral thesis in Christian education, and Faye was completing a master's degree in Social Work. The Moon family lived a fully immersed Korean life north of Seoul in a home without insulation, central heating, a refrigerator, or a washing machine. Faye joined the Monday Night Group in part to connect to like-minded people in the expat community and gain support for her situation. She eventually took a position in her field of study, working as a social worker in a drug rehabilitation program at the Yongsan U.S. Army Headquarters. She took the job with mixed feelings, as she felt the U.S. was not doing enough to challenge Park's military regime. People like Faye Moon and Marion Kim, both married to Korean activists, provided a much-needed local perspective to the Monday Night Group meetings and work.

Reverend Moon participated alongside other seminary professors in activities calling for democracy. Under government pressure, his seminary fired him from his position. He took the opportunity of this lapse in employment to start Galilee Church with other people involved in the movement. He and his brother, Timothy Moon (Moon Ik-hwan), took part in the formation of *Minjung*, a liberation theology that said God was found in the struggle of ordinary people. Reverend Moon taught the Monday Night Group about *Minjung*. I understood it meant "the people," or "the masses," and that it tied God directly to the human struggle for justice. *Minjung* had its roots in Korea's hierarchical history, when commoners were treated as non-beings by their rulers and the wealthy *yangban* class.

I was eight years old when the Monday night meetings began in earnest. They rotated from our house to other members' houses to make it difficult for the Korean CIA to monitor their activity. Their presence in our home spanned many years. I knew they were getting together to do something about the abuses of Park Chung-hee's government. I knew they were concerned about the conditions of the factory workers and the arrest and torture of those who criticized Park. I knew they were my parents' closest friends. Over the years, I came to understand more.

At some point, it became clear to me that the Monday Night Group's interpretation of what it meant to follow Jesus was not the same one I learned at Camp Mount-O-Pines, our missionary summer camp, where we made God's Eyes instead of Tiger Eyes, memorized Bible verses as if our lives depended on it, and learned to recite the books of the Bible in order as if that would make everything okay in the world.

The people of the Monday Night Group taught me to look at the Bible as a tome of social justice. They seemed less impressed by the massive Billy Graham Crusade outside of Seoul than they were by the work of the Korean activists they were trying to support. They were inspired by the words of people like Desmond Tutu, Dorothy Day, and Gandhi. They said "God" instead of "He" when they read the Bible and sang hymns. This was not Vacation Bible School.

Though we didn't know all of the neighbors in our residential circle, we knew a couple families well. Our next door neighbor, Mr. Miller, the other *miguksaram* among us, first came to Korea as a U.S. Navy officer at the end of World War II. He later returned and worked for many years in business. He became most renowned for starting a sea-side arboretum that held the largest collection of species of plants in the nation. Ajumoni was often whispering to me about Mr. Miller, with a new tidbit to share each week from an over-the-wall chat with his maid.

We knew Kim Chan-kuk's family the best. Dean Kim was head of Yonsei's Theological Seminary. His family made us feel welcome right away when we moved into the neighborhood, bringing over food and inviting us into their home. We came to know them well, spending time together in our neighborhood and taking skating trips outside of Seoul. Their daughter, Song-hae, had lived in the U.S. as an exchange student. After Song-hae returned, Mom hired her to teach me to play the piano. I didn't like to play the piano, and I don't think Song-hae was so keen on teaching me, but we all loved her kind, globally-minded, and learned family.

One day Song-hae's mother, slight, friendly Mrs. Sung, arrived at our front gate in tears. "I came home today and my husband was gone," she told Mom. "I have no idea where he is." Earlier that week, Dean Kim answered a question raised by one of his students about whether it was moral to dissent against the government. His answer, "It sometimes can be done," got him arrested. The government gave him a two-year sentence.

My parents told us many good people like Dean Kim were taking on the government at great risk. Reverend Moon and his colleagues co-drafted a statement on the need for true democracy in South Korea. After the statement was read in a public place, he was arrested and put in solitary confinement to await trial.

The Monday Night Group, their regular meetings and their ongoing work, was in many ways just a normal part of the routine of my life. Where's Mom? Oh, she's going on a train ride with Faye to visit Mr. Moon in prison. Oh, she and Linda Jones are going to visit the manager of a computer company across the city to see if he will agree to eye exams for the workers. But these people and the actions of those they supported had a profound and lasting effect on how I understood the world, and how I came to understand Christianity.

One day, when Dad was walking downtown, he kept seeing the same man wherever he went. Dad tried to make eye contact, but the man quickly looked away. Later that day, Dad saw the man talking into a walkie-talkie hidden in a rolled up newspaper. Dad told us the story that evening. He stood up in middle of the living room, rolled up a copy of *The Korea Times*, and held it up to his mouth. He glanced around the room a few times, his eyes darting back and forth, and whispered conspiratorially into the paper funnel, "I am following Rice *Moksa*. He has just entered a tea house."

The situation wasn't exactly funny, but gallows humor went a long way in our home.

After Reverend Moon was imprisoned, plainclothes policeman followed Mrs. Moon everywhere she went, from morning to night. Mr. Matthews had a minder, too, a KCIA man who moved his office into a building near Mr. Matthew's workplace. In what was perhaps a less than typical tactic, he began to take Mr. Matthews out to tea each day. They got to know one another. They became friends.

The startling fact was that President Park had over three hundred thousand agents all over the country monitoring people's activities. The Korean CIA intimidated, arrested, and tortured many who spoke out against the government. A couple of agents may have broken the rules and enjoyed a cup of tea with people, but they were notoriously brutal. Many Koreans suffered physically and spiritually because of them, including the Moon family.

Around this time, the Monday Night Group invited the Canadian ambassador to our house to talk about the human rights situation. As the ambassador and the rest of the group left our home at the end of the evening, my mother noticed a uniformed man up the telephone pole. He had been listening in on their conversation. The next day another man showed up at the gate announcing he was from the telephone office and he needed to fix our phone. There was nothing wrong with our phone.

He entered our living room, unscrewed the receiver, placed a small object into it, and then screwed it back together. He departed without fanfare, calling politely as he left, "The phone is fixed now, Ma'am!"

Soon after this, I noticed my parents having hushed and vague phone conversations. "The piano teacher is coming to stay with us for a few weeks," Mom said, quietly and deliberately over the phone, in an overly-pronounced, self-conscious voice. "The library books have arrived," Dad said in a similarly stilted way. One day I realized my parents were talking in code. Our phone was being tapped.

Cho Chi-sung, a friend of my parents, was a minister who worked with factory workers in the Yong Dong Po industrial area. He answered his phone one day and heard one of his previous conversations played back to him on tape. Any Korean person monitored this closely was in serious danger. For me, a tapped phone line was merely an odd quirk to home life. I did wonder if some of my conversations were on a cassette tape in a dark government office somewhere. Would I someday pick up the phone and hear my own voice saying, "Jennie, are you coming over to spend the night?"

Around this time, a college student from Dad's Kyung Hee University group came to live with us, and ended up staying off and on for two years. His name was Chang Chang-ki, but he asked us to give him an English name, so we called him Chucky because it sounded like Chang-ki. Chucky came from a traditional home in a small village. He performed so well on the college entrance exam that he got into one of Seoul's most prestigious universities. Chucky's handsome face, easy laugh, ability to yodel, and quickly learn English made our guest into a brother, and he became like a son to my parents.

Given Poe-bae and her mother, Chucky, Mr. Pak, and various other people had lived with us off and on over the years, given the history of our house as community center and fellowship hall, it wasn't surprising when another man came to live with us one day.

What was surprising is that he stayed in the basement. He didn't sit in the living room like our regular guests did or eat dinner with us like Chucky did. I later found out that he was an activist on the run from the government. He had a mimeograph machine in the basement and he was printing out anti-Park leaflets. His code name, "The Piano Teacher," explained some of Mom and Dad's strange phone conversations. I knew, instinctively I think, that I wasn't supposed to mention his presence in our home to anyone outside the family. He was a shadow figure. I saw him once during the few weeks he stayed with us, when he surfaced for a quick conversation with my parents. He came and went in the dark of night, and I never saw him again.

As all of this was transpiring, my brothers and I played flag football in the yard using Dad's black dress socks as flags. I did my best to follow Chris's carefully calculated running patterns. We played highly competitive games of Horse at the basketball hoop Dad put up in the small area between our front gate and the car port. We ate dinner together each night, enjoying Ajumoni's very respectable rendition of spaghetti and her first class version of Korean chicken stew.

One winter, Chris convinced us to participate in a Strat-O-Matic baseball tournament which, given Chris's highly competitive nature and penchant towards bursts of anger, turned out to be a lot more stressful than one might ever imagine a baseball board game might be. After three weeks of walking on eggshells, the tournament culminated in the tantrum of all tantrums when Dad beat Chris in the finals.

There would be some tricky days ahead, but my life was not made unsafe or difficult because of my parents' participation in the human rights movement. With their father in prison, the Moon children felt the difficulty of this time, as did the children of Marion Kim. But I never talked about the Monday Night Group with anyone outside of our family, including the children of other Monday

Night Group members. I knew not to talk about this part of my parents' life, the meetings, the people hiding in our basement, or our tapped phone. But I know that we, the children of the Monday Night Group, were affected by the presence of these people in our homes and lives. I read that when the Basingers returned to Iowa and had people over, one child or another would whisper in Mrs. Basinger's ear, "Mom, is this the Monday Night Group?"

I once described my parents' political involvement to a work colleague in Seattle. She said, in a less than positive way, "Wow, they were *radicals*." She said the word 'radicals' like it was a disease. It sounded so funny to hear that word spoken about my parents. Radicals. My parents, and the Basingers, and the Krauths, and the Moons, the Matthews, all of them, were in many ways about the most normal people you could ever meet.

If the Korean CIA had been monitoring our home life more closely, they would have seen a handsome, salt-and-pepper bearded man with deep hazel eyes and a kindly voice reading books to his children, making Bilbo Baggins, Aslan, and the White Witch of Narnia sound as enchanted as they were written. They would have seen that same dangerous man stick napkin rings into his eye sockets at the dinner table and hold them there while he made a crazy face at each of his children.

They may have seen this troublemaker of double-jointed fingers dot his daughter's nose with shaving cream, then apply Nivea to his calloused, dry hands as he blurted out Tom Swifties, "'I can't find my tuba,' Tom tooted! 'The boat is leaking,' Tom said balefully!" Sometimes he slipped them in while Mom was trying to be serious. It drove her crazy. "Randy, stop thinking up puns. I have something I need to tell you."

If Lady Luck, as we called Mom, had been under constant surveillance, they would have seen her eating peanut butter toast in her fuzzy blue robe, or pulling the exact *Mille Bornes* mileage card needed to beat her unlucky children, once again. They might have seen her bargaining for strawberries at the local market, chatting with the lady who sold her flowers in Sinchon Rotary, or bundling up her children to reluctantly skate on the frozen rice paddy down the hill in sub-zero temps, and then cheerily skating circles around them as they contracted mild cases of frostbite. They may have seen her donning her goggles and swim cap for one more life-giving swim in the Yellow Sea. These were my radical parents.

MINJU HOEBOK

"I have nothing against (the words produced by the established church),
and I have produced a substantial quantity of them myself.
But suddenly I was in the middle of a situation where the church
which I represented had no words . . .
It occurs to me that the church would do well to find itself
from time to time in situations like that—
when all it can do in the name of Jesus Christ is to cry,
because injustice has burned a hole in its heart."

—GENE MATTHEWS, *MORE THAN WITNESSES*

All signs indicated it was an ECF night. Thirty extra pairs of shoes were scattered in the entryway. The ambient temperature in the house had increased ten degrees. The Ecumenical Christian Fellowship was deep into the third verse of their cheerfully meaningful theme song, singing, "Here in ECF, here in ECF, I receive Christ as my saviooor! Here in ECF, here in ECF, I receive Christ as my Looord!"

Once in a while I joined in, taking my place in the circle of floor cushions in Dad's Upper Room, feeling the particular warmth that only a gathering of humans in a small, under-ventilated space can generate. I sat next to Dad, leaning my head against his shoulder as he led the meeting. I was comfortable there, born into the bosom of fellowship, student meetings, and meaningful togetherness. And I loved my Dad.

I loved to hear Korean roll naturally off his tongue. He had to work to turn the thin pages of his Korean hymnal with his heavily calloused, work-worn hands. Dad had the mind of a theologian, but he had the heart and body of a woodsman. He sang hymns loudly and proudly in English and in Korean. The students listened closely to him as he spoke, almost hanging on his every word. They laughed at his corny jokes. He listened intently to them, engaging them in deep discussions about faith and life. Many of the traditional Korean ministers we knew used formal language ending in a flurry of *shimnidas*, but Dad tried to keep things down-to-earth when he could, like the American he was and always would be.

I was more often downstairs during ECF meetings, watching *Barnaby Jones* or *Gunsmoke* on the American Forces TV channel, trading stamps with Mark, or doing homework. From down below, we non-worshippers heard loud choruses of hymns sung in harmonious voices. Moments of silent worship were punctuated with raucous laughter. This was nice. But sometimes Dad broke the meeting into small groups. Suddenly our rooms were not our rooms anymore. They were Conference Rooms A-C. A line formed for the bathroom during meeting breaks. In these moments I began to wonder, *could we ever just live in a normal house?* Then, just as my indignity peaked, the students spilled out of Dad's study and descended the stairs to leave, calling out greetings in the friendliest voices, *"Anyong, Lidgie! Anyong Maga!"* It was impossible to remain piqued for long. They were so warm and kind to me. They were just so nice.

Like the translation work he was doing at Christian Literature Society, ECF was a big part of Dad's work. Like any activity Mom and Dad were a part of, many of the members became life-long friends. Each year we dressed up to attend the annual ECF Christmas party to sing and eat plates of carefully prepared, beautifully presented dinners. But Dad did other work, too.

One non-ECF evening, while Mom was away on an orphan flight, Mark, Dad and I left the house to eat dinner out on the town. Until that moment the day had no reason to stand out, no cause to be memorable. A dinner at Chosun Hotel's Yesterday Restaurant was always a special treat, but as Dad preferred more basic fare, we were probably heading to Sinchon for a bowl of *pibimpap*.

We started out from home, taking our usual steps down our residential hill to catch a taxi on the main road. Smells of soy bean paste stew wafted from behind neighbors' walls. Clothes hung on lines. Was that Song-hae practicing the piano? It was just a typical day in Yonhi Dong.

I don't remember where we ended up that night, because we never got there. As we reached the bottom of the hill, two men approached us, materializing out of nowhere it seemed, and began to talk to Dad. As they talked I looked past them and saw a black car idling a few yards away. It was all so strange. After they spoke for a few minutes, my father told us we needed to return home.

Ajumoni opened up the gate, puzzled as to our return, and the men waited just outside. Once safely inside, Dad told us in his calm voice that he was being taken in for questioning by the immigration office. Ajumoni cried out in shock. *"Moksanim, musowo!"* she said. I'm scared!

The only other time I had seen her face look so petrified was the day after Dad thwarted a burglar from getting into our house. She wasn't even there when it happened, but she kept looking outside the window all week, wide-eyed, saying, *"Ayuuuu!"*

Since Dad didn't want Ajumoni involved or implicated in any way, he immediately sent her home. He called a missionary friend to come pick me and Mark up and take us to his house. That's all I remember of that day. Dad filled in the details for me years later. As he spoke a full and tragic performance filled in around my short and for so long inadequate draft of a one act play called "Dad Gets Arrested and Eight Innocent Men are Put to Death." This is what happened to lead up to Dad's arrest.

Earlier that year, another of Park's emergency decrees gave the government the power to silence, arrest, and imprison those who objected to his rule. Reporters who demanded freedom of the press were fired. In April of 1974, the government announced what they referred to as a vast communist plot. Newspapers reported the arrest of over one thousand people. My parents talked in particular about eight men who were being held as ringleaders of the so-called People's Revolutionary Party (PRP), accused of plotting to overthrow the government by inspiring student demonstrations. A number of months after the arrests, eight women made contact with Methodist missionary George Ogle. They heard Mr. Ogle's name spoken at Sodaemun Prison, where many political prisoners, including their husbands, the supposed PRP leaders, were being held. A few people there told them Mr. Ogle might be able to help them. By this time their husbands had been sentenced to death by a military court. They were hoping for a retrial in a civilian court.

George Ogle had worked with industrial workers for ten years, ministering to those who toiled in steel, textile, and lumber mills, machine shops, railroad yards, and glass factories. He and colleagues from the Korean Methodist Church visited men severely injured in shop accidents. They conducted labor education programs. Some colleagues worked in factories themselves to best understand how unsafe, filthy, and poorly managed they were. By the 1970s, the Urban Industrial Mission had worked with thousands of laborers and union leaders. Accused of communist leanings, their work was under police scrutiny and KCIA surveillance, and they received many threats.

After a two-year furlough, Mr. Ogle took a position as Professor of Labor Relations at Seoul National University, and his family moved to Seoul. By this time he was well known in human and labor rights circles. I looked up to the Ogle family for a number of reasons. They had lived in Korea for a long time. The Ogle kids were raised in part away from the foreign community, in a Korean-style home in the center of Incheon, and they spoke Korean well. Like my parents, the Ogles were kind and reserved, but if you listened to them carefully, the words that came out of their mouths cut to the heart of social justice issues.

Every few weeks my parents called out cheerily as they left home, "See you later, kids! We're going to the Christian Building for a prayer meeting!" That meeting was not quite what I had always imagined it to be. Apparently a lot more was going on down there than rounds of "Kumbaya." Those concerned about the human rights situation were meeting to give voice to their concerns. Over the year, the gathering grew from a few people meeting in a small room to a large group that met in a five-hundred-seat auditorium. Many who came had loved ones in prison. With riot police stationed outside the building and in the lobby, and plainclothesmen roaming about, the families of jailed Christians and students gave testimony to their situation. Much like in South Africa's Anti-Apartheid movement, more could be said under the guise of prayer.

A week after the eight women came to his home, Mr. Ogle stood up at this meeting and spoke a prayer, saying, "Christ is often mediated to us through the most humble and weakest of our brothers and sisters. Among those now in prison are eight men who have received the harshest of punishments. They have been sentenced to die, even though there is little evidence against them. They are not Christians, but as the poorest among us, they become the brothers of Christ. Therefore let us pray for their lives and souls. Probably they have committed no crime worthy of death." He prayed for an open, civil, and fair trial to be granted. As he spoke, a few people in the back of the room wrote down everything he said.

The next day, KCIA agents came to George Ogle's house to arrest him. They took him on a wild ride to their headquarters, where they aggressively interrogated him through the night. They demanded he name everyone he knew. They asked him about the work of the Urban Industrial Mission. They told him he had no right to question the government.

Early the following morning, after signing a piece of paper saying he would not give sermons about the eight men, Mr. Ogle was released. About a week later, an official from the U.S. Embassy, acting as an intermediary, told Mr. Ogle he must apologize or risk being thrown out of Korea. Mr. Ogle wrote a letter giving an explanation of his work, but not a full apology. Within two days he was taken to the Office of Immigration, where an officer told him there was a problem with his visa. They told him he had to leave Korea.

I knew people were being arrested. I knew factory workers didn't have rights, some newspapers told lies, and a lot of people worked too long, too hard, for too little money. I knew that many people who spoke out against Park were tortured and put in prison. The violence of the DMZ axe murders had frightened me. The national tragedy of the first lady's assassination had deeply saddened me. But the reality of deportation shook me like nothing else. This hit home. Could my family be deported, or as the Monday Night Group liked to joke, "exported" from Korea? Would we have to leave if that happened? Could life as I knew it really end in an instant, like it had for the Ogle family?

Mr. Ogle's deportation scared me. But it mobilized the Monday Night Group to act more fervently in defense of the eight men. Over the next months, members of the group accompanied the wives to Sodaemun Prison. They brought money, long underwear, blankets, and food. They contacted international journalists and congressmen about the situation. They spoke out in any way they could.

On the day the final verdict was to be announced at the Supreme Court downtown, many people gathered outside the courtroom. Inside the courtroom were family members, a few Korean journalists, a representative of Amnesty International, and a number of people from the Monday Night Group. Everyone was hopeful for a reprieve. The members of the Supreme Court filed into the room, sat down, and promptly read out the verdict. It took them just minutes to confirm a sentence of death.

The courtroom exploded. The wives cried out in shock. A few banged their umbrellas on the backs of seats, sending spindles in all directions. A few sprawled across courtroom benches, wailing "It's all lies!" Louise Durst lay on the floor and had be carried out by police. She later said, "I had to do something." Mom ran out of the building in shock. The wives, in various stages of disbelief and anguish, were ushered out of a side door, forced onto a bus, and dropped off outside of the city so they couldn't talk with journalists or cause a scene outside of the court building.

Early the next morning, Mom was walking through an underpass near Seoul Plaza Hotel. She happened to run into Jim Stentzel, a journalist and a member of the Monday Night Group. Jim said,

"Have you heard what happened, Sue? I heard the men were hung this morning. That can't be right!" They rushed to the *Tonga Ilbo* building, where the daily paper was always posted behind thick glass. There, with a crowd of citizens, they confirmed the news. The men were hung early that morning.

Nothing had prepared Mom for this moment. Even ten years of living in South Korea, after all she had seen at House of Grace, in orphanages, in sweatshops, and in factories, nothing had prepared her for this. This is the kind of news that buckles one's knees. This is the kind of news that knocks the air out of one's chest.

That same morning, Gene Matthews received a phone call from the twelve-year-old daughter of one of the men. Thirty-five years later, I heard him tell the story on a U.S. radio show. His always humor-filled voice choked up. "The girl asked, 'We heard my father has been executed. Can this be true?'" Gene Matthews rushed to a nearby office where he confirmed the news. When he called the girl back they both broke down in tears.

A few days later, Reverend Moon spoke at the Thursday Prayer Meeting, holding nothing back. A number of Monday Night colleagues met together. It was all too much—the imprisonments, the torture, the deportation, and now the swift execution of eight innocent men. The international press hadn't picked up on the story. Only a few people outside of Korea knew what had happened. Many people in South Korea believed the government account told in newspapers, that the men were anti-government communists. The Monday Night Group knew they needed to do something. The rest of the world had to know what was going on.

That night, the women of the Monday Night Group sewed black hoods and wove thick plaits of heavy rope. The next afternoon, seven Monday Night Group men congregated nervously at a tea house in downtown Seoul. They gathered their resolve, then began to walk towards the U.S. Embassy. They entered in through the front gate, their foreign faces allowing them unimpeded passage.

Once on the property, they donned hoods and nooses and began marching silently in a circle. They pulled out signs that read, "Must the U.S. Support Oppression of Human Rights?" "Does this mean nothing to you?" "Is this the result of quiet diplomacy?" They demonstrated for fifteen minutes. Dad later told me it felt like they were there for hours.

The men were asked to come inside the embassy, where a U.S. official listened to their concerns. Thirty minutes later they were released to go home. They were hopeful that maybe the world would take notice. By this time the Monday Night Group was savvy. Someone had leaked the time of the protest to *Newsweek,* and a photographer was there to take a picture.

It was that evening that Dad took us out to dinner. I had no idea what he had done that day. After he was arrested, my father was taken to the immigration headquarters and escorted into a small, inner room, where he was questioned until late evening. They asked him to name names. They threatened him with deportation. They asked why he was meddling in Korean affairs, why he was protesting, and who the other men were with him. They yelled at him, saying, "You can't do this as foreigners! You're here as missionaries! You shouldn't be political!" Dad said as little as he could and gave no names. After a few hours of intimidating interrogation, he returned home shaken but unharmed.

Decades passed before I fully processed what happened that day, that week, and in those years. I was worried when Dad was taken in. I will never forget the moment those two strangers walked up to us. I was worried when I watched Dad whisked away by government men. But I knew foreigners were treated differently than Koreans, and I knew my Dad would be okay. I broke down the first time I put all of the pieces of this story together. I cried for the innocent men. I cried for their wives and children. I cried because I understood the multiple layers and lessons of those years, the ones I couldn't process as a little girl, when birthday parties and soccer games dominated my life. I cried because not everyone's Dad came home.

So many things bonded me to my Korean brothers and sisters. Seoul was my home. But some things made me different. As an adult, I learned to carefully weigh my dire childhood fear of deportation against the reality that some parents disappear forever. I learned to weigh the distressing idea of being forced to say a quick and permanent good-bye to Ajumoni against having to make a call to a man across town and ask, "Was my father executed this morning?" I weighed my fear in seeing Dad taken in for questioning against the sadness of Young-me and Tae-gun Moon, whose father was not home because he was in solitary confinement in a prison far away. And I knew there was no comparison to be made. I could never take what I had been given for granted, or forget what happened in Korea.

Some time after Dad's arrest, our family gathered in the living room. Dad was holding an international edition of *Newsweek*. In the Asia section was a photo of a group of men protesting in front of the U.S. Embassy. They were wearing nooses and hoods, and carrying large signs. We all crowded around. Dad pointed to the picture. "That's me, there," he said. "I think that might be Bill Basinger. I think that's Gene Matthews." A short article described the protest and the reasons for it. *The Korea Times* and the U.S. military newspaper, the *Stars and Stripes*, wrote articles about the protest, too.

Dad and Mom always said they were doing what anybody would do in their position, having heard what they had heard and seen what they had seen. Without one bit of false humility, they told me the brave people were the wives who banded together like sisters when their husbands were suddenly, one day, forcibly taken from their homes and made into scapegoats because of a government's desire to stoke anti-communist fervor. The brave people were the reporters of the *Tong-A Ilbo* newspaper who fought government control and kept on telling the truth, occupying their offices when their colleagues were fired. They were people like Rev. Stephen Moon who had the audacity, after two years in prison, eighteen months of which was spent in solitary confinement, to develop a new theology called "Joy on the Way."

They were people like Chun Tae-il's mother, who spoke out on behalf of sweatshop workers for the rest of her days, carrying on her son's legacy. They were the factory women who formed human walls against riot police in order to fight for the right to unionize, who risked their only way of making a living to tell people about the broken, unfocused microscopes they looked through all day.

They were the women who walked alongside Faye Moon, who spoke out when their husbands were put on trial for pro-democracy statements, who defiantly and creatively protested outside of court, stitching purple V-shaped "Victory Shawls" as they prayed for democracy. Purple—the Christian color of suffering—the color of *mugunghwa*, Korea's national flower. *Minju hoebok*, they chanted with each four stitches. *Restore democracy. Minju hoebok. Minju hoebok.* With every ten thousand stitches, a purple shawl was finished, and another story was told. The list of sacrifices in South Korea was endless.

A few memories of this time always stayed with me. A pile of purple shawls in the corner of Mom's room, soon on their way to the U.S., sent surreptitiously through Faye Moon's U.S. military APO mail box to raise funds and awareness for the democracy movement. The story of the chaotic scene at Mr. Ogle's home on the day of his deportation. The gold ring I heard so much about, the one Mr. Ogle was handed as he was ushered from his house into a government jeep. The ring that was passed from hand to hand through the crowd of supporters, given to Mr. Ogle by one of the PRP wives because she was worried he would land in the U.S. with no money. And that picture of Dad in *Newsweek*.

Twenty years later, during a family visit to Korea, after taking a leisurely walk from City Hall to the peaceful neighborhood of embassies and tree-lined lanes behind Toksu Palace, Mom and I suddenly found ourselves in front of the Supreme Court building.

"This is where the trial was held," Mom said, tears suddenly streaming down her face. "This is where the eight men were given their final sentence."

How can anyone enjoy a nice hotel lunch after this?

When I look back on this time of my life, I mostly see a normal kid growing up, doing what normal, safe kids do. Watching TV. Having sleepovers with friends. Listening to pop music. But I see something else, too. I see a girl beginning to weigh the words of one group in her faith community against the next. I see a girl who feels sad for the Sewing Lady, the woman with a kind but worried face who comes to the house to take on sewing projects, a lady whose husband has just lost his life for no reason. I see a little girl who is paying attention, who is feeling more than she knows she is feeling. And maybe that is why, forty years later, I'm telling you this story.

I never met any of the eight men. I saw a picture of them once. They were lined up in handcuffs, standing in court. Among the group were a lumberyard foreman, a bathhouse manager, a high school teacher, and a bookkeeper. Most of the wives were home-makers of limited education. They were just eight ordinary, inno-cent men who didn't come home one day. That happens some-times. My Dad came home.

US Missionaries: America Must Fight ROK Repression

Seven American missionaries wearing black hoods and straw ropes around their necks staged a silent rally in the US Embassy compound Wednesday to demand clarification of US policy toward "deterioration of human rights in Korea."

They said their protest was sparked by the hanging last week of eight Korean political prisoners they say were unjustly executed by the government of President Chung Hee Park. "We ask for a clarification of US government intentions regarding the deterioration of human rights in Korea and request that it continue its economic and military assistance to the republic of Korea only to the extent that such assistance contributes to the realization of freedom and human rights" they said in a statement.

The missionaries held up three placards that read "Must the US support oppression of human rights?" "Is this the result of quiet diplomacy?" and "Is this nothing to you?"

"We are aware that the US State Department has expressed deep regret over the executions and the manner in which they were carried out," the statement said. "It seems inadequate to continue merely expressing regret, however, as they Korean government gives no indication that it any longer pays attention to such words." The seven were invited into the Embassy building for a one-hour talk with officials. The Rev Gene Matthews, 42, a Methodist missionary from Wapello, Iowa, said the officials listened 'cordially.'"

The 8 prisoners were among 22 former members of the outlawed PRP convicted last year on charges of plotting to overthrow Park's government and replace it with a Communist regime.

More than 100 students, church leaders and other prominent citizens, including former President Yun Po Sun and dissident poet Kim Chi Ha also were convicted in connection with the alleged conspiracy.

—*Stars and Stripes Newspaper*, April 17, 1975

Everyone Wakes Up at a
Different time in the Morning

My parents were heartbroken about the hanging of the eight men. They were distressed to hear Father Sinnott was going to be deported from Korea, too.

One day I mentioned a growing concern to a close friend.

"You won't believe it," I said. "I hear some missionaries are angry with my parents for their political work!"

Her response caught me completely off guard.

"I totally agree with them," she said swiftly. "My parents feel the same way."

I quickly dropped the discussion about politics and missionaries. I should have known better. How could I have been so naive?

Mom and Dad varied their conversations whether they were eating in the dining hall of Taechon Beach lodge, worshipping at Seoul Union Church with fellow missionary families, meeting with ECF students, or eating dinner with the Choi family. They knew not to talk openly about politics with everyone they knew. They genuinely got along with and spoke highly of people from all of our communities. They tried to see the best in people. We counted as friends missionaries who measured the worth of their time in Korea in "saving souls" and those who measured it more by the efficacy of facilities they had established for the poor and disenfranchised. Mom and Dad counted as friends conservative *yangban* ministers and pro-democracy poets.

In spite of inevitable conflicts in our diverse community, most missionaries made a concerted effort to focus on what we had in common instead of on what divided us. Like one might do at summer camp. The fact was, I didn't really know what made a Presbyterian a Presbyterian or a Lutheran a Lutheran. I'm not sure I can tell you that now. That I had been part of a mission community my whole life didn't mean I knew the difference between a Nazarene and a Southern Baptist.

I knew there was a strong tendency towards evangelism in some denominations and a tendency towards works in others. I knew not everyone was picking up protest signs. I knew that some of my friends couldn't play cards or go to school dances, but I saw other friends live with what seemed to be a lot of leeway, including me and my siblings. My parents always encouraged me and my brothers to think for ourselves.

One summer, after Chris came back from a week at Camp Mount-O-Pines, I became aware of a series of hushed conversations. Mom later told me that Chris said he had given his life to Jesus at a campfire one night. This announcement was not met with celebration, nor was it met with any scorn. It was just something Chris had gone through. I felt like my parents wanted each of us to forge our own way in life, to find our own path, even when it came to our spirituality.

On the other hand, after a sleepover at the Patten's house, Mr. Patten, enthusiastically lovable son of Oregon loggers turned Korean seminary president, drove us to school in the back of his pickup. As the truck dodged darting pedestrians and honking taxis in northern Seoul, Mr. Patten shouted out Bible verse numbers. Becky, Rachel, Naomi, Debbie and I were supposed to shout back the memorized text through the din of traffic.

I didn't have their facility with John and Matthew, Corinthians and Romans. We didn't focus time on verse memorization in our home. But I accepted we were all somewhere along a scale of faith and works, liberal and conservative, somewhere between "I've got the joy, joy, joy, joy down in my heart" and *Minjung*. And I shouted out John 3:16, as I still can today. *For God so loved the world that he gave his only begotten son. . .*

Our missionary community had grown close over the decades. We knew one another better than we knew our relatives. We were all we had. We shared church and school life and competed in historic tennis tournaments together. We staged epic musicals at Taechon, a Southern Baptist missionary a King of Siam I will never forget; a Methodist lady belting out enthusiastically, as waves crashed on the Yellow Sea, "You Can't Get a Man with a Gun!"

I didn't dwell on what divided us because so much that was fundamental to who we were united us. We shared an inseverable bond of living in Korea that spoke more to me than denominations and nationality and even religion ever could. Who else knew about Taechon Beach cinnamon rolls and Seoul Union Club french fries? Who else shared the memory of a sunset Vespers service, a school carnival in a Quonset hut gymnasium in western Seoul, and dear people like little Mrs. Grubb, who stood up at Vespers each Thursday evening in her flowered dress to make an announcement about the seashell contest?

For a few years Dad became involved in something he called the "charismatic movement." I gathered this meant people were laying hands on people and calling on the power of the Holy Spirit to heal, which sounded very dramatic. One time Dad talked more openly about one of these "laying on of hands prayer sessions." Mom looked at him with quiet disapproval and he didn't say more. Mom believed firmly in a social gospel, in a faith of action, beliefs informed and influenced in large part by her college days at St. Lawrence, a school founded by Unitarians. Mom was not into charismatic movements.

Dad once told me, with his usual quiet and reflective reserve, about a transformative spiritual experience he once had after a long period of depression. I could tell his faith in God made a dramatic difference in his life. His faith had transformed him. It led him away from a life in business and to this life we were living. I knew he was happy when an ECF student "accepted Jesus into his heart." He told me he saw a change in the faces and lives of those who "walked with God." He said he saw a new light of hope in their eyes, in the understanding that no matter what terror or sorrow life brought, no matter if they worked in the worst factory or in the halls of powers, they were adored by a loving God.

Dad formed his thoughtfully-crafted, meaningfully-delivered sermons around stories about regular people. One of my favorite sermons was about a tiny, wrinkled, and energetic old lady named Fanny Zigenfus, a woman Dad used to visit in a nursing home in Connecticut. Another sermon was centered around a man named Arlie Gregor, a coal miner who befriended my parents when Dad served his first permanent church position in a mining town in Ohio. Arlie took Dad down into a coal mine one day so he could see what it was like to serve a shift underneath the earth. These kinds of people impressed Dad. I think he saw God in them.

But Dad was still too Rice to value talking about something over just doing it. Mom was too Belden to go on about her personal faith journey. Mom once attempted to employ the strategies she was learning in Parent Effectiveness Training classes and gather the family together for an overly earnest family meeting. She met so much eye-rolling sarcasm from my brothers that it made her cry a little bit.

When my turn came to pray before dinner, I blurted out the carefully crafted, one-sentence-long supplication I had perfected over the years. I was inspired by my brothers, who had come before me, and gave similarly short invocations. "ThankyouJesusforthisfoodandforthisdayamen."

During family dinners we discussed things that happened at school that day. Dad and Chris talked about who might win the World Series. Sometimes we were treated to an obscure detail about the Battle of Waterloo or the Mongol Conquests, intricacies of world history that Mark somehow knew so much about. An earnest discussion of the Bible and Jesus in our hearts was just not in the language of our family dynamic.

In spite of an ability to get along with and accept one another in our tight community, some missionaries said the actions of the

Monday Night Group were jeopardizing the visa status of missionaries. They quoted Romans 13, which they believed instructed Christians to be subject to governing authorities. A number of them wrote to the U.S. mission board complaining about the political involvement of the Monday Night Group. Some called them communist sympathizers. They complained that because of this political activity, missionary families now had to be fingerprinted every six months instead of every two years.

I never thought this was so terrible. I enjoyed taking the trip downtown as a family, walking into the immigration building to line up, get inked, and have a serious-faced man roll my finger smudge onto a piece of paper with my name on it. Someone was keeping track of me. That seemed very nice. I appreciated being watched out for. One can grow accustomed to a little tyranny.

The Monday Night Group responded to the criticism with a tract outlining the reasons they felt their faith demanded their involvement in the struggle. They asked, "Do guests sit quietly even if they discover that their host has become ill or is dying? Why do guests have the right to "meddle" in the most crucial aspect of life—religious—but not the human?"

So much about who I was expected to become as the child of missionaries was declared in uncertain terms. Be a light unto the world! Do unto others as you do to yourself! I was taught to serve God, not money. I was told to let my light shine, to "praise God from the mountaintop!" I knew "It only takes a spark to get a fire going" and that I needed to "pass it on." Ron Moore, talented song-writer and missionary kid from the generation before me, reminded us to "Seek the kingdom...cause nothing else will last."

I knew the reverence of Toksu Church, where the heads were always bowed lower in prayer than mine, the prayers prayed more fervently. The songs and the story of *Godspell* moved me deeply when the musical was performed at SFS. I can still sing the words to every song. When we watched the movie *Run Baby Run* in sixth grade we learned Christianity had the power to bring even former addicts and gang members like Nicky Cruz to turn his life around. I also knew people living out a Christianity that prompted them to pick up protest signs and call for school integration.

The people who were angry with my parents were the people who helped raise me. They were my family. They had all came to Korea to bring the "Good News." But what was the good news? Was it just a matter of theology and denominational belief? I was living in world founded on faith, on belief in things not seen, on following God's will even if it meant moving across the world. But what exactly was God's will?

Be kind to others. Love thine enemies. Feed the poor. Heal the sick. Protect the weak. The lessons sounded so simple when I heard them in Sunday school, but in a place like South Korea, what did it mean to protect the weak? What did it mean to love your enemy? If a person took these words seriously, how far would they go?

Somewhere during middle and high school, in part because of the Monday Night Group, and perhaps in part due to a genetic disposition to questioning in my blood line of sensible lawyers and gentlemen farmers, I began to question a mission focused on evangelism. Did I know what was best for another community or country? For a missionary kid to admit this is like coming out. But I was beginning to see God, and spirituality, as bigger than nationality, and even bigger than religion. My spirituality would be another layer of identity to sort through after we left Korea.

My parents didn't talk about the Monday Night Group at Toksu Church or with ECF students. Mom couldn't help but sometimes sneak in a quiet but short but firm statement during the open prayer time at Seoul Union Church.

"We pray God will embolden those who are struggling for human rights in Korea."

The words dropped like a lead balloon. A few seconds of uncomfortable silence always followed.

ECF students tended to be more conservative, although my parents learned in a few quiet conversations that a number of them were involved in protests. In the late 1960s, a student from their Kyung Hee University group appeared at the front gate one day with a friend.

"Mrs. Rice," he said, catching his breath from running, "we were just at a demo. The police are looking for us. Can we stay here for the night?"

"Of course you can!" Mom replied. "Come in!"

After they were safely inside he opened up his gym bag. "Mrs. Rice, don't worry. We have this to protect us." He pulled out a thick metal pipe. Mom's eyes were as big as saucers.

A few years later Mr. Choi saw Mom. "Mrs. Rice," he said openly, "you looked so scared when I pulled out that metal pipe."

"I was!" Mom said. "I was thinking, 'Is that small pipe really going to protect you?'"

Mom had a way of quietly pushing boundaries. We loved our rustic summer getaway, but the fact our beloved Taechon might be a bit of an enclave was hard to defend. We called the other end of the beach, the beach next to town, the "Korean Beach," as if ours was not a Korean beach. I did have to chuckle, though, when I read one scholar on Korea refer to "those missionaries and their speed boats." When it came to speed boats, there were, I believe, three families who had them of maybe one hundred families. I thought of the watering can we used to take showers and the musty cots we happily slept on, year after year, and the fact I never once stepped foot on a speedboat for sixteen years. But sometimes I think a stereotype is easier to talk about than a more complicated reality.

Mom loved to invite our Korean friends to Taechon. I still think fondly of Poe-bae's visit, and of the teeny, tiny ruffled white bikini she made by hand. I don't think Mom did this deliberately as some act of defiance. I think she just thought, "Poe-bae will love the beach!" and "Hong-chun will be fun to invite!" in much the same way as she thought, "Liz will love skating!" and "Mark will love skiing on a remote countryside hill with a frayed rope tow!" And maybe there was nothing magnanimous to this gesture of hers. But maybe, when a community is made up of mostly foreign people enjoying a place, and mostly Koreans working for those foreigners, inviting a Korean friend to enjoy that place is a gesture that needs to be made.

A few years ago I saw Dorothy Ogle at a reunion of Korea missionary families. Since these reunions began over a decade ago, we flock eagerly to the hills of North Carolina to spend time with the only people who understand a world that so naturally held a teen hangout along the Yellow Sea called the Peanut Butter Revival and a school within driving distance of the DMZ. I love these people for many reasons. I love them mostly for our shared love of Korea. I love them because they are my family.

Mrs. Ogle was preparing a talk about her ongoing work on Korean reunification. I sat down and asked her if she was resentful about the heavy criticism they faced for their involvement in human rights work. I was trying to work this out in my head.

Mrs. Ogle turned to me, and in her firm but quiet voice said, "Liz, an old Filipino proverb says, 'We all wake up at different time in the morning.' Many of the people who didn't understand what we did back then have changed their minds. And the people who criticized us did wonderful work in Korea. They had a real impact on the people they worked with."

Her spirit of forgiveness and understanding moved me. After we talked, I went up to my room and thought about what she had said. I thought about the sharp divisions between conservatives and liberals in the U.S., between faith and works, Democrat and Republican, and the chasm that I could feel between the beliefs of my dear friends in Seattle and my dear friends of Taechon Beach. I thought about the disparaging statements I heard as an adult, comments from friends and strangers alike about "those terrible missionaries." I knew what they said was true. Missionary history is fraught with horrible acts. But I knew a different side to the story.

Then I thought about some of the people in my dear mission family, who, though I know love me like a sister and a daughter, may look at parts of my life and feel I have strayed from the path. I thought about the conflicts between missionaries who were trying their best to live out their faith, each so sure that what they believed was God's Truth. And I knew I would always feel somewhere in the middle of all of this. Somewhere between *minjung* and the Ten Commandments. Between Seattle and Seoul. Between Seoul Union Church and Toksu. Between Korea and the U.S.

Once, when I was in elementary school, I looked down an alleyway as I walked through a residential area of the city with Mom. I saw a woman in a long white robe entering an old house.

"Who is she Mom. What is she doing?" I asked.

"She's a *mudang*, Liz, a shaman healer," Mom explained calmly. "She's probably entering that home to try and heal a sick family member."

Fascinated, I asked more. Mom told me the *mudang* entered into a trance. Sometimes she could be called to a home thought to be inhabited by evil spirits. On other days she might visit a village weak from famine. There were many things Mom didn't say. She didn't say, "She has no powers, Liz. She is a sham." She didn't tell me the lady was misguided or tell me she was going to be damned because of her beliefs. She didn't try to talk her into being a Christian. I'm sure that didn't cross her mind. The Ouija board in our closet was a sign that Mom might have believed in the power of the spirit world, too.

Among the papers my father gave me during the writing of this book is a copy of a church bulletin. Church bulletins have featured prominently in my life. I have scribbled on and made airplanes out of thousands of them. Bulletins written in English, in Korean, bulletins from a foreigners' church in Seoul, from churches in Lewiston, Oklahoma City, Michigan, Mississippi, and Vermont. I always crossed off each portion of the service as it passed.

Welcome and Announcements. *Check.*

Doxology. *Check.*

Old Testament Reading. *Check.*

It gave me that satisfying feeling things were moving along.

The bulletins usually had pretty pictures on the front—lilies, Jesus with sheep, a mountain pass with a Bible verse over it. But this bulletin had just words on the cover, like what lay within was a serious matter too important for a picture of the Son of God tending to farm animals. This service was being held to officially appoint and send into the world the missionaries, including my parents, who were leaving that year to serve in countries across the globe.

What words, I wondered, were chosen to prepare my parents for all they would face in Korea? Was there any reading, or song, or Bible verse that would have been adequate? How do you tell someone that soon, everything they know about the world will change?

I read the Words of Commitment that formed the last part of the service:

Do you promise to be zealous and faithful in maintaining the truths of the gospel and the purity and peace of the Church, in whatever field to which you may be designated and whatever persecution or opposition may arise to you on this account?

I do so promise.

Go ye therefore and make disciples of all nations. And as ye go, preach saying the kingdom of heaven is at hand. Heal the sick, cleanse the lepers, raise the dead, cast out devils: freely ye have received, freely give.

Then I read the words of the closing hymn, "Christian, rouse and arm for conflict, Nerve thee for the battlefield," and I imagined my parents earnestly singing each word. Mom in her reserved, self-described "monotone," Dad in his proud baritone voice, their faces young, their hearts wide open. And I thought of a battlefield of overcrowded sweatshops and drafty factories. I thought of a front-line of brothels full of young girls from the countryside.

A few memories from this time remained with me long after my ability to recite the books of the Bible faded away and I forgot the precise order of the Ten Commandments. A slow walk up the stairs with my mother to a Peace Market sweatshop. Dad organizing a house project for the older man with TB who came to our house each week to ask for work. Watching Mom change the diapers of a baby who I did not want to take my place. Listening to a group of good-hearted, modestly dressed people plot Park's overthrow in our living room. Simple acts, done with love and kindness.

I don't know what my parents imagined our life in Korea was going to be like when they attended that appointment service in 1966. But I know they never expected this. These were the stories I carried with me into an elite American college. I carried them with me when I temped in Boston, when I worked in inner city Jackson, Mississippi, and when I worked in a clinic in the township of Lusaka, Zambia. I carried them when I tested software at Microsoft and when I worked with refugees in Minneapolis. I couldn't stop carrying them with me.

The actions of my parents and the Koreans they supported taught me that if someone in need comes to the door, I need to do something. My childhood taught me to make no swift judgments. To never judge a person by their title, gender, hairdo, or religion. Everyone wakes up at a different time in the morning.

THE LAND TREMBLES

When the humidity and searing heat of summer of 1979 lifted, autumn arrived as it always had, with high skies, cooler temperatures, and bright red and yellow trees lighting up the mountainside. Colder nights and shorter days were a sign that winter *kimchi* making season was on the way. The harvest festival of Chusok was soon to begin, with people all over the country making preparations to travel home to bow at the gravesites of their ancestors. Ajumoni was cleaning the house, frying egg-washed fish, and calling me a cheese *chaengi*. Since our house was no longer available for rent after a year-long furlough in 1978, we moved back to the SFS hill, into the house we lived in when I was two years old.

The regularity of Korea's four seasons and the constancy of rituals like fall *kimchi* making and New Year's Day celebrations represented the aspects of Korea that never seemed to change. Seasons paid no attention to the arrests of neighbors or the complicated dynamics of an expat community. For my family, change was most felt in the departure of my oldest brother from Korea.

The personalities, preferences, and motivations of each of my very different brothers was evident with one look into their rooms. Chris lived an organized and purpose-driven life upstairs amongst his many sports and academic awards. He was fully engaged with life in Korea, but he was most inspired by the speeches of Abraham Lincoln and the baseball stats of Willie Stargell, Roberto Clemente, and Jose Martinez.

Mark had the smaller of the two downstairs bedrooms, right next to the front door. Since Mark and I had always been close, more friends really than siblings, I spent most of my free time in his cozy, enchanting, not-so-private *ondol* palace. In Mark's room marionettes came alive, fake rabbits appeared out of hats, and new worlds were created as chairs and blankets became great forts and castles.

I can still smell the blend of incense, leftover pie, and, I don't know, maybe sulfur? that combined to make up the mysterious odor that emanated from Rick's dark, palatial teenage haven. Rick had the only western style bed in the house. After making sure he was gone, I crept in, parting the long door beads to tip-toe through a menagerie of clothing and magazines. Once settled comfortably onto his luxurious bed, I listened to "Stairway to Heaven" and "Landslide" through expensive, Japanese-made headphones. Rick's collection of Fleetwood Mac, Led Zeppelin, and Pink Floyd albums were not Itaewon knock-offs. These were originals purchased during furlough. This was impressive stuff.

Entering Rick's room was like visiting a museum under questionable management. The bookshelves were lined with war relics and tins of chemistry powders and other unknown substances. Teenage sloth permeated the space. I loved Rick's album collection, but some of the music felt beyond my reach. Johnny Winter's albino skin, black clothing, and long, bright yellow hair made me understand Rick knew about a world I knew nothing about. My days were still full of *Pippi Longstocking* books, Bravo Cones, and kindly teachers. My big moment of rebellion was furtively looking through *Mad* magazine with Debbie and Jennie.

One day, I saw Ajumoni crying in the kitchen, talking with my parents. Our normally settled house was feeling very unsettled. Rick left a stove burner on all night after coming home from a late evening at a rice wine bar. My big brother was living with us as a shadow figure. He wasn't at the dinner table anymore. He didn't go to Taechon Beach or walk to school with us. Chris, Mark, and I once arrived at SFS after our usual, cheery fifteen-minute walk through Yonsei to see Rick pull up to the front door of the high school building in a taxi. He nodded to us and smiled, cool as ever. "Hey guys."

To be honest, until that morning I wasn't sure Rick was going to school. Rick wasn't thriving at SFS. He loved Korea in his own way, but it wasn't home. It's hard to tell, sometimes, if the things that happened to each of my siblings would have happened anyway, whether we were in Korea, in the U.S., or anywhere else. But part of me believes Rick suffered from our move to Korea in a way the rest of us didn't. By the time Rick was ten years old he had lived in six different homes.

One day, or so it seemed to me, Rick left us. He and my parents decided he should try finishing high school in the States. He was not there, and then he was really not there. Since I was only eight when he left, for a long time it felt like there were just five of us. For a few months a sadness hung in the air. My parents didn't talk about what happened. It was as if they were too sad, or too tired, or they just didn't know what to say. I later found out Mom and Dad felt terrible about what happened to Rick. Dad carried that pain for years. I think he still carries it. It would take a long time for my big brother to return to us.

In 1978, Chris graduated from SFS as student council president and one of the stars of our winning basketball team. He was off to Middlebury College, our Rice family legacy school. One by one, my brothers were leaving.

That October came the shocking news that President Park had been assassinated. I don't remember how I heard the news, or who told me. I just remember walking around in a daze. Park had been president for eighteen years. I was surprised he was mortal.

A Korean friend later told me his perspective on the day. When he arrived to school, his teachers were crying, so he cried. The school sent the students home early. When he arrived home, his mother and all of her friends were crying. Feeling obligated, he cried again. When he turned on the TV, all the newscasters were crying. By the end of the day he was exhausted. South Korean grief was a collective event. Grieving required.

The irony that Park was shot by the head of his own KCIA was not lost on anyone who knew anything about South Korean politics. I knew not to expect an orderly constitutional line of procession to play out. During a Korean funeral, order and procedure was critical. When meeting a new person for the first time, custom governed every move. When Korean friends married, the bride and groom had to follow tradition and bow in a precise, deep way to their parents. But I knew not expect order and procedure when a presidency was at stake. In the realm of Korean politics, anything could happen. Every Korean republic up to this point had begun or ended in an uprising or military coup.

The following days were strangely quiet with anticipation. In this tenuous state, with this vacuum of leadership, anything could happen. My parents hoped Park's death might finally usher in an era of democracy. Maybe this was the time the country would break free from authoritarian rule.

School reopened a few days later and our SFS community went back to classes and assemblies and sports practices as if nothing had happened. A friend later told me they remembered participating in a drill to practice evacuation, but I remember nothing of this. Did I treat the drill with that much nonchalance?

Within a few weeks, in a day-to-day way, my life slipped back into routine. I spent free time with my best friend, Cathy, talking about how amazing the latest Led Zeppelin album was. We saved up our allowance to hop in taxis to loiter in the lobbies of fancy downtown hotels, rubbernecking wealthy foreigners and sneaking into basement bars. I went back to the same life I was living before Park was assassinated, with a bit less surety of the semisolid ground I had long walked upon. I had learned to compartmentalize events like coups, assassinations, departures of brothers, and furloughs in New York and Oklahoma. Although a delicate opera of politics and power played out behind walls across the city, I knew I would likely never be in the line of fire. I felt safer in Seoul than anywhere else I would ever live. Korea was my grounding place, come what may.

But signs of change were in the air. My family had lived in Korea for a decade and a half. Mom and Dad, who originally committed to Korea for one five-year term, had stayed and stayed. Rick and Chris were living in the U.S. and Mark was soon to leave for college. Our family balance was starting to tip. Soon I would graduate from high school, leaving just Mom and Dad in Seoul. I didn't know it then, but the land I had learned to walk on was beginning to tremble beneath me.

A Line in the Sand

The moon is rising, the moon is rising,
ganggangsullae, ganggangsullae.

The moon is rising from the east sea,
outside the east window, ganggangsullae.
Whose moon is it? Ganggangsullae.

Ganggangsullae, ganggangsullae.

om was sitting next to me on the couch with tears running down her face. Newly elected President Jimmy Carter was walking from the U.S. Capitol to the Executive Mansion, holding hands with his wife and daughter. Mom said, through sniffles, "Honey, he's the first president to walk instead of ride from the Capitol to the White House."

Mom loved what Jimmy Carter represented. She couldn't help but have admiration for a man of the people and a champion of human rights. She was sure he would do something about the abuses of the South Korean government.

A few months after Park's assassination, the prime minister stepped in as acting president. Then another army general, head of Security Command Chun Doo-hwan, was named to lead the assassination investigation. One day a gossipy taxi driver told me Chun lived somewhere in our neighborhood. This was interesting news. Maybe I had run into him or one of his family members buying snacks at the corner store. I tried to figure out which house he lived in when I walked through the tonier Yonhi-dong residential areas, trying to imagine behind which thick, high wall he spent his evenings.

Soon our neighbor, Chun Doo-hwan, took control of all intelligence activities. He shook up the leadership of the KCIA. Almost overnight he grew into a giant. This is how South Korean politics worked. People watched and waited for the one who had the most will for power, the person who pushed harder than anyone else and forced his way in. In December, Chun took full control of the government in a military coup.

Unlike President Park, with his strong cheekbones, thick hair, and hard-set jaw, Chun Doo-hwan was bald and pale. While I gave Park a tiny bit of begrudged admiration, I had a feeling nothing good could come from having Chun in charge. I heard the coup d'état unfolded, erupted, or whatever coups are wont to do, down the road from Yongsan Army Base, near one of our favorite shopping neighborhoods of Itaewon, where knock-off sneaker stores and fine tailor shops catered to tourists and U.S. military personnel.

I was in a taxi a few weeks later as we passed the building where the main confrontation was said to have occurred. I tried to imagine how it had transpired. I heard of a gun fight, of a series of small battles, of the invasion of Chun-loyal troops and their arrival into Seoul to take over control of the military. If I went only by what I saw that day, Park was alive. The neighborhood showed no signs of conflict. Nothing. People were bargaining down the price of produce and riding along in buses as if nothing had happened. As we passed the area where everything went down, I thought, "Hmm. A coup happened here. Interesting." And I proceeded on to purchase pirated pop music records.

The assassination of Park Chung-hee brought a renewed call for democracy from college students and opposition leaders all over the country. Protests began again as colleges opened in the spring. We watched as our neighborhood campus of Yonsei came alive with clouds of pepper fog and flying Molotov cocktails. The students demanded an end to Chun's imposed martial law and the return of freedom of speech and assembly. They demanded the government hold a free and fair election. By mid-May of 1980, one hundred thousand people demonstrated at Seoul Station. Chun extended martial law into the rest of the country.

Kwang Ju was the regional home of opposition leader Kim Dae-jung. South Korea's larger cities had long overshadowed Kwang Ju in size and importance. The southwestern province was known for its agriculture, its spicy food, and its strong politics. Because of the province's long history of exploitation by Seoul powers, the region had seen little of the country's economic advancements. Kwang Ju was Kim Dae-jung's hometown, and many people there supported their champion of democracy. The only time I went to the province of Chollanamdo was during a high school hiking trip, when about twenty of us climbed Mount Chiri, the second highest mountain in South Korea. Other than that one trip, I didn't know a lot about the area, other than the fact Cho-ssi came from the region, and that it seemed a lot different than coming from Seoul.

College students in Kwang Ju began to protest against the closing of their university and the extension of martial law. Demonstrations that started on the campus moved into the city. Within days, office workers, housewives, and market workers were joining in. Something significant was happening. Those divided by politics and social class were coming together. Parents of protesters brought food and water. Local police put down their weapons and joined in. Taxi drivers led a formation of buses and trucks into the main shopping area of the city. Within one week, ten thousand people were demonstrating downtown. They robbed police stations and military depots of arms. They burned down a TV station reporting misinformation. Then the movement surged again, with fifty thousand citizens eventually calling for an end to martial law and the release of Kim Dae-jung.

Chun struck back with force. He ordered military into major cities to "secure peace and order." He sent the most seasoned paratroopers from the DMZ into Kwang Ju to take back the city. On May 27, troops from five divisions moved in. Specially designed clubs broke students' heads. Soldiers stabbed citizens with bayonets. Government forces shot indiscriminately into the crowd. Within hours, the paratroopers defeated the civilian militias. Government and news sources said a couple hundred people had died. Based on reports of foreign press, the death toll was in the two thousand range. A people's movement was quickly silenced. The bloodshed shocked the citizens of Kwang Ju.

Mark was casually chatting on the phone one day when he picked up a stack of snapshots sitting on a side table. The pictures were there, out in the open, as if they were a pile of cheery Christmas cards to glance through. To his horror he saw photos of men being beaten, military police dragging people through streets like sacks of rice, and women screaming in terror. Blood was everywhere. Someone had passed these pictures along to my parents to give evidence of what was happening in Kwang Ju. This was how news was spread in Korea, and this was what one might find in our living room on an otherwise uneventful day.

TV news reports were distorting the facts and downplaying the loss of life. A missionary from Kwang Ju said to Mom, "You all were always talking about how bad the situation was in Seoul. You should see what happened down here in Kwang Ju. Now we understand what you're talking about."

Mom couldn't believe President Carter had let this happen. A U.S. navy ship was docked off the west coast of the peninsula, not far from Kwang Ju. In order for paratroopers to leave the DMZ area for this big of a mission, they had to have U.S. approval. Why hadn't the U.S. stepped in? Did U.S. leaders approve of Chun's violent response to the protests in Kwang Ju?

Over the years I had amassed a number of artifacts from the U.S. I hoarded dollar bills, U.S. flag decals, baseball pennants, and a felt blue Union army cap from a furlough RV trip to Gettysburg. These were not just keepsakes. This was a *collection*, kept in a special shoe box in my closet.

One day I hung an Uncle Sam picture on my wall, not understanding at all what it represented. He pointed at me every morning, saying he wanted ME for the U.S. Army. Once middle school began I made regular trips to Itaewon to purchase pirated Michael Jackson, Earth, Wind & Fire, and Eagles records. The album covers were single-colored cardboard copies of the original. The center song labels were poorly typewritten and misspelled. The vinyl warped easily during the humidity of summer. But these warped records and AFKN, the American Forces Korea Network radio station, were my connection to the wonderful world of western music.

In the back alleys of Sinchon, Milky Way bars and Frosted Flakes cereal boxes were laid out on makeshift tables, teasing me with their American packaging, English lettering, and high price tags. On Halloween I got my greedy hands on as much American candy as possible. Deprived of American food, we knew to show up at the homes of expat families with access to the PX. I hoarded Milky Way and Butterfinger bars for months, allowing myself tiny bites of chocolate and nougat like sips of water on a desert hike.

One Halloween, Mark and I rang the gate bell of a home where we heard a foreigner had just moved in. A Korean lady we did not know opened the gate to find me dressed in a white sheet with two holes in it and Mark dressed as a pumpkin. She shrieked and slammed the gate, then ran back into her house, still shrieking.

In the early 1970s, in what felt like a miracle of culinary global-ization, the confectionery company Haitai began selling a packaged ice cream product called the Bravo Cone. Then Orion introduced a packaged corn and wheat-based cereal glazed with sugary syrup, called Jolly Pong. When you grow up eating plain puffed rice from a clear plastic bag for breakfast, the availability of a bright yellow, shiny package of Jolly Pong written in bouncy lettering is a break-fast sea-change of epic proportions. I measured South Korea's prog-ress by the availability of bad versions of Western food.

We were so impressed when someone's maid could make french fries. Mark would return from Jimmy Rhee's house looking smugly satisfied. "Mrs. Lee made french fries for us." I thought these crispy potato sticks so exotic and American, so special. Only recently did I wonder why we didn't just make them. We had potatoes. We had oil. We had salt. We had a kitchen. Somehow, french fries kept their mystique for sixteen years. Even for my parents.

The States was the home of 3 Musketeers candy bars, french fries, the slam-dunk, Evel Knievel, and Muhammad Ali. In the 1976 Summer Olympics, the U.S. came in third behind the powerhouses that were the Soviet Union and East Germany. While the U.S. earned thirty-four gold medals that year, South Korea earned one, its first gold medal in Olympic history. From homogeneous, developing, gray concrete, Confucian South Korea I couldn't help but be infatuated by a country in which you could wear whatever clothes you wanted to wear, dye your hair, eat french fries, and make a living out of jumping canyons on a motorcycle.

When you grow up collecting decals of a country, when you pay five dollars for one bar of candy from this country, when you visit it just enough to keep it exotic, you don't know of it as a real place. The complex role the U.S. played in Korea was only complicating this relationship more.

What good was the power of the U.S. if it was not used to stop the killing of innocent people? How did the U.S. government determine what being a "partner" to South Korea meant? What good were the rabbit warren neighborhoods of bars and brothels that sprung up around bases, with U.S. soldiers so ill-trained in cultural matters, who seemed to know so little about a people and a nation that had been formed thousands of years before their country was even an idea?

In spite of the friendly soldiers we had over to dinner in our first years in Korea, my interaction with GIs was largely superficial. I mostly saw them in the shopping and brothel districts that formed around U.S. army bases. I hated the way they acted in these neighborhoods, how they talked down to store owners older than them, how they acted like they owned the streets. I hated how loud they spoke, and how many of them spoke to Koreans in Konglish *pan-mal*. I hated they had done nothing about Kwang Ju.

We are different from the people on the army base, I thought to myself. *My parents respect Koreans. My family has Korean friends in our home and in our lives. I would never think of talking to an elder in the tone I heard come out of some soldier's mouths. I always use respectful language with store owners or bus girls or anybody older than me.*

I drew a line in the sand. Maybe it's human nature to draw a line in the sand. Maybe we all come to understand which side we stand on. I had developed loyalties in fifteen years. To Onni. To Ajumoni. To the staff at House of Grace. To the Choi family. To people too countless to name. I not only learned Korean history, I embraced the stories to my bosom. Like a good patriot, I admired the bravery and craft of Yi Sun-sin. I felt my heart stir when I heard the refrain, *ganggangsullae*, when I heard women sing the harvest moon song under moonlight. I loved this ancient melody that was turned into a song of battle when Admiral Yi commanded women to dress in military uniforms and dance on Mt. Okamae, causing the Japanese to overestimate the strength of Korean troops. I was resentful about Japanese colonization and angry about the way so many young Korean women had been forcibly taken from their homes and made into sex slaves for Japanese soldiers. I was resentful about the centuries Korea paid tribute to the powerful nation of China. When I measured the ills of South Korea against the good, the good always won. But I began to question the decisions and actions of the U.S.

Was the U.S. really complicit in Japan's original occupation of Korea in 1905? Was the celebrated liberation of Korea by the U.S. in 1953 only prompted by the strategic value Korea held in the region? Why, in 1945, did leaders of U.S. troops make key and long lasting decisions about a country they knew little to nothing about? Why was it that the U.S. government sometimes called intervention "meddling in local affairs" and other times "just and necessary?" I benefited from the generally positive perception of Americans even as I began to question whether it was deserved.

In 1981, nine months after the Kwang Ju uprising, Chun Doo-hwan was invited to the U.S. as the first head of state of South Korea to visit a U.S. president. On that day Ronald Reagan spoke of the "great bond of freedom and friendship" with Korea.

This was the president of the country to which I would one day, soon, "return." This was the country where people said to me, upon my arrival there, "Welcome home." It's always nice to be welcomed anywhere. I appreciate those words. But it felt so strange to be welcomed home to a place I didn't really know, to a land that wasn't really mine, to a place that, in many ways, I was beginning to resent. I could never make the U.S. home in the way Korea was. It just wasn't possible. There were too many things that tied me to Korea, too many onion skins of belonging to ever shed.

WHAT CAN I TAKE WITH ME?

Dad started a garden of healthy green squash and large orange pumpkins in a plot of dirt next to our driveway. Part lumberjack, part poet and theologian, Dad loved to counsel people and he loved to chop wood and carry water. His green thumb thoroughly impressed our Korean friends. They were surprised to learn honored *moksanim* had hearty farm skills. Some friends were still surprised we ate *kimchi*, as though we had not been living in Korea for fifteen years and eating *kimchi* with them during all those years. "What!? *Samonim* you like *kimchi*??"

Mark and I spent as much of the summer as we could at Taechon, tanning ourselves on small, scratchy towels, searching Back Bay for rare Scotch bonnet shells, and sitting on the long concrete wall to watch the sun fall into the ocean as fishing boats glided home for the night. Some nights, as dusk fell, my friends and I walked the long, sandy road into the tourist and fishing village to eat fried shrimp, drink OB beer, and dance to "Bahama Mama" in temporary tented bars. (Sorry, Mom and Dad).

Mark and Paul clinched the finals of Taechon's annual Rook tournament, thumping a Southern Baptist missionary couple in the finals. As the summer came to an end, Mark flew to the U.S. to begin his freshmen year at Middlebury College. Only Mom, Dad, and I were left in Seoul. In a year I would graduate from high school, and presumably, I would go to college in the U.S., too.

Looking back, I can see that within our world of longstanding mission tradition in Korea, it seemed assumed that we, the children of calling, would leave Korea after high school. We would make new lives in the places our parents or ancestors came from, or be called to other places, as if we would just move from one life, from one country to the next, seamlessly. As if we were on a mission, too. As if Korea was not *really* our home. If young people came back to Korea it was to do good work there. Not because it was simply their home. It felt like that reason wasn't deemed good enough.

A few missionary kids did come back to Korea after college. Some of them appeared to be purpose-driven and focused, working in the Peace Corps, teaching English, or finding teaching positions at SFS or other international schools. But more than a few of them appeared to carry a rootless restlessness, a melancholy-happiness, like they were so relieved to be home again, but were searching for something they couldn't find. Sometimes I got the feeling a few of them were *not making it*. Like living successfully in the U.S., or wherever we were supposedly "from," was a test we all hoped we would pass but had no idea how to study for.

Regardless of what lay ahead for me, so much had changed in fifteen years. I was almost sixteen. Mom and Dad were in their late forties, and Dad's beard was showing wisps of gray. Mom had moved on from her 1960s wigs, and her style, always spot on, was now '70s casual. Seoul had changed, too. The middle class was growing. Pedestrian overpasses were erected all over the city, which meant we could choose whether or not we wanted to take our lives into our hands and dart across the road, or trudge up and down the steep stairs. We even had a restaurant in Sinchon that sold American hamburgers, although Dad did point out that the menu at The Western boasted a hamburger and a beef burger, which he thought begged a few questions.

Seoul's population had doubled since we first arrived, to eight million. More people owned and drove a private car. We even saw a women taxi driver now and then. The success of the Hyundai Pony, Korea's first mass-produced car, was a symbol of national pride. Then, in 1981, we got news we never thought we would hear. Seoul was chosen above Nagoya, Japan to host the 1988 Olympics. We couldn't believe it. Korea beat Japan in something on the world stage? We were witnessing South Korea's industrial and modernization explosion, one that would be unparalleled in the world.

On the other hand, it felt like some things would never change. Ajumoni was still shuffling around the kitchen. SFS was still a thriving international community. Mrs. Riemer was still teaching Bachelor Survival to the high school boys and Mr. Schneider still held court in his history classroom, his tailor made suit jacket of the finest cloth draped over his shoulders. We still had a nightly curfew and monthly air raid drills, and one Korea was still two. After all of the Monday Night fact sheets, student and people's demonstrations, imprisonments, hanging of innocent people, the uprising at Kwang Ju, and the deportation of foreign activists, another dictator's portrait was hanging on our police station wall. It appeared like South Korea was settling uncomfortably into many more years of authoritarianism. In this way, it seemed like life would go on as it always had.

In the fall of 1981, my father got a call from the director of the counseling program at Presbyterian Hospital in Oklahoma City, offering him a position as hospital chaplain. With this offer, my brothers living in the U.S., and I soon to depart for college, my parents began to wonder if it was time to leave Korea. Dad was restless for a new challenge. The deeply impoverished country my parents first set foot upon in 1966 was transforming. Many people still lived hand to mouth, but South Koreans had risen up out of rubble and were rebuilding their nation.

Mom later told me she wanted to work in Korea until retirement. She felt bad leaving. But she was open to moving to the U.S. To Mom, life decisions were always about the work she could do in a new place. She thought she might be able to start a counseling center for immigrants and refugees arriving to Oklahoma from

places like Vietnam. She knew many Korean women were struggling in their new lives, living in the U.S. with military husbands.
Dad was excited about the possibility of chaplaincy work.

My parents asked me what I thought about leaving. So I spent a
few days thinking. As serious and as well-informed thinking as an
eleventh grader can conjure up. My best friends at that time, a year
ahead of me, were either in the U.S. or about to graduate from SFS
and go to college. Mark, a freshman at Middlebury, seemed to be
happy there. Chris left Middlebury College during his junior year
to work for an urban Christian community development organization in inner city Jackson, Mississippi. Rick floundered for a
couple years, until the timely intervention of our relatives and the
tough love of Uncle Jim, a former Marine, who one day grabbed
Rick's long hair, told him to get off the couch, get a haircut, and
enlist in the Army.

When we saw Rick at the airport two years later we walked right
past him. He was thirty pounds lighter, his once long, curly locks
were shaved close, and he was wearing a neatly pressed army uniform. In the services Rick found the structure and focus missing
from his life. By 1981 he was a few years into an Army career,
soon to travel between the Philippines, Germany, and other places
he couldn't tell us about involving parachute landings, deep scuba
dives, and foraging for snake meat in the jungle.

I was anxious about moving to the U.S., but it wasn't totally foreign to me. Because of our 1970 furlough in New York, I knew
about Hibbard's (or was it Hubbard's?) and Tops Grocery. Because
of a 1978 furlough in Oklahoma, I knew about Izod shirts, *The
Brady Bunch*, *The Partridge Family*, Taco Bell, Taco Mayo, and
where to take refuge during a tornado when you live in a cheaply
made tract home. I wasn't naive to the challenges of living in the
U.S. I experienced a few months of severe culture shock during my
eighth grade year in Oklahoma, a feeling I can only describe as a
dull, throbbing pain of not belonging; a sickly, gut-punch feeling

of ungrounded-ness that prompted me to miss school a lot and overeat. But furlough was only one year. I could do anything for a year. And by the end of that year in Norman, I was happy. I made great friends.

When I thought about moving to the U.S. I imagined exciting, important things, like how in the States I could *drive a car, eat at McDonalds*, and *go to shopping malls*. If we went back to the U.S. we were likely to live in Oklahoma, where I had, in the end, done well. So I told Mom and Dad I was okay if they wanted to move. I left the decision up to them.

By January of 1982, the middle of my junior year of high school, everything was set in motion. Our travel itineraries were finalized. We were packing boxes and barrels and sorting through sixteen years of life. We were trying to decide what to bring with us and what to leave behind. Just like when we left the U.S. in 1966, there were choices to make. Only this time I was awake to what was happening.

Should we take our rattan living room furniture with us? What about Mom's *I'm OK—You're OK* book, our "Arirang" records, and Dad's books on church history? What about the maple dressers my grandparents once owned, the furniture Mom and Dad brought with us to Korea sixteen years before? What about our *yos* and *ibuls*, the sacred bedding Ajumoni had stitched and restitched for years, that now held the shape of our bodies?

For a while, these surface decisions made the deeper questions avoidable. What about Ajumoni? Could I take the soil of Saddleback with me? Could I put some Yonhi-dong dirt into my pocket so I could always find my way back home? What about the things I could not take, street corners and snack shops, the people I could never carry with me?

About a week before we left, my parents and I were finishing dinner. My father reached to the side of his plate and began to casually open a neatly wrapped gift from a friend. The gift was just one of many he and Mom received in the final months as a gesture of thankfulness. Koreans were masters of gestures of thankfulness. Over-the-top masters.

As Mom and I chomped and chatted, Dad opened the box and pulled out an expensive watch. Then my father did something I had never seen him do. He hung his head and began to weep.

"It's too nice," he said. "It's just too nice."

For what seemed like ten seconds Dad looked at the watch and said, over and over again, "It's just too nice." Dad was no macho man, but I had never seen him cry, even when my grandmother died. It seemed that for Dad, everything that had happened over the last decade and a half was held in the gift of that watch. The watch held the kindness of Reverend Choi and his family, who came to the airport our first day to welcome us into their country. Who painted a scroll of Chinese characters for my family, equating our rainy September day arrival to Korea with blessings of unseasonal rains.

It held the humor and difficulty of two years of language school, and his first trip to Sinchon Market, when he fumbled with *won* bills and spoke only a few words of Korean. It held the kindness of Onni, Mrs. Kim, Cho-ssi, Poe-bae's mother, and Ajumoni, these women who had carried his children, prepared his *ramyun* lunches, and cleaned his home. It held the earnest fervor of the college students of ECF, and the joy and tears of the Monday Night Group. Maybe it even held the tragic story of eight men hung for no reason.

I think my father realized in that moment all he had gained living in Korea. I think he understand what he was going to lose by leaving. My father would be able to grieve the loss of South Korea. He would one day move on.

It would prove so much more complicated for me. There would be countless layers of loss to grieve, so many things, great and small, to long for. Something dear to me, something fundamental to my identity, was coming to an end. Some people called it "going back home." But we were leaving my home. And I was about to unravel.

Missionary friends stopped by to wish us well. These were my aunts and uncles and cousins, but I didn't know if I would ever see them again. We were from Korea but we were from all over the world. We were home but we were not home. Within ten to fifteen years many of them would be gone from Korea. How could a simple 'good-bye' hold all of that?

On the day we left, Ajumoni came to our house with Myong-ju and Un-ju. I have a picture taken that day. We're sitting together on our living room couch. We're crowded in like we don't want to separate from one another. I'm sitting next to Ajumoni. I look sad but hopeful. Ajumoni is smiling, but her eyes are red with tears, as if she knew better than I did what our leaving meant. I wish I hadn't let go of her hand and walked away. Something broke in me that day.

We said our final good-byes from the car. We drove down the hill through Yonhi-dong, past our neighborhood bakery, past the tea shop, the old police station, and the tire repair store. We drove further west towards Kimpo, past the Catholic martyrs' statue.

I imagine Ajumoni walking down the hill towards her home. I imagine her opening the door to her apartment, wondering what would come next. We were more than Ajumoni's employment. We had become her family. But we were more than her family. We were her means of making a living. Now one family was two, with a vast ocean to divide us. Ajumoni and I, in very different ways, were headed into a time of change and insecurity.

I don't remember leaving Kimpo that day. I want to remember this. I want to tell you I stood in the terminal and the people I loved were all around me, patting at my arm, calling, "*Aigo, Lidgie, aigo.*" I needed someone to tell me to say good-bye. I was living a life that felt so rooted. I was secure and grounded. I was a member of a long-standing, rich community, and a citizen by soul of a country I loved. In the face of leaving Korea, I somehow thought this life would go on forever.

For sixteen years, Korean ways washed over me like blessings of unseasonal rain. The dawn sounds of Buddhist monks chanting at the temple up the hill said, *You live in an ancient place, with people who believed in things a long time before your people came along.*

The clank of dishes in the homes a few feet away told me, *You live in a place where people live near to one another, where being close together is more important than privacy and comfort.*

The repetitive megaphone announcements belted out from three-wheeled trucks reminded me, *You live in a country of persistence and hard work.*

The middle of the day sounds of heavy traffic, the pounding of never-ending construction projects, the buses stopping and starting, these told me, *You live in a city of hope, alongside people who literally rose up from ashes.*

The calls for justice, the cries for democracy in the face of billy clubs and tear gas, these told me, *You live amongst people who will sacrifice everything for what they believe.*

And the late night sounds of Seoul told me that even in my crazy, neon-lit, industrializing city, tranquility could settle on the gray concrete buildings and old palaces like heavy fog. And all of this said together, as one great unified chorus, *This is where you come from. This is where you belong.*

THE UTICA INCIDENT

나는 누구인가?
(명상원)

Who am I?

In January of 1982, life as I knew it ended with a single plane flight. The day became pivotal, a before and after moment, like the day of a serious, life-changing car accident. But the damage was not immediately evident. My injuries lay beneath the surface, a slow internal bleeding that only began to reveal symptoms over time.

My last year of high school, spent in a large public school in Oklahoma, went remarkably well. I missed my brothers, but I enjoyed living at home with just Mom and Dad. We had an easy relationship. And, remarkably, we finally lived in a house my parents actually owned! Our historical red brick home in an older area of Oklahoma City was cozy, and our neighborhood was diverse. I missed SFS and Korea, and of course I missed Ajumoni, but graduating with friends from an eighth grade furlough year made Norman High School bearable, and actually, quite fun. I caught up with cultural references I had missed out on. I made new friendships and reignited old ones. It seemed I was "making it" in the U.S.

The time came to pick a college. It seemed that, for the most part, Rices went to Middlebury. Dad, Chris, and Mark went to Middlebury. My great-grandfather, grandfather, great uncle, various cousins, and an aunt and uncle went to Middlebury, too. So I decided to go to Middlebury. This was my well thought-out reasoning. I didn't think to meet with an admissions counselor. I'm pretty sure there were no books like *Colleges that Change Lives* or *Choosing the Right College* lying around the house.

Actually, I don't remember having one conversation with my parents or anyone else about the various factors one might consider when picking a college, such as big or small, city or countryside, conservative or liberal, or the make-up of the student body. Mom and Dad were kind of loose about these types of choices. I knew I didn't want to attend a Christian college, I knew that didn't fit me, but beyond that, I was wide open. Although I knew Chris left Middlebury early, I never connected his restlessness there with anything I might experience. I was happy when I was accepted into my family's legacy school.

At first things seemed to be going well. I made friends in my freshman dorm. I learned how to pump cheap beer from kegs. I bought a t-shirt that read "Club Midd." I familiarized myself with sports I didn't grow up with like field hockey, ice hockey, and lacrosse. Political science, art, and history courses were challenging and interesting. Middlebury was living up to its academic reputation. Classmates who came from private schools, which was most of my classmates, were much more academically prepared than I was for conversations about Plato's cave and the complex undercurrents of T.S. Eliot's *The Waste Land*. I had a lot of catching up to do. But this was fine. I had always enjoyed meeting an academic challenge.

Then, over a period of months, something strange happened. A deep well of loneliness began to grow inside of me. I began to feel disconnected from reality. I thought about death and the randomness of life. Nobody knew it, but I was coming apart inside. I had chosen a college whose student body represented the most high-income, mono-cultural environment I had ever lived in. I was in a tiny town in a small state in a country I knew little about. I was a thousand miles away from my parents, living far away from the two people who had always grounded me from Seoul to Oklahoma to Lewiston. My nuclear family was now my primary tie to Korea. They were my umbilical cord to a former life. Months, then years passed without any significant contact with Korea. One year away was like a furlough. I could do that. Two years away was like a furlough that was going on too long. When three years passed, I realized our life in Korea was over. The loss was unbearable. I didn't know who I was without Korea. I was not making it.

I was in a political science class one day when a student said something about what a weak president Jimmy Carter was. Everyone except the professor nodded nonchalantly, like, of course we all know this. I was so surprised. People thought Mom's dear, kind-hearted Jimmy was a terrible president? Even though Mom didn't understand why Carter had turned a blind eye to what happened in Kwang Ju, she still respected him. I couldn't believe how many people admired Ronald Reagan.

I was naive about the greater world outside of Korea. I was naive to the reasons many people got degrees. People went to college to get a good job and make money? Not everyone was bound by calling? The world did not move by chants for democracy? I was an agnostic-leaning missionary kid with a heart for social justice. I was a Middlebury legacy more at home on Saddleback than in the Green Mountains. I was a Democrat in a world of Republicans. I was by definition a citizen of the U.S. I looked and talked like I came from the U.S. But I belonged in the international club. I needed a host family.

I was supposed to be a chameleon because of my global upbringing. I was supposed to get along with almost anyone, adapt to any place. SFS students came from over thirty different countries. I adapted to life in Norman, Oklahoma after Korea. That was not exactly a seamless move. A friend of mine who grew up in Norman once told me she thought it was hard for people from *Tulsa* to fit into Norman. Maybe I wasn't that adaptable after all. Maybe I was tied to a certain way of living in the world, too.

When I tried to tell Mom I was unhappy during college, she said, "But honey you loved Middlebury!" She just couldn't see me that way. Then she added, "I had a hard time at St. Lawrence, too, Liz. There were a lot of people there from big cities."

I thought about how going to college in the same state she grew up in might not be a totally fair comparison, how this might not be apples to apples, and about the cheerful stories she still tells of her Kappa Kappa Gamma sorority sisters, and the class reunions she still attends, sixty years later.

I grew silently angry with my parents. My dear parents, with their kind hearts, social work degrees, and counseling certificates, who dropped me off at the bus station in Utica, New York before college to make my way to Middlebury on my own, forever known after this as "The Utica Incident."

Mom and Dad took classes in "active listening" and "parent effectiveness." They listened first hand to the stories of factory workers and biracial teens. I was rootless and untethered, but they were once again heads down, focused on healing the spiritual needs of cancer patients and drug addicts in Oklahoma, working to find housing for immigrants from Vietnam. How could I be having problems? I had everything! I was one of the world's fortunate ones. The cobbler's children had no shoes.

My parents were doing their best, but these furloughs based solely on work assignments and advanced degrees gave little regard to the importance of creating any familial or cultural connection to the States. Our furlough year in Oklahoma, during Mark's eleventh grade year, was horrible for him. Mark is one of the most charming and funny people you could ever meet and he came out of that year at Norman High School with one friend. After Mark graduated from SFS he flew back to the U.S. on his own to begin college. Compared to that my drop-off at the Utica bus station looks like helicopter parenting.

With each year away from Korea it began to feel like my childhood was a setup. Mom and Dad took me to Korea as a baby. They told me it was our home. They worked to turn *them* into *we*. They sent me and Mark to Korean nursery school and kindergarten. They moved into a Korean neighborhood. They gave their hearts to Korea. We stayed for sixteen years. And then we left. And I was supposed to just move on? I no longer had a home in South Korea and I didn't have a home in the U.S. I felt dropped into a country I didn't understand and I was living an adulthood I didn't want to live. I didn't know my own relatives and the lady that felt like my grandmother was across the world. Almost every relationship from the first sixteen years of my life, other than those with my immediate family, was gone. My international school friends were scattered around the world like non-native flowers, trying to thrive in new environments with no email or social media to connect us.

My parents had six months of training before going to Korea. They sat through lectures about culture shock and acculturation. They knew they would have to acclimate. They understood things would be hard at first. Six months of training is extravagant for people who are moving to another country for work, but most adults, whether trained or not, know to at least prepare for culture shock when they move to another country. Expat kids had fourteen hours and a few packages of free peanuts to prepare us for our life's most dramatic and fundamental change.

My expat community, these people who spent their lives making fundamental, generational, cultural, and geographic shifts, had no language for our experience. I don't remember talking about culture shock or cross-cultural identity with my parents or with any counselors, teachers, or administrators. It wasn't until I left college that I learned there was something about my childhood that might make my adulthood challenging. I didn't hear about reverse culture shock until I was in my twenties. At that point, I didn't know where I was supposed to be feeling culture shock and where I was supposed to be feeling the reverse of it.

Instead of feeling a sense of accomplishment, I graduated from a prestigious college with a feeling a leaden emptiness. I was thankful for the education. I knew many people didn't have these kind of opportunities. But I felt completely dislocated from the experience. I smiled in all the photos. I sipped gin and tonics as if everything was terrific. My New England genes kicked in and I deemed it more important to appear happy than to be happy. Dad felt bad enough for becoming a minister and going to Korea. My grandfather counted his years at Middlebury as his best. I couldn't add another generation of disappointment to his plate. But the devastation of the loss of Korea was leading into a long episode of dislocation and deep depression.

Something dawned on me after I graduated from college. Something that seemed obvious to my classmates. I was supposed to make a *choice* about what I was going to do next. I had no idea what I wanted to do. I was operating under an assumption that everyone heard a *call*, and that if you answered that call, life unfolded mysteriously and miraculously into richness. I had learned about how to live life from the most influential adults in my childhood, the people of our mission community. I was missing key information about how to be an adult in the non-missions, non-expat world. As I watched my classmates move into rewarding careers and graduate school programs, I waited for my call as if it was going to fall on me like rain. But the call wasn't coming. Maybe calling wasn't magical, after all.

Without direction, and with few connections from my prior life, I worked at a Vermont bakery. I did temp work in Boston. I moved so often that, by my thirties, I had lived in more U.S. states than most people who grew up in the U.S. had. My life was turning into a series of short-term attempts to find community and calling, discovering over and over again that I didn't know how to live a regular life.

I struggled to develop the depth of relationships I had in Korea. I tried to move on, as if my childhood was something to get over. I carried on as if I *had* to move on from Korea, as if my desire to live in my home country was somehow unreasonable. No matter where I went, no matter which state I lived in, or what work I did, the most fundamental part of me, my Korean side, was unseen and unrecognized. But that part of me wouldn't go away. She was dormant, but breathing. She was on life support, refusing to pass over.

After a couple years of taking different jobs to make ends meet, and a month long Outward Bound trip I financed on a scholarship, I decided to join Chris in Mississippi to live and work in the low-income African-American neighborhood of West Jackson. I was in a community of calling again. People of different races were coming together to address the injustices of the neighborhood we lived in, a legacy of slavery, Jim Crow laws, and racism.

I changed in Jackson. I learned about African-American history. I committed to the cause of racial reconciliation. It seemed I had found a place to use the cross-cultural skills and social justice lessons of my childhood. Even the most stubborn agnostics who listened to Arthur Phillips and the interracial Voice of Calvary Church choir sing the gospel song, "I'll Tell It," had to feel the deep spiritual power that lived in that space.

I experienced some hard, bring-you-to-your-knees moments, too, the ones that inevitably come with crossing hardened lines. But I made many dear friends. Mississippi opened my eyes to understand the U.S. in new and complicated ways. Many Americans had suffered, too. The DMZ wasn't the only divide in the world that mattered. The focus on purposeful social justice work was the missing piece of my college experience. When co-workers called for "justice to roll down like waters," the *Minjung* inside of me awakened. But the longer I stayed, the more I couldn't reconcile my core beliefs with the organization's conservative stance on social issues. In spite of those many Sunday school lessons, I just didn't believe Christianity was the only path to spiritual awakening. So I moved again.

In our intermittent phone conversations, it seemed that Jennie and Debbie were faring better than I was. They had attended Christian colleges where they were around people familiar with our kind, classmates who at least understood missions and calling, who knew there were blondes and brunettes who might know a lot more about Nairobi than New York. I heard about friends settling down in the countries of their passports, or elsewhere, making new homes and starting families. I later found out that many of them were facing the same challenges and struggles I was, but we were so isolated from one another, too spread out to reach out and say, "What in the world happened?"

Seeing my nuclear family during these years helped. When we got together for holidays we used Korean words. We said *uyu* instead of milk and *paji* for pants. When we knew a family member was calling we answered the phone, "*Yoboseyo?*" We ate short grain rice and gobbled up *kim*, the crispy, salty seaweed squares that I can unbiasedly assert nobody makes better than Koreans. We grilled *pulgogi* and tucked greedily into Mom's sesame-laden *chapchae* noodles. We laughed about things that happened in Korea. We talked about the people we knew and missed. We reminisced about Taechon Beach and Seoul Union Club and Ajumoni and Cho-ssi. Half of my parents' house decorations are from Korea. Just the other day I asked Mom, "Do you have any rice paper? I want to try out my *tojang* seal."

She looked at me and said, "Are you kidding?" She headed directly over to one of many small Korean chests they own and pulled out a thick roll of white paper, one of many. Then she added, "Do you want the ink stone, too?"

In many ways, we are fundamentally defined as a family by the experience of living in Korea. But nobody talked about wanting to go home. Nobody said, "I miss Ajumoni so much my heart hurts." I began to realize something, something that maybe should have been obvious to me. Although my parents were deeply attached to Korea, although they loved Taechon and Saddleback, their deepest childhood attachments were to a lodge in the Adirondacks, a town called Lewiston, and a cabin along Ontario's Severn River. I took their commitment to South Korea as a statement of belonging. I made magic out of their story of acculturation. I made magic out of calling, thinking of their move to Korea, away from their country and family, as seamless. I projected my story onto theirs. But they didn't go to Korea at the age of nine months. I did.

I didn't know they had a falling out with a Puk Ahyon-dong neighbor, or that they sometimes missed the U.S. in the early years. I don't remember a time before they spoke Korean. By the time my memories began, my parents had Korean names and bowed to people as if they grew up bowing to people. Dad had a traditional personal seal *tojang* he pressed into red ink to sign official documents. Mom tucked into salty *myolchi* anchovies as if she always had. I didn't remember a time before Korea, and I assumed everyone felt the same way I did.

I would never understand Korea like a Korean person did, but so much about that country was a part of my flesh and blood. Korea was my starting point. Before I spoke, I knew Korea. Before I could feed myself, I knew Korea. I absorbed concepts like *nunchi* into my skin. I am always quietly gauging other people's moods in interactions. I learned the body language of respect and reserve unconsciously. I instinctively feel titles and speech levels to be important. I can never sit down at a table before my Korean elders do. The fact of my age in going to Korea made it so Korea was home. It made my transition from the U.S. to Korea not a transition at all. But it had another effect, too. It made the leaving much harder. I needed to learn to look at my family's experience in Korea honestly. Maybe my story was not their story. Maybe each of us, my parents and my three brothers, carried our own balance of belonging and identity. Maybe each of us had our own story to tell about Korea.

During a move from Boston back to Vermont, in the aftermath of another decision made much too quickly, from a place of unrooted loneliness, I suddenly felt unsure where my body ended and where it began. In that moment the world became a timeless place, and I understood this might be what a breakdown felt like. I was untethered and ungrounded, suspended in mid-air between two lives. Years passed without any contact with Ajumoni. From state to state, and job to job, I grieved for my childhood as if I was grieving the loss of a mother. I was going through reentry shock without knowing it, and I was doing it in some of the most intense places.

I grew dizzy in large supermarkets. I felt like I was walking on a swaying boat as I picked out cereal and pasta. I had difficulty swallowing a drink in public, my throat closing up tight as I tried to take a simple sip. Underlying anxiety took over my life. I had no context for my own despair and no way to understand the depth of my loss, even to myself. I kept feeling I needed to do more with my life. What was an existence devoid of rich community and shared purpose? What good was a life without a deep sense of calling? What was I doing testing software?

There was Before Liz and After Liz. Before Liz was the Lidgie Ajumoni knew. She was the Liz who knew how to hail a cab in Yonhi-dong, eat Jolly Pong cereal and USO french fries, and talk easily with the friendly *ajossi* at the corner store. She was the Liz who could bargain for socks in Namdaemun and walk downtown Seoul without a map. I didn't know who After Liz was. Was I Mississippi Liz? Was I Boston Liz? I certainly wasn't Middlebury Liz. Who was I if I could adapt to West Jackson, Seattle, and Lusaka, Zambia? Or maybe more importantly, who was I not? And who was I without Korea?

Sometimes time passed and I felt like I was finding my place. I tried to be thankful for my childhood instead of mourning its loss. I found meaningful work in the nonprofit sector. I earned an advanced degree in Public Administration. I took Korean classes to keep my first language alive, to lessen the *changpi* I carried for not speaking it more fluently. But even in days of growing fulfillment, my grief and longing could return in a memory, a smell, or a chance encounter. I dreamt about Korea like I was dreaming of a lost loved one. For a few minutes, in the waking time of early dawn, Korea was real again. When I realized I wasn't really home, I was heartbroken

My family always used humor to get through tough times. Mom and Dad taught me to take life seriously, but not take myself too seriously. They would be talking about a difficult situation and then, in the next minute, see an absurd side to it all and begin a long, drawn out period of hilarity. But none of my old coping mechanisms were working. The pain went too deep. So I pushed my depression down. I pushed it deep inside of me. I tried to wish the anger, the loss, and the sorrow away. But internal bleeding doesn't stop on its own. Grief doesn't go away by ignoring it. It just digs in deeper.

WHERE ARE YOU FROM?

"I'm trying very hard to love the mangroves."

—POET MARY OLIVER,
On leaving her long-time home of
Provincetown and moving to southern Florida.

Where are you from? It seems like such a simple question. But then, many things seem simple on the surface. I recently read about something called "ambiguous loss." This is loss someone goes through when someone they love is missing but never found. A person who experiences this kind of loss is said to go through partial stages of grief but is never able to go through them all. They don't know exactly what they're grieving for. It's suffering without closure. Processing grief requires a starting point. We need an ending or to know there is no ending. It becomes a problem of human cognition. We simply do not have enough information.

My life in Korea had ended. But Korea was there. We lost contact with Ajumoni. But Ajumoni was alive. My expat community was spread out all over the world. But those people were alive, too. So what exactly was I grieving for? Was it for the empty cabins at Taechon Beach? For the cracking concrete of the unused tennis courts? For the way, one summer, after years of missionaries slowly leaving Korea, the lodge remained shuttered? Was it for a lady who was more a grandmother to me than my own grandmother? Was it for a persevering widow who delivered eggs to our door? For the people who held me as a baby, walked with me as a toddler, and taught me as a teen? Was it for the vibrant, rich community I was realizing I would never get back? Was I grieving the loss of myself?

People I met from Boston to Seattle told me, in attempts to be helpful, "Well, you know, you can't go home again." This was terrible news! This is like telling someone who lost a dear loved one, "They're in a better place now," or saying, "Why don't we all just get along" about race relations. I don't think some of them know enough to say this, I think to myself, these people *who are home*,

who have been rooted in the same country, or town, or neighborhood, or even the same house for twenty, thirty, or forty years.
These people who say, nonchalantly, every few months, "I'm going
home for the holiday!"

I couldn't believe my ears when I first heard someone say, "Home
is not a place." How could home not be a place? What in the world
did that mean? Was a profound connection to geography, cultural?
Was I operating under a fundamentally different set of values than
the people around me? Was this Korea's influence, the result of
growing up in an country rooted in the love of motherland? Did I
have a profound, inner soul-pull of the people of *kohyang*, a people
whose country's founding mythology was based on a real mountain, a place that existed, a place they still knew?

Throughout these years a thought stayed in the back of my
mind that gave me hope. *Someday I will return to Korea to live.*
This hope, on some difficult days, kept me alive. The eighteenth
century physicians who worked with displaced military and navy
soldiers prescribed, "no remedy other than return" for the afflic-
tion they called "nostalgia." They noted a return to health even if
patients were given a "fraudulent promise" of return. I was resting
my hopes on a fraudulent promise.

I know this seems like the obvious answer. Just go home! I don't
know how to explain it, and I think it's complicated, but something kept standing in the way. Other than that summer during
college, when I found Ajumoni, I had never lived in Korea without
my family. Going without them was a big step. Did I want to live
that far away from my parents? I felt shaming guilt about not being
with Ajumoni and I anticipated even more Korean daughter's guilt
if I moved across the world from Mom and Dad.

There was also fear in returning after so long. Was Korea still my
grounding place? What work could I do there without a Korean
passport? I couldn't just show up without a work visa. I'm not
a citizen of my home country. My conversational Korean could

easily get me around Seoul, order *pibimpap*, and carry me through pleasant conversations with friends, but it wasn't going to get me far in a job that required fluent Korean. And as I considered this, as I tried to make the U.S. work, I grew more homesick, until nostalgia ached inside of me. And somehow, ten years passed.

I saw a documentary once about children who grew up traveling around the world on a boat with their parents. When asked about this experience, they kept saying, quite cheerfully, "It doesn't seem different to us!" I think a child is genetically predisposed to believe that there is nothing unusual about her life unless someone tells her it is so.

People who were curious asked me, "What was growing up in Korea like?" I really appreciated when people asked me about my childhood. I love asking people about where they come from, whether it's a farm in Minnesota or a city in Europe. I'm so interested in human roots. But I didn't know what to compare Korea to. I didn't know where to start. What is growing up in Boston like? What about Wyoming? What about living on a boat? To begin to talk about something with any eloquence we have to step away from it, to see it from afar, to understand what about it is this way or that way. I had to learn to talk about my childhood from some distance, to understand what people wanted to know, to realize the answer, "It was just my childhood," wasn't adequate.

"Where are you from?" people asked so casually. It's a question I can't answer with any hint of grace. I've seen friends I grew up with literally sigh after being asked this. When people ask *where are you from*, I think they want to know, *How do I categorize you? How do I understand who you are? What will you bring to this interaction, this friendship, this job, this country.* Essentially, they are asking, *Who are you?*

My answer usually depends on my mood, on who is asking, and on what I think they are asking. Sometimes I tell people where I currently live (which is not technically where I'm *from*). Other times I add, "But I grew up in Korea," the 'but' making it sound like I'm adding on an addendum of identity, when really this is the main story. Claiming my cultural identity requires a back-stepping on my part, an explanation, a justification.

I worked over the years to make the answer sound nonchalant, off the cuff.

"Well, my parents are from Niagara Falls. I'm living in Seattle right now. But I grew up in Korea."

I don't know why I tell people where my parents come from. I think it might be because I think some people *want* me to feel I'm from the U.S., or to be from somewhere I look like I'm from. A more complex reality seems tiring to some people. Usually, by Seattle, I've lost them. They've moved on to a more straightforward conversation.

Sometimes I answered, "I'm from Minneapolis," or "I'm from Seattle," even when I had only lived in those places for a few years. The problem is, as soon as I said this the assumptions began. And they were usually wrong. I can't claim Minnesota or Seattle as where I'm from. I certainly can't claim Niagara Falls, either. I wasn't formed by those places. But if I say, "I'm from Korea," people often laugh, or they say something like, "Ha ha, you don't look Korean." Ha ha.

I recently heard a TED talk by writer and photographer Taiye Selasi, called "Don't ask where I'm from. Ask where I'm a local." Her words struck me to my core. "Last year I went on my first book tour. In thirteen months I flew to fourteen countries and gave some hundred talks. Every talk in every country began with an introduction. And every introduction began, alas, with a lie.

'Taiye Selasi comes from Ghana and Nigeria. Or, 'Taiye Selasi comes from England and the States.' Whenever I heard this opening sentence, no matter the country that concluded it . . . I thought, but that's not true . . ." In examining this idea of identity, Selasi goes on to say, "What if we asked, instead of 'Where are you from?'—'Where are you a local?' This would tell us so much more about who and how similar we are. Tell me you're from France, and I see what, a set of clichés? . . . Tell me you're a local of Fez and Paris, better yet, Goutte d'Or, and I see a set of experiences. Our experience is where we're from."

She's right. There has to be a better question. There has to be a better way of defining ourselves. Lately I've been asking people, "Where is home for you?" Maybe I will start asking, "Where are you a local?" Because what Taiye Selasi is saying cuts to the essential limitation in asking people where they are from. The reply often doesn't answer the question. Who we *are* is so much more complex and interesting than that answer can ever convey.

Selasi continues, "I've got a friend named Layla who was born and raised in Ghana. Her parents are third-generation Ghanaians of Lebanese descent. Layla, who speaks fluent Twi, knows Accra like the back of her hand, but when we first met years ago, I thought, 'She's not from Ghana.' In my mind, she came from Lebanon, despite the patent fact that all her formative experience took place in suburban Accra. I, like my critics, was imagining some Ghana where all Ghanaians had brown skin or none held U.K. passports. I'd fallen into the limiting trap that the language of coming from countries sets—the privileging of a fiction, the singular country, over reality: human experience."

When she said this I immediately thought of the look I have seen on people's faces when I say I'm from Seoul, Korea. The one that says, "You're not really from Seoul, Korea." One lady I met listed all the reasons she thought I wasn't really defined by that experience. "Well, you probably went to an international school, right?" "Well, you came back to the U.S. a lot, right?" Why, I wondered, did she want to take this part of me away?

When I told people *why* I grew up in Korea I could see the stereotypes pop into the thought bubbles above their heads as soon as the words "missionary kid" left my mouth. They were creating

scenes about my life based on *The Poisonwood Bible*. In fact, many
people suggested I should read that book. Why would I want to
read that book? I started to add information right away, scram-
bling to try and tell a more complex story. "Well, my parents were
good missionaries," I would say to try and win points. "They were
into social justice and worked for democracy."

It's not like that was necessarily interesting or impressive to
everyone, either. But I knew people were making assumptions
about my parents and about me in every direction, and I hated
that. Some people assumed my parents were narrow-minded Bible-
thumpers. I hated it just as much when people assumed my parents
were saints, and assumed I was a Christian. I'm extremely proud of
my parents, but who they are is not necessarily who I am.

When I did try and talk about Korea there was too much to tell.
Where do I begin? Any childhood, any country, is too complicated
to describe in a casual conversation. If I talked too long about the
tear-gas demonstrations, I felt the need to remind people I was playing on the tennis team and eating Barbie-shaped birthday cakes. If
I talked only about my international school, I felt I should explain
how intertwined my family was with Korea, and how affected I
was by my parents' democracy work.

I knew I couldn't combat the single imagery of the TV show
M.A.S.H. by talking about the long history of intricate dynasties,
but I began to take it as my job to defend Korea, to think of ways
to casually mention how Koreans had made some of the world's
finest ceramics and spun beautiful silk. I wanted to tell them about
the old palaces and the thirteen-storied pagodas. I wanted to talk
about the astounding perseverance etched into the eighty thousand
hand-carved wooden blocks of Buddhist scripture stored in the
open air at Haein Temple. It was difficult to check my annoyance
when I was asked, more times than I should have been, "Did you
eat dog meat?" when what I really wanted to tell them is how beautiful the Sorak Mountains are in the fall, when the leaves change to

yellow and red. It's not as easy as you might think to fit celadon into a casual conversation.

I tried to think of the best way to describe Koreans, like anyone can describe a people. As I started to talk about the crazy street life, the shameless shoves of five-foot-tall middle-aged ladies in train stations, I felt I should also explain these were the same people who played refined court music of the stringed *kayagum*, seated quietly in flowing silk *hanbok* dresses. Or how a country with white-gloved, starch-bowed store clerks who bowed deeply to customers at the entrances of fancy department stores was the same place that birthed variety shows with wacky, slapstick comics who contorted their faces into expressions like Jerry Lewis. The thing is, I can't explain Korea. I don't know how to talk about Korea as if I was a visitor there. And I think that's what people were expecting me to do. To talk about it like I might talk about a week-long trip to Puerto Vallarta or a year long work project in India.

How do I talk about a twelve-year relationship with Ajumoni and what she meant to me in a casual conversation? Or the impact of a place like House of Grace? Or the lessons of the Monday Night Group? Or the impact of a demarcation line of tragedy called the DMZ? So what I learned over the years was that it was easier to not talk about Korea at all. It's not that I wanted to go on for hours, to dwell on this one part of my identity. I just wanted to talk about my childhood like everyone else did. I wanted people to see me for who I was and not who they thought I was. I wanted people to not assume I was the "we" or the "them" they talked about.

"Well, coming from the States, Liz, you know how *we* are."

Do I? Am I included in your we?

"Liz, let me tell you how we Koreans think," says a new Korean friend.

Am I excluded from your we?

I can so easily picture the shell-shock look on the faces of a few new Korean-American friends when I, their white American friend, said *aigo* and cooked a decent *toenjang* stew. I was used to my Korean-American friends from SFS who understood we American- and Euro-Koreans in the same way we understood them. We knew that in many ways we were two sides of the same coin, that we both carried some measure of influence from the rituals and the people of each of our places. We were not shocked or surprised about our cross-cultural identities. One day, a Korean-American friend who moved to Korea during middle school told me, "Liz, your family is sometimes more Korean than mine is."

The thing is, I am missing fundamental information about Korea. There are basic things I missed out on completely. I often don't know if a Korean name I haven't heard before is male or female. Since I related mostly to Korean adults after the age of five, I'm not good at speaking informally with people my age. In fact, I'm terrible at it.

I know Korean holidays, I love Korean holidays, but I never visited my relatives at Chusok or bowed to my parents during the New Year. Can I speak from an identity I didn't come to by genetics or ancestry? Can I claim a feeling of belonging when I am missing key information, if I am not fluent in the language? Can I even say I feel half Korean?

And so I say, "I'm from Minneapolis." "I'm from Seattle." "I'm from Vermont."

But I'm not really from any of those places at all.

I recently read an article about cultural variance. The researchers proposed that wide differences exist almost everywhere we look, even if we don't recognize them as such. Culture, they said, affects our spatial reasoning, the way we infer the motivations of others, the way we categorize, use moral reasoning, and how we define the boundaries between self and others. How we behave and how we see everything, they proposed, comes down to psychological tendencies handed down through thousands of generations. It's all dependent on how we learned to live within our culture.

What is our belief about gift giving? Is a gift a burdensome obligation or a thoughtful item given with no attachments? What do we consider fair? When, if ever, is lying okay? How do we tolerate differences and react towards deviant behavior? Is our internal sense of self-worth dependent on our community status or our educational and financial achievement? Do we value social harmony over self-expression? And maybe this is what lays at the heart of my story.

From the moment I was born, I began to understand how the world was ordered. Along the way, I learned what to value and what was deemed right and wrong by those around me. In the presence of Cho-ssi and Horace Underwood I began to understand how to eat, how to welcome people in, how to grieve, and where my people should bury our dead. From the Choi family, and in our annual mission meeting, I learned how to live in a house, with a family, a community, a country, and the world. From Yonhi-dong to Taechon Beach I used all of the senses I was given to understand who I was. I didn't think about this. I grew into who I was naturally and unconsciously, like we all do. And one day I realized something. I didn't learn how to be an American. I learned how to be a Korean.

I could never sit down before my Korean elders at a restaurant, even if I was in St. Paul, Minnesota. My reaction to 9/11 felt so disconnected from most of the Americans around me. Of course I was saddened and horrified, but I didn't feel personally attacked. It was not a life-changing event for me. Mark watched the Twin Towers fall from his apartment in New York City. That night he rolled up his mat and walked to yoga class, surprised to find out it was canceled. It's not that he didn't care. Mark was trained to move along after a shocking incident. He was wired differently.

In the U.S. my belief in the power of fate, in the power of picking out a book or a stack of *won* bills from a table, looked like giving in. The level of importance I placed on interpersonal relationships seemed to get in the way of "getting things done." My frequent use of the word "we" made it sound like I wasn't a strong person on my own. I do believe in the self-evident truth that we are all created equal, but does this mean titles and social hierarchy are inherently bad? Was it was really okay for me to forge my own singular identity apart from my parents, like many of my American friends seemed to so easily do? Was personal freedom really as great as so many people in the U.S. seemed to think it was? What about the importance of the group? For a long time, the feelings of guilt I had about not doing enough for my parents, about not seeing Ajumoni, had more to do with my Confucian upbringing than even I understood.

When I was in my late 20s I heard a man named Dave Pollock speak. He said there was this person called a Third Culture Kid. He said all of us in the room were that person because we were raised in a culture outside of our parents' for a significant part of our development years. He began talking about concepts like "unresolved grief." He said we were "hidden immigrants" who had relationships to all the cultures we were part of while not having full ownership of any. The list of "pitfalls" he posted on the white board left me speechless. It read like my own checkered history of living in the U.S.:

- Deep loneliness
- Feeling trapped in the past
- Overly critical of passport country
- Habitual anger and bitterness
- Depression

It would be an understatement to say this was a watershed moment for me. Maybe my reaction to moving to a country in which I was a foreigner, but looked like I belonged, was within the range of normal. Maybe my longing for the people and places of my childhood was a logical part of my life journey. Maybe I just needed to learn how to manage the aftermath, to embrace my not-so-easily-labeled, global heart.

The only way to stop internal bleeding is to first understand what is causing it. I began to explore concepts of cross-cultural identity and the hidden immigrant. I read about what it meant to belong to a particular place, to a particular geography and set of customs. I learned about the aftereffects, good and bad, of my kind of upbringing. I spoke up about my identity struggles and grief for Korea, with mixed success, in therapy sessions. One therapist looked at me with a quaint little frown face and said, "Awwww!" Another exclaimed dramatically, in a way I actually appreciated, "Oh my God, Liz! Understanding your cultural identity is like researching children who were raised by wolves."

I read about the struggles of new immigrants, displaced peoples, and those who had lived geographically-rooted lives but still felt a deep connection to place. *American Childhood. I'm A Stranger Here Myself. The Language of Blood.* These were just a few of the books on my bookshelf, an altar to questions of belonging and identity. I thought about the thin, blurred lines of distinction in my childhood. Yes, some lines were firm and fixed. I can't imagine Ajumoni shopping comfortably at the PX, and I can't see Reverend Choi bowling at the Seoul Union Club. But I can picture Mom sitting in a hole-in-the-wall restaurant with her friend, Hong-chun, slurping down dumpling soup. I can envision Mark in a conga line at Ewha kindergarten. And I can easily see my dear *chingu*, blonde-haired Jennie, squatting in the alleyway outside her Seoul home, tossing *konggi* jacks into the air with her best friend, Yun Sun-i.

Is Jennie American? Is she Korean? Is she some combination only she will ever fully understand? What is cultural identity, after all? Is it really paperwork and documents? Can our identity be explained by an official stamp? Or even the genetics of our grandparents? Or is it the games we played? And the food we ate? And how we learned to eat it? Maybe our cultural identity is made up of ordinary, even mundane aspects of our childhood that gave us a point of view, a lens, an angle from which we began to see ourselves and the world. And maybe this never fundamentally changes.

Fifty years passed last month since my family first landed in Seoul. And South Korea is still my geographical, cultural, and spiritual compass point. Even with my U.S. passport. Even if I have not lived there for so long. Even as Spanish is replacing the Korean left inside of my brain. Even with my American parents. Even if. Even with. Even if.

In 1996, after ten years away from Korea, I knew that if I wanted to get up from the trail I needed to begin healing. With a lump in my throat and a pit in my stomach, I organized a trip to Seoul. In some ways returning to Korea felt like going to the scene where the life-changing accident occurred. But it got to the point where returning to Korea was the only thing I could do. I knew this trip wouldn't answer every question I had. I knew healing was going to take a long time. But I knew this was where I needed to start.

I made the decision to go when I accepted my parents weren't going to live in Korea again. I made it when I understood it was time for me to make my own way. Unlike a lot of people in this world, I can go home. I needed to see Ajumoni. I needed to make sure my childhood wasn't just a dream. I needed to wake up in the city that raised me, for the neighborhoods and people of nighttime dreams to become flesh and blood, concrete, tile, and steel. I needed South Gate to appear in front of me like an old friend. I had to reach out and touch the old city wall, to make sure it was real.

When the Korean peninsula materialized through the plane window, all of the pain and longing of ten years welled up inside of me, and I cried like a grandmother once again laying her eyes on the old country. I was finally somewhere I had a history. I was finally home. I could finally, for a moment, put away all of my questions of belonging.

GETTING UP FROM THE TRAIL

*"I exist...as the tension between all my "versions,"
for that tension, too (and perhaps above all), is me."*

—V. HAVEL, *LETTERS TO OLGA*

It's 3 am, and I'm wide-awake with jet lag. Even though I know this means tomorrow will be a tiring day, I don't care. Our *yos* are lined up neatly in a row, the lights of Seoul are flickering outside the window, and humid air fills my lungs. Even the bathroom is familiar. The smell of wet tile, the low sink, the simple faucets, the water that trickles out of them. The bright red plastic pail on the bathroom floor looks like the one Cho-ssi used. I've missed all of this too much.

Seoul will soon pulsate with activity. A gong will chime at Chogyesa Temple and the old grandfather will wheel his cart into place down the road and begin to roast the first chestnuts of the day. The well-stocked *supa* will open, the corner store down the alley is stocked with bottles of Chilsung Cider, Choco Pies, and banana yogurt cups, the snacks of my childhood. A twenty-minute walk will take me to the tourist neighborhood of Insadong, where Mom used to shop for calligraphy supplies. These are just a few of one thousand signs telling me I am finally home.

The large, six-story brick building we're staying at during our family visit is a multi-function property serving the Korean Presbyterian Church. The building sits on the old mission compound in East Seoul. The only mission home from that era that still stands is used as administrative offices. I can see it from my room, along with a short segment of the old compound wall that has remained. These are remnants of a bygone era, a time of Moffetts and Kinslers, outside men and *ajumonis*, a history unknown to the people who buy lattes down the alleyway. Along with the city outside the window, the history of that compound and those people is a part of me, too. My brothers once ran these roads in Scout uniforms. But that story is over. That chapter was written and that era has passed. We were part of a rooted community whose time in Korea was limited. Sometimes I think TCK childhood is a lesson in being free of attachments.

My family's 1996 trip to Korea was a significant turning point for me. That visit broke through my stubborn grief. I returned to the beloved places of my past to find old comfort there. The first time I saw the shoreline of Taechon Beach after ten years, I wept. I walked the grounds of Kyung Bok and Toksu Palace. I visited Admiral Yi, who still stands proudly in the heart of Seoul, in my favorite part of the city. I roamed the halls of SFS and greeted the cafeteria ladies and school guards.

I sat in the community room of House of Grace and ate a lunch of cold *naengmyon* noodles with Director Han and the young women who, like so many before them, are making a second home in a place of temporary safety and refuge. We shared meals with missionaries still living in Seoul and enjoyed festive reunions with former ECF students. We found Mrs. Kim, my first caretaker, walked through Yonsei and Sinchon, and hiked South Mountain. And, most importantly, we celebrated the reunion of Ajumoni's family with ours.

Every few years I kept doing all of this again and again, until Korea became real, until the places and people of my childhood became a part of my present and not just a part of my nostalgic past. In each visit I gained a better understanding of where I begin and end. Each landing on Korean soil was a step towards moving forward, a way to remember where I came from in order to move on. To spend time on that land was like taking in the oxygen my body needed.

Over time, from Seattle to Minneapolis, from Vermont to Zambia, I began to feel a central *Lizness* return in me, emerging from my *maum* as my grief passed through each stage. My disparate parts began to feel whole again. I realized the Korean part of me could never slip away, whether it was seen and acknowledged or not. Instead of fighting my identity struggle, I gave into it. And as I did all of this, blessings of understanding, grace, and forgiveness washed over me.

Nobody wants to sit by the trail too long. You sit by the trail when you don't want to move forward, and you can't figure out how to get back to where you came from. You sit by the trail when you're too weary to do anything else. But one day, I had to stop sitting by the trail. It doesn't do any good to hold a place with one-dimensional nostalgia. Homesickness can distort a complicated picture. Grief can stick us in time and sorrow like mud.

In 1996, I returned to a country that still felt like it belonged to me. But even then, signs of major social change were plain to see. I noticed more than a few high school students with dyed hair. I noticed less conformity in dress and more varied body sizes. Just south of the Han River, a new center of finance and economic power and neighborhoods of expensive, high-rise apartment buildings were emerging in a place I still envision, in my child's eye, as farmland. Overall, most people seemed to be enjoying a higher status of living.

The biggest change of all was watching the City Hall clock tick past midnight. Democracy had come, martial law was over, and the curfew was a relic of the past. In the mid-1980s, an intense two-year protest campaign of confrontations between the people and the government finally brought the downfall of the Chun administration. In 2002, South Korea's Presidential Truth Commission officially announced the PRP case a fabrication of the Park government and issued an apology to the families of the eight men. In 2003, my parents and a number of Monday Night Group members and other foreigners involved in the democracy movement were invited back by the government, through the Korean Democracy Foundation, to honor them for their service to Korea.

Once on the government's list of "subversive" foreigners, they were honored at a Blue House luncheon. In 2008, my parents and their colleagues published a book about their story, called *More Than Witnesses: How A Small Group of Missionaries Aided Korea's Democratic Revolution.*

Now, decades have passed, and in a place like South Korea, ten years of change compresses into two. Nelson Mandela once said, "There is nothing like returning to a place that remains unchanged to find the ways in which you yourself have altered." It's more difficult to know who you are when you return to a place that is sometimes unrecognizable. Seoul has spread miles beyond its old borders. The Han River, the river that long marked the southern edge of the city, is now in the middle of glass skyscrapers and tony urban sprawl. Our old YMCA camp and remote picnic sites have become neighborhoods of trendy coffee shops and luxury department stores. Spreading clusters of fifty story apartment buildings line up all over the country like gray dominoes, reminding me South Korea will never be the same.

Today Seoul is a highly developed, world-class city. South Korea boasts the world's highest Internet speeds. The country has one of the largest economies. Once an international aid recipient, Korea is now an aid donor. But there is a story behind all of this progress. A tale of eradicated neighborhoods and uprooted communities. The loss of patchwork districts of endless alleyways, where one corner was never the same as the next. I heard somebody say people describe locations in Seoul by saying, "It's close to where building x used to be." I read about an older Korean woman, who, having seen South Korea for the first time in twenty years, kept saying, "Too much building, too much building!"

Puk Ahyon-dong, like so many other old neighborhoods, underwent a mass forced eviction a few years ago to make way for redevelopment. The last photos I saw of our dear old neighborhood were of broken down walls, crumbling structures of quickly abandoned homes, and forsaken personal effects scattered through the streets like strange archaeological artifacts.

South Korea has the second highest suicide rate in the world, due in part to the intense pressure for students to academically succeed, and the high poverty rate in the elderly population. The old system in which grandparents were taken care of at home by their children has largely disappeared. Many Korean friends say they are living in a society increasingly run on the steam of status-conscious materialism. Young people are working fourteen hours a day and seeing little in advancement. Subway stations walls are plastered with plastic surgery ads showing dramatic before and after transformations a little bit of time under a surgeon's knife can bring. I almost can't reconcile this Korea with the Korea of my youth. Artist Minouk Lim is one of a number of people addressing the "human cost of modernization," who, through her art, is mourning and ritualizing the dislocation of a society that has lived through a time of such fundamental and irrevocable change.

I don't want to romanticize Korea's difficult past. The standard of living in South Korea has increased significantly. There is a lot to love about new South Korea. Great international food. A thriving art and music scene and a revitalized Korean arts movement. There's a lot more green space. And less pollution. Cheongyecheon Stream, once surrounded by stilted hovels, then covered over for decades by an elevated roadway, is now a beautiful downtown park. Ironically, South Korea has all of the food I was so dramatically longing for as a teenager. We really do need to be careful what we wish for.

But I'm from another era. Like an émigré returning to the old country, I use 1970s words people tell me aren't used anymore, like the heavily stressed *bbotteri* for battery. I use titles when I don't need to, or I use outdated ones. A few years ago I was on a bus trip to a remote Buddhist Temple with Myong-ju and Un-ju.

Feeling bored, Myong-ju said, "Let's sing a song!" I launched into "Arirang," and Myong-ju and Un-ju simultaneously groaned.

Jennie participated in a workshop in Seoul a number of years ago. The facilitator asked everyone to write down the sounds that made them think of Korea. People called out their list. "Cell phone rings." "Subway doors closing." Jennie said, "Magpies. The clanking of the metal scissors of the taffy man." Everyone looked at her blankly.

I can't help but be nostalgic for some aspects of old South Korea. But then, after I accept Korea is not the same anymore, I stumble into a crowded marketplace of blood sausages where ladies are frying mung bean pancakes. I walk through downtown to take photos of Kwang Hwa Mun, the newly renovated gate into Kyong Bok Palace, and I pass at least five groups of people engaging in quiet protests, one for peace, another against the current administration, another an ongoing sit-in by relatives of the Sewol ferry disaster who are asking the government to reveal the full truth behind the tragedy.

On another trip, I go to a *noraebang* karaoke house with Ajumoni, Myung-ju, and Un-ju and we sing our hearts out and Ajumoni dances to old Korean pop songs with abandon. I join old friends for dinner and we sit cross-legged at a low table at a hole-in-the-wall restaurant. People are everywhere, neon lights are lighting up the sky, thirty small dishes are on the table, the meat is being cooked in front of us, the waitress is cutting sizzling beef with scissors, and everyone around us is with friends, and it all feels so singularly Korean. And I think in these moments, that maybe in some ways, Korea will always be Korea.

Just the other day I got a note from Chris, now living in Korea. "Liz, familiar Korea still shines through the cracks. During my morning run at six am I saw a group of *halmonis* planting cabbage and chatting up a storm and a *haraboji* and *halmoni* trash pick up brigade wearing yellow vests and white gloves with red rubber palms, where the highlight seems to be long breaks and also chatting up a storm."

I've come full circle one thousand times. I keep coming full circle again and again, as if the circle will never complete. And maybe it never will. A few years ago I returned to Korea with my parents to celebrate the 50th anniversary of House of Grace. Mom was invited to speak at a commemorative event and I wanted to be there to support her.

House of Grace, now called Ae Ran Won, adapted as society changed, with programs supporting single mothers to keep their babies. The agency continues to work to change government policies and address the social stigma that still makes the lives of single mothers in South Korea so difficult. The organization operates from a large, three story building on the same land where the original three simple traditional homes once stood.

Although we had arrived with a reasonable social schedule, within a couple of days, after Mom made and received what seemed to be fifty phone calls from her rented cell phone, our itinerary became a jam-packed, exhausting, life-giving few weeks of reunion meals, commemorative events, and outings.

One day, as Mom and I were heading out for another social engagement, Dad called to us from a fetal nap position on the bed. "Please don't accept any more engagements," he pleaded in a mock-serious voice. "Lock arms. You can do it." I thought of the countless lonely days I spent in the U.S., where for some reason I could never get this kind of communal traction.

The third night into our visit, the cleaning lady in the building we were staying at noticed I had stacked three quilts onto my mattress. Although the bed was off the floor, I felt like I was sleeping on a slab of concrete.

After seeing my quilts of comfort and shame, she asked me, in Korean, "Do you want . . ." and then she used an English sounding word . . . "*cush-on?*"

I paused, responding carefully and hopefully. "*Cush-on mwoy-eyo?*" What is cush-on?

She left for a few minutes, walking purposefully down the long hallway of modest, comfortable guest rooms. When she returned carrying a large foam pad, I was almost giddy with excitement. My childhood *yo*, I reasoned to myself, was much more comfortable than this. But my weakness shamed me. As I lay down on *cush-on*, I thought, "I'm not very Korean anymore." Then, later that day, I went over to Ajumoni's house and I saw they were sleeping on high beds with soft mattresses.

During the second week of that trip, we embarked on a three-day excursion outside of Seoul to visit a Buddhist Temple with Ajumoni's family. On the first evening, I found myself in the shameful position of explaining delicately, to the bewildered and disappointed face of Myong-ju, that no, Mom, Dad and I were probably not up for a two-hour visit to the *jjimjilbang* bathhouse spa after a four-hour drive to the countryside followed by a two-hour dinner.

"Geez." I thought to myself as I lay in bed that night. "I've grown soft."

A couple years ago I began living in Central America with every expectation I would fit in easily. I anticipated feeling a sense relief living internationally again. Although I didn't speak any Spanish at the time and had only been to Central America once, I was counting on my chameleon TCK skills to kick in. I often feel like I'm coming home when I travel the world. I think it's in the familiarity of everything from soccer on television to the metal storefront doors that roll down for locking. I find comfort in disordered chaos. I love a city where life is lived on the sidewalks. I'm at home in definable cultures. I prefer humble nations. I don't mind sticking out like a sore thumb.

I made the transition into a six-month public health work stint in Zambia pretty smoothly. I was more comfortable in the city of Lusaka than I ever was at Middlebury College. There was the way the clinic staff called one another brother and sister, the importance of relationships over tasks, the formality in greetings, and the respect shown to elders. There was the way my friend, Darlingtone, said to me one day, "Liz, don't say 'my mother.' In Zambia we say 'our mother.'" And I thought of *uri*, the important "our" language of Korea. *Uri nara.* Our country.

There was the familiar, earthy smell of garbage fires in the evening, and the way things worked out even when I couldn't imagine how they could. Deep friendships were easy to make in the expat community. So when I moved to Costa Rica, I moved with the expectation everything would go smoothly. I felt that, in a way, I was returning to a place where my international soul could breathe.

Within the first few weeks I shocked myself twice on the same lamp. I reset the clocks every morning expecting them to stay set, until I realized the electricity went off and on each night. Then I contracted a raging, heat-and-humidity-induced eye infection. I found myself in conversations I swore I would never have, commiserating with recent arrivals, my impatience and expectation that everything should work smoothly boiling over, "But why doesn't the gas man *come* if he says he is on his *way?*"

In these moments, away from the U.S., the fullness of my identity comes into full focus. At these poignant junctures I know I will never be firmly this or that. The *miguk* part of me wants the gas man to show up on time and the grass to be mowed like a golf course. Sometimes she needs to lay down alone quietly after many hours of communalism. In Korea, away from the U.S., my undefinable cultural identity settles comfortably into its old, illogically familiar ways. I balance easily into the mixed-up person I am, part *miguksaram*, part *hanguksaram*, neither and both, and something in-between. After two weeks of eating Korean food I'm starving for a plate of lasagna.

As I've grown older, I've come to understand why growing up in Korea made it difficult for me to live in the States. It had to do with growing up in a country shaped by communalism, in a place in which Confucian ethics always trumped personal freedom. It had to do with taking on a small country mentality, not big country thinking. I'm not used to my country winning everything. I think it's also because I was *supposed* to fit in in the U.S., to feel like it was my home, and I just didn't. I rubbed up against that reality every day. And because the U.S. had and has such a complicated role in South Korea, I came to question what the U.S. stood for. I can't unsee the impact of those army bases.

I do think growing up in Korea helped me adjust to living in Costa Rica and Zambia. I really don't mind if a driver uses a cell phone with one hand and drives with the other, as long as they are driving relatively carefully. I figure we're taking risks all the time. While I always use a seatbelt in the U.S., I sat in the back of taxi cabs for fifteen years, careening through the streets of Seoul without once wearing a seat belt. We can't prevent everything horrible from happening.

I once told an American friend of mine that my Mom was knitting while sitting in the passenger seat during a road trip. She wrinkled her forehead and said, "Isn't she worried she'll impale herself with the knitting needle if she gets in a car crash?" I thought about all of the turn of events that had to happen for Mom to get impaled with a knitting needle and the car to crash, and I said, "I think if she gets into a crash the knitting needle is the least of her worries." I still can't stop laughing when I think of that conversation.

I understand there isn't just one way to do things. I'm rarely culturally surprised. On the other hand, just the other day I found myself in a long, earnest conversation with a new American arrival about lawn mowers and how we wished the grounds crew of the university we live on would mow our lawns more often. I'm not sure anything says *gringa* more than an obsession with lawn care.

Another full circle moment happened a few years ago, when one fall, after Mom wrote a letter to her Vermont senator, Ajumoni, Myong-ju, Un-ju, and her two grandsons were granted visas to visit us in the U.S. I was so excited to see Ajumoni, but I was worried she might feel some shock landing in the U.S. for the first time. When she emerged from the gate at the airport holding her hand over her mouth, I thought she was overcome with emotion. As I leaned in to give her a hug she giggled, covered her mouth, and said, "I haven't brushed my teeth!"

A couple of weeks later we took everyone berry picking at a local farm. Myong-ju and Un-ju and I were chatting as we filled pint boxes with large, ripe blueberries. I couldn't see where Ajumoni had gone. Then I looked down the lane of bushes and saw her moving around the ground in an area of weeds. She called to me with delight, "*Lidgie, iri wa! I namulun aju masissoyo!*" Come, Lidgie, these plants are delicious! She was picking dandelions to fry up later.

No matter what continent she is on, Ajumoni is still the same delightful person she has always been. She is slowing down now. Ajumoni is now Halmoni, and she is growing older. Every year I feel a greater urgency to see her. I will always live with a sadness that I have not been able to see her more, that I am not part of her daily life. Sometimes I just want to take a cab across the city to sit down on her bedroom floor and simply pass the time together.

These days, when I visit Korea, I take time to learn more about the stories I didn't know well or fully understand as a young girl. I visited the grandmothers at the House of Sharing, the home of the survivor "Comfort Women," who live to tell their story of capture and sexual slavery by the Japanese. I navigated the Peace Market to find the statue commemorating the life of Chun Tae-il, to honor the worker who immolated himself there. As I knelt down to read the brass plates inscribed with his story, I noticed the stares of passersby who were likely wondering why this *miguksaram* cared so much about a 1970s garment worker. Could they imagine he is one of my heroes?

I took the bullet train from Seoul to Kwang Ju. I wanted to visit May 18th Memorial Park, to pay my respects to those who lost their lives during the Kwang Ju Uprising. Though my family had little personal connection to that part of the country, I felt I needed to do something to honor the people whose actions eventually led to democracy for South Korea.

Half an hour into the train ride, I realized it was a terrible idea to take a bullet train through Korea. I take trains because I want to see the countryside, because I like a slow pace of travel and life. I don't take trains to go hurdling past country villages and farmlands. I loved the train ride to Taechon *because* it was slow. Taking a bullet train in South Korea was a terrible idea, something I never want to do again.

An hour into the trip I heard an announcement that a ferry full of high school students was sinking off the coast not far from where we were located. At first it sounded like most of the students were rescued. It was unclear what had exactly happened, but it didn't seem too serious. By the time we arrived in Kwang Ju, I felt terribly sick with stomach discomfort. Through a series of miscommunications and mishaps, I toured one commemorative park carrying my heavy backpack. The heat and humidity of Kwang Ju made my load feel like the weight of a large stone, as if I was carrying the heaviness of May 18th, as if the heartbreak of a crushed people's uprising and a sinking ferry full of young people was settling into the pit of my roiling stomach.

Over the next few days it became clear that very few students had been rescued from the ferry. Over the next few weeks the grief and anger of the nation erupted as the horrific tragedy of the Sewol incident unfolded. I had a difficult time following the complicated analysis of what many pointed to as the causes of the accident—a mix of greed and social ills that came together to contribute to a national heartbreak, and the culpability of President Park Geun-hye, former President Park's daughter, who was now, inexplicably to me, head of South Korea. Who is today, two years after the Sewol incident, embroiled in a scandal that may bring her rule to an end.

I was too far removed from the problems of modern Korea to understand what was exposed by the Sewol tragedy, or to understand how in the world the daughter of Park Chung-hee had been elected president. But I did understand Korean grief. Here, again, my country was awash in mourning. I felt like I knew the sobbing parents who gathered at City Hall. I could feel the pain of the grandparents who wailed along the seashore, as close as they physically could to their unrecovered grandchildren. So when a thick collection of yellow ribbons began to fill up the walls along the entrance to Cheongyecheon Stream Park, I placed mine there too, to join my prayer with the others, to express the deep sorrow I shared with my Korean brothers and sisters, the grief that lay so heavily on my Korean heart.

During that visit I stayed at a place called the DMZ Peace Life Valley Center, a peace and ecological retreat and teaching center in South Korea's northeastern province. One side of the village is lined with fields of green peppers and rice. The other side is lined with deep army bunkers and military training centers. This is the legacy of a nation still split in two.

I awoke at dawn to the sound of a Japanese monk chanting and drumming on the hillside. He was facing North Korea, the land where his grandfather died and his mother and father once lived. He shared his story with us the night before in the director's open-aired, traditional home. As we sipped from a shared bowl of maple sap, the monk told us his grandfather called to him in a dream and told him to go to South Korea to pray for reunification. The monk was living and working at the center. He spent each morning facing north, chanting, drumming, and praying for peace. I felt him to be, like me, a person of place, and a placeless person.

I got out of bed, dressed, and walked outside to listen. I wanted to take some strength from the drumming and chanting of a Japanese man who felt certain it was his life's task to simply do this. Within a few minutes, an army helicopter circled overhead. For a moment, the propeller noise drowned out the invocation. So close to the 38th parallel, I thought about Onni and her brother, and the people who are still separated from their families, sixty years later.

The Boundary Railroad Station, Torasan, is one mile from the southern boundary of the DMZ. The station was reopened in 2000, when South and North Korea made tentative plans to connect the two countries by rail. In 2004, the track was built. In 2007, the first train since the Korean War crossed the boundary line carrying delegations from North and South. For a short time freight flowed back and forth from the Kaesong Industrial Complex, until increased tensions brought an end to economic cooperation. Today Torasan is South Korea's "Last Station," a symbol of disappointment for those who seek reunification. The track with the destination of Pyongyang is closed.

What heartbreaking loss those generations carried. And I knew that even in my dislocation, even in my homesick-driven grief, I was given so many blessings in this life. An intact family. Safety. Security. A home country to love and cherish. Korea.

As I looked away for a moment, I noticed a decorative stone along the path that wound through the center. On it was carved a simple question.

나는 누구인가?
Who am I?

Perhaps there is no way to ever settle this question. It's impossible to take all the influences of my childhood and bend them towards one single line. The influence of American parents who played badminton and picked up protest signs. The story of a

Korean widow who called me cheese *chaengi* and taught me it was okay to lament. The conviction of a theologian named Moon Tong-hwan, who wrote a treatise called "Joy on the Way" during one of his family's most difficult days. An American man named Horace Underwood, who once said, "Korean blood flows through my veins." A country of rice candy and riot police. A childhood of *yonton* stoves and country club dinners.

I share this story with Mark, who at the age of four became Maga. Who learned to squat low on his haunches, his feet flat, his knees high by his chest. Who still sleeps on top of his bedspread with a quilt over him, as if he is sleeping under an *ibul*, as if he is still napping peacefully on the floor of Ewha Kindergarten.

I share this story with Chris, who loves Duke basketball and Abe Lincoln, and returned to South Korea last year, to the place he calls his motherland, to work for peace and reconciliation, continuing my parents' legacy.

I share this story with Rick, my American to the core brother, our patriotic soldier, who knew long before I did how hard it is to leave home, who can still eat a huge bowl of *kimchi*, and always carried what he saw in Korea with him.

I share this story with Na Soon-Hui and Na Ui-son, my dear parents, who gave me my Korean heart. Now in their 80s, they are still counseling the mentally ill, visiting shut-ins, chopping wood, raising goats, taking Spanish, volunteering, and counting the years in Korea as their most precious. I think they are beginning to understand they raised a little Korean girl.

I share this story with the children who did not go to Korea by calling. For my infant playmates who rode into Seoul in a mission-issue jeep. For my grade school classmates who took the hand of a parent and stepped off the plane and onto the tarmac of a foreign airport. For those friends of mine, like Jennie, and Debbie, who were born to soil that was not theirs by birthright or passport, but became their motherland nonetheless.

Maybe I'm just a patriot like my grandfather was. Because nothing will ever stop me from loving Korea. The thud of black riot police boots falling on asphalt didn't stop me. The need for a place like House of Grace didn't stop me. The axe murders and the infiltrating commandos and the DMZ didn't stop me. Living away from Korea for five, ten, then twenty years has not stopped me. Nothing will ever keep me from believing that at their best, the largess of the Korean heart cannot be surpassed.

So if you ask me now, "Where are you from?" I will reply, "I come from Korea."

I'm the ten month-old baby who laid on Onni's back.

I'm the five-year-old girl who walked the streets of Puk Ahyon-dong with Cho-ssi.

I'm the international school kid with foreign friends with Korean hearts.

I'm the thirty-year-old woman crippled with homesickness in a Seattle garden.

I am all of my names. I am much more than my eye color and passport can ever tell. I am Belden and Rice, *han* and *mi*, East and West.

Now when I lift up and away from this divided land, away from the people who taught me my essential truths, from the society that gave me my sense of place in the world, I know I need to say good-bye. Now I take a moment for a ritual of separation. I take a moment for a ritual of thanksgiving.

Good-bye Saddleback, I call from the airplane window.

Stay in peace, Ajumoni.

Good-bye kohyang.

Saranghaeyo – I love you.

Annyonghi kesipsiyo—Stay in peace.

And tetani kamsahamnida—one thousand thank yous, for raising me, for loving me, and for teaching me how to weep and laugh in the same long breath.

The Korean National Anthem

Until that day when
the waters of East Sea run dry
and Mt. Paektu is worn away,
God protect and preserve our
nation.

Three thousand li of splendid rivers
and mountains, filled with Roses of
Sharon;
Great Korean people, stay true to
the Great Korean way!

As the pine atop the near Namsan
stands firm,
unchanged through wind and frost,
as if wrapped in armor,
so shall our resilient spirit.

Three thousand li of splendid rivers
and mountains, filled with Roses of
Sharon;
Great Korean people, stay true to
the Great Korean way!

The Autumn sky is void and vast,
high and cloudless;
the bright moon is our heart,
undivided and true.

Three thousand li of splendid rivers
and mountains, filled with Roses of
Sharon;
Great Korean people, stay true to
the Great Korean way!

With this spirit and this mind, give
all loyalty,
in suffering or in joy,
to the love of country.

애국가

동해물과 백두산이 마르고 닳도록
하느님이보우하사 우리나라 만세.

무궁화 삼천리 화려강산
대한 사람, 대한으로 길이 보전하세

남산 위에 저 소나무 철갑을 두른듯
바람서리 불변함은 우리 기상일세.

무궁화 삼천리 화려강산
대한 사람, 대한으로 길이 보전하세

가을 하늘 공활한데 높고 구름 없이
밝은 달은 우리 가슴 일편단심일세

무궁화 삼천리 화려강산
대한 사람, 대한으로 길이 보전하세

이 기상과 이 맘으로 충성을 다하여
괴로우나 즐거우나 나라 사랑하세

무궁화 삼천리 화려강산
대한 사람, 대한으로 길이 보전하세

Acknowledgements

I would like to thank my family for their love and support throughout this long process. Dad, your wisdom and insight, both in our long conversations and in the detailed and thoughtful letters you sent to your parents from Korea, has been an inspiration to me, and served as a backbone for many of the details in this book. Your willingness to always listen to my story, even when it was hard for you to do so, means more to me than I can ever express.

Mom, your encouragement to keep on writing kept me writing. Thank you for your continued example of embracing life to the fullest and your compassion for the least of these. Thanks for the time you took to talk with me about your important work with women in Korea.

To my brothers, thank you for companioning me during our childhood days and for your shared love of Korea.

Thank you to our family who remained in the U.S., who faithfully sent presents to us on Christmas and helped in so many ways when we returned for furlough. Thank you for doing for your best to understand your crazy relatives who lived in Korea.

Yanine, there are no words to express the joy you have brought into my life. Thank you for believing in me, even when I didn't, and for always reminding me this story needed telling.

To Cathy, thanks, *chingu* for all those hilarious downtown Seoul moments, your unwavering love and support throughout the years, for taking the time to do painstaking editing, and for your willing-ness to put your artistic talent to work on the cover of this book.

Jennie, thank you for companioning me on this, our journey of TCK grief and thanksgiving, and for your open and loving heart.

To Barbara Schaetti, thank you for your continued support, your dedication to understanding cross-cultural identity, and for taking the time to read many versions of this story. Thanks for always giving me the honest, constructive feedback I needed to encourage me to continue writing.

Thanks to Donald Clark for his work in researching and docu-menting life in the Korean mission field in *Living Dangerously in Korea: The Western Experience, 1900-1950*, a book that informed much of my understanding of the early days for the Korean mis-sionary community, and helped me distinguish myth from reality.

To the Monday Night Group, the impact of your actions on my life was profound. Thank you for deepening my understanding of what it meant love a country that was not your own, for your ded-ication to the cause of South Korean human rights and democracy, and for the time you took to write your stories down in *More than Witnesses*, a book that helped me better understand what you were all doing in our living room.

A special thank you to Minouk Lim for inspiring the title of this book and for her important work in keeping records of, and inventing rituals for, moments of separation.

To my first book group in Minnesota, thank you for putting up with sub-par work and for trying to understand a story you did not live. I hope this version reads a little better.

Many thanks to the readers who gave me feedback and helped focus the story along the way: Sue and Randy Rice, Jennie Rader, Catherine Breer, Yanine Chan, Barbara Schaetti, Ruth Porter, Kelly Teamey, Beth Underwood, Chris Rice, Kay Rader, and Cynthia Dawdy.

Notes

Front Pages

"Nietzsche was said to have wept . . ." This quote, a portion of which became the title of this book, was taken from an article in *Walker Magazine* of Walker Art Museum, written by artist Minouk Lim (June 1, 2012). I first saw Minouk Lim's work at the Walker Art Museum in Minneapolis. I was deeply moved by her art and her story. In the article, Lim was reflecting on what motivates her as an artist. "Today, under the changes caused by globalization, places are counted only as space; individuals are merely a resource or networking. Nietzsche was said to have wept as he embraced a downtrodden horse, but I want to weep, embracing places. Nevertheless, I also want to fight against the sense of powerlessness caused by melancholy, whether it is the feeling that overwhelmed Nietzsche, or any other kind. So I am inventing rituals for, and keeping records of, moments of separation."

http://www.walkerart.org/magazine/2012/minouk-lim-walker-art-center

1 Sitting By the Trail

Photo: First birthday dress. November, 1966. Photo credit: Sue Rice.

"We all know the story . . ." Said to be the dying words of Chief Poundmaker (Pitikwahanapiwiyin), Plains Cree Chief from 1842-1886. "It would be so much easier just to fold our hands and not make this fight . . . to say, I, one man, I can do nothing. I grow

afraid only when I see people thinking and acting like this. We all know the story about the man who sat beside the trail too long, and then it grew over and he could never find his way again. We can never forget what has happened, but we cannot go back. Nor can we just sit beside the trail."

"Liquid architecture . . ." In describing the work of artist Minouk Lim, Walker Art Museum curator Clara Kim referred to Seoul as "an urban landscape that changes before your eyes—a city of a kind of liquid architecture that gets destroyed as quickly as it gets built." http://www.minouklim.com/index.php?/reviews/clara-kimminouk-lim-notes-from

2 Compass Point

Photo: Arriving at Kimpo Airport on a rainy evening in 1966. Mom is carrying me in her arms and Dad and Mark are behind us. Photo credit: Rev. Choi.

"There are two kinds of people . . ." Thanks to co-producer James Mirabello for permission to use this quote from the film *First Lady of the Revolution.* "*First Lady of the Revolution* is the remarkable story of Henrietta Boggs, who fell in love with a foreign land and the man destined to transform its identity. Her marriage to Jose 'Don Pepe' Figueres in 1941 led to a decade-long journey through activism, exile and political upheaval and, ultimately, lasting progressive reforms. *First Lady of the Revolution* is not only a depiction of the momentous struggle to shape Costa Rica's democratic identity; it's also a portrayal of how a courageous woman escaped the confines of a traditional, sheltered existence to expand her horizons into a new world, and live a life she never imagined." For more information, visit www.firstladyoftherevolution.com

3 Santokki

Photo: With Mrs. Kim and her daughters at their home down the hill. Photo credit: Sue Rice.

4 The Van Lierop's House

Photo: Mr. No loading furnace coal into the Van Lierop's house. Photo credit: Randy or Sue Rice.

"A piece of toast . . ." Clark, Donald N. *Living Dangerously in Korea: The Western Experience, 1900-1950.* Norwalk, CT: EastBridge, 2003.

5 The War That Never Ended

Photo: Outside our Puk Ahyon-dong house with Cho-ssi. Photo credit: Sue Rice.

6 Puk Ahyon-dong

Photo: With neighborhood friends in Puk Ahyon-dong. Photo credit: Sue Rice.

7 Weeping Upon Places

Photo: Pukchon Hanok Village, Seoul. Circa 2012. Photo credit: Elizabeth Rice

"The lesson you draw . . ." Bryson, Bill. *I'm a Stranger Here Myself: Notes on Returning to America after Twenty Years Away.* New York: Broadway, 1999. Print.

"In the year 1782 . . ." Hamilton R. History of a remarkable case of nostalgia affecting a native of Wales and occurring in Britain. *Medical Commentaries, for the year 1786.* Edinburgh 1787.

8 Furlough

Photo: Article from the *Niagara Gazette*.

9 Ajumoni

Photo: Ajumoni. Photo credit: Sue Rice.

10 Finding Kim Gap-kil

Photo: Samcheong-dong, Seoul. Circa 2012. Photo credit: Elizabeth Rice

11 Inches and Li

Photo: Celebrating my birthday with SFS friends Debbie, Jennie, and Pam. Photo credit: Sue Rice.

12 Under the Divided Sky

Photo: Rick, assessing his readiness for battle, or possible, a camping trip. Photo credit: Sue Rice.

"Korea is one . . ." From an article written in *Pyongyang Times* in 1972, when a basic arrangement to unify North and South Korea was agreed upon but never came to fruition.
Kwak, Tae Yang. "The Nixon Doctrine and the Yusin Reforms: American Foreign Policy, the Vietnam War, and the Rise of Authoritarianism in Korea, 1968—1973." *The Journal of American-East Asian Relations*. Spring-Summer 2003: 51-52.

"Here in Korea . . ." Morehead-Young, D. "Rip-Roaring ROK Crowd welcomes Johnson." *Stars and Stripes,* November 2, 1966.

13 The Beheading Hill
Photo: The 83rd Annual Meeting of the Korean Presbyterian Mission, 1977. Photo credit: unknown.

"Like Confucianism . . ." Moffett, Samuel H. *The Christians of Korea*. New York: Friendship Press, 1962. 82-83.

14 I Call Their Names Quietly in my Heart

Photo: Mom with staff members of House of Grace. Photo credit: unknown.

"My dear baby . . ." Dorow, Sara. *I Wish for You a Beautiful Life: Letters from the Korean Birth Mothers of Ae Ran Won to Their Children.* St. Paul, Minnesota: Yeong & Yeong Book Co, 1999. By permission of the author.

17 Minju Hoebok

Photo: *Newsweek* article about Monday Night Group protest.

"I have nothing against the words produced . . ." Stentzel, Jim (Ed.) and the Monday Night Group. *More Than Witnesses: How a Small Group of Missionaries Aided Korea's Democratic Revolution.* Mequon, WI. Nightengale Press, 2008, p. 211.

"Christ is often mediated to us . . ." Stentzel, Jim (Ed.) and the Monday Night Group. *More Than Witnesses: How a Small Group of Missionaries Aided Korea's Democratic Revolution.* Mequon, WI. Nightengale Press, 2008, p. 87.

US Missionaries: America Must Fight ROK Repression. *Stars and Stripes,* April 17, 1975.

18 Everyone Wakes Up at a Different Time in the Morning

Photo: Visiting Chang Chang Ki outside his base during his required years of military service.

20 A Line in the Sand

Photo: May 18th National Cemetery, Kwang Ju. Photo credit: Elizabeth Rice.

21 What Can I Take with Me

Photo: Insadong, Seoul. Photo credit: Elizabeth Rice.

22 The Utica Incident

Photo: A decorative stone at DMZ Peace Life Valley Center, Inje, South Korea. The words read, "Who am I?" Photo credit: Elizabeth Rice

23 Where are you From?

Photo: Buddhist temple, Seoul. Photo credit: Elizabeth Rice

"I'm trying very hard to love the mangroves . . ." Mary Oliver. "Listening to the World." Interview by Krista Tippett. *On Being*. Krista Tippett Public Productions, American Public Media. 15 Oct. 2015. Radio.

"No remedy other than return . . ." Austin, Linda M. *Nostalgia in Transition, 1780-1917*. Charlottesville: University of Virginia Press, 2007.

"The fraudulent promise of return . . ." Austin, Linda M. *Nostalgia in Transition, 1780-1917*. Charlottesville: University of Virginia Press, 2007.

Selasi, T. (2014, October). *Taiye Selasi: Don't ask where I'm from, ask where I'm a local* [Video file].
Retrieved from:
http://www.ted.com/talks/taiye_selasi_don_t_ask_where_i_m_from_ask_where_i_m_a_local

24 Getting Up From the Trail

Photo: Reunited with Ajumoni, now Halmoni.

"I exist . . ." Havel, V. (1989): *Letters to Olga: June 1979 — September 1982*, (trans. P. Wilson), New York: Henry Holt & Co.